THE VISIBLE EMPLOYEE

THE VISIBLE EMPLOYEE

**Using Workplace Monitoring and Surveillance
to Protect Information Assets–
Without Compromising Employee Privacy or Trust**

Jeffrey M. Stanton
and
Kathryn R. Stam

Information Today, Inc.
Medford, New Jersey

First printing, 2006

The Visible Employee: Using Workplace Monitoring and Surveillance to Protect Information Assets—Without Compromising Employee Privacy or Trust

Library of Congress Cataloging-in-Publication Data

Stanton, Jeffrey M., 1961-
  The visible employee : using workplace monitoring and surveillance to protect information assets — without compromising employee privacy or trust / Jeffrey M. Stanton and Kathryn R. Stam.
    p. cm.
  Includes bibliographical references and index.
  ISBN 0-910965-74-9
1. Electronic monitoring in the workplace. 2. Data protection-- Management. 3. Information resources management. 4. Supervision of employees. 5. Privacy, Right of. I. Stam, Kathryn R., 1966- II. Title.
  HF5549.5.E37S73 2006
  658.3'14--dc22

                                                                                          2006006265

President and CEO: Thomas H. Hogan, Sr.
Editor-in-Chief and Publisher: John B. Bryans
Managing Editor: Amy M. Reeve
VP Graphics and Production: M. Heide Dengler
Book Designer: Kara Mia Jalkowski
Cover Designer: Lisa Boccadutre
Copy Editor: Pat Hadley-Miller
Proofreader: Bonnie Freeman
Indexer: Sharon Hughes

To Judy, Abe, Arlene, and Walter—JMS

To Terrin, David, and Deirdre—KRS

Contents

Foreword

While technological controls are necessary for protecting the information resources of a firm, human and behavioral controls are also vital. After all, a *computer* has never been arrested for committing a computer crime. Given the increased reliance on information and communication technologies by the business world and society in general, *The Visible Employee* is a timely and much needed resource. Clearly a deeper understanding of surveillance and workplace monitoring is necessary, as are techniques that organizations can use to secure and control employees' use of technology. But how do employers protect the privacy rights of the employees at the same time? Balancing privacy and security often emerges as an enormously challenging task.

In its thorough analysis of the behavior of employees and the attitudes of managers, information technology professionals, and employees towards information technology use and abuse, *The Visible Employee* illustrates four classes of control structures in organizations:

1. Technical controls: Although the authors do not delve deeply into technical controls, they clearly recognize these are essential.

2. Formal organizational authority: The book highlights the significance of organizational responsibility structures and authorities. Defining responsibility and authority is worth the effort, especially given the virtualization of work. It is paramount to define where the buck would stop in case of any breach. Related to responsibility and authority structures is the issue of trust, which this book treats in a rather elegant manner. The authors consider trust as a kind of a psychological contract between the organization and the employees, the breakdown of which results in disgruntled employees—which may be the greatest threat to an organization.

3. Informal authority/culture: The book also discusses the development of a sustainable organizational security culture. Although touted as a principal means to manage information

security, culture is indeed an elusive concept, as the research presented in the book clearly suggests.

4. Monitoring and enforcement: The technical, formal, and informal controls can realize benefits only within the scope of a good regulatory environment. Monitoring and enforcement enable conformity with the behavioral rules of the organization. This fourth class of controls is important, and the authors of *The Visible Employee* rightly point to the need to proactively implement these controls.

The Visible Employee makes a call for a balanced and considered approach to the protection of information assets, and it sets an interesting and useful context for advancing research in behavioral aspects of information security. High-integrity behavior in organizations is a primary antecedent to good information security and assurance practices.

Gurpreet Dhillon, PhD
Professor of Information Systems
Virginia Commonwealth University
Author, *Principles of Information Systems Security:*
Text and Cases
www.security-professor.com

Acknowledgments

This book would not have been possible without the assistance of the many dozens of PhD, master's, and undergraduate students involved in the Syracuse Information Security Evaluation (SISE) project between 2001 and 2005. Chief among these, both in overall contribution and leadership qualities, is Isabelle Fagnot, who was the project leader for the Central New York Secure Business Initiative and assistant director of the SISE project in 2004 and 2005. Other important contributors to the SISE project include Indira Guzman, Carissa Smith, Tyler Blanchard, Freda Perry, Alana Edmunds, Vibha Vijayasri, Cavinda Caldera, Patty Manti, Saira Haque, Slav Marcinkowski, Nasriah Zakaria, Norhayati Zakaria, Ashley Isaac, Mikhiel Advani, Farhan Qazi, and Tatyana Poletsky. To all of these students and to the many others we have failed to name, we offer our appreciation for your efforts and dedication.

Thanks to Dr. Paul Mastrangelo, Dr. Jeffrey Jolton, and the rest of the folks at Genesee Survey Services for their assistance in survey data collection and their more general support of the whole behavioral information security research program. Our initial financial support from the Society for Industrial and Organizational Psychology Research Foundation would not have been possible without their collaboration. Thanks also to Dr. Shiu-Kai Chin and Roger Trabucco at Syracuse University's CASE Center for their financial support of the Central New York Secure Business initiative. To Dr. Roman Markowski, we owe an enormous debt of gratitude for his assistance with the technical aspects of the Central New York Secure Business initiative. Thanks also to Dr. Jon Gant, who helped out with this initiative.

Thanks to Rachelle Hollander and Sheila Slaughter at the National Science Foundation for their assistance, question answering, and encouragement during our applications for and administration of research grants from the foundation. Note that financial support for the data presented in this book came from two different awards: SES-9984111 and ITR-0312078. The National Science Foundation does not necessarily support any of the findings or conclusions presented in this book.

We cannot name, but nonetheless do greatly appreciate, the contributions of the hundreds of employees, managers, and information technology professionals who agreed to be interviewed and/or complete surveys for our research project. We hope we have told their stories faithfully and constructively.

The School of Information Studies at Syracuse University provided a friendly and supportive home for all of our research, and we offer our gratitude to Debra Eischen and Kathy Benjamin for their assistance with locating and placing the many internship students with whom we worked, as well as Dr. Bruce Kingma and Dr. Raymond von Dran for providing the infrastructure to make all the research happen. We appreciate the help of Deirdre Stam and Judy Stanton with proofreading. Thanks to Christiane Spitzmueller for the reuse of her master's thesis data and to Dave Molta for access to the *Network Computing* survey data.

Finally, to all of our colleagues mentioned here, we take full responsibility for the accuracy and completeness of the data and analyses presented in this book. All of their help made this book possible, so they share in the accomplishment, but we must retain full ownership of any and all mistakes.

Preface

Contemporary organizations are awash with information. From files to formulas, from e-mail to essays, almost every organization creates, processes, and distributes huge amounts of information. For many organizations, data are the red blood cells of the organization, carrying informational oxygen to all parts of the operation. Organizations cannot survive without information and can become severely crippled if that information becomes damaged or if it seeps out at the wrong places. Unfortunately, security threats affecting organizations' most important forms of information have grown rapidly over recent years, and this growth shows no signs of abating. Information in organizations is difficult to protect, and although some organizations succeed with protection strategies, many organizations are insecure and many of the people in these organizations are alarmed about this insecurity.

Thousands of technology experts focus their talents on improving information protection in organizations, and their efforts have led to a raft of technical solutions to difficult security problems. In *The Visible Employee*, however, we focus on the human element in information protection, and in particular on the roles that members of the organization play in ensuring information security. Employees have a responsibility for creating, maintaining, and handling much of the organization's information. When employees do a good job and handle information appropriately, the organization remains healthy and can fulfill its mission. If and when employees handle the information badly, everyone and everything around the organization may suffer as a result of lost productivity, lost revenue, legal liability, and financial disaster. As the major creators, consumers, managers, and distributors of information for the organization, employees play a critical role in ensuring the continued success of the enterprise.

Because of the importance of the employee role, organizations go to greater and greater lengths to ensure that employees handle information appropriately and effectively. Just as information technology facilitates the handling and processing of information, information technology also facilitates *watching* the information handlers and processors at work. Monitoring, surveillance, filtering, logging, and tracking are all words that have been used to describe the myriad processes that organizations have put in place to help understand if, when, and how employees are doing their jobs and handling the organization's lifeblood carefully.

The Visible Employee is all about these techniques—how organizations secure and control employees' uses of information systems. The book describes how monitoring and other techniques are used in the pursuit of information protection and how employees, managers, and information technologists view these techniques. These analyses and the recommendations developed from them are based on data collected over a period of four years (2001–2005) in a variety of organizations: interviews and surveys with hundreds of employees, dozens of managers, and scores of information technology professionals. The goal of the book is to educate and enlighten. We believe there is no way to close the Pandora's box on information technologies; what we must do instead is use them in humane, fair, effective, and profitable ways. Based on extensive data collected from managers, employees, and information technology professionals, this book provides processes for supporting information protection that can benefit organizations and everyone who is affected by their information management successes and failures.

CHAPTER 1

An Introduction to Information Protection and Employee Behavior

In most organizations, information flows at the heart of workplace activities. The effective management of information requires information technology, and that technology is therefore crucial to organizational success. Information technology comes in many forms—networked personal computers, personal productivity devices, software applications, the Internet, and more—but one thing all types of information technology have in common is that their effective use depends upon human users. People put the technology to work in managing information, and people are ultimately responsible for whether information technology succeeds or fails. Within organizations, these people are the employees who use the technology to get their jobs done, serve the needs of customers, and keep the organization running.

Almost all organizations that use information technology in any substantial way are also struggling to maintain effective information security. In an increasing number of organizations, information is among the most valuable assets they possess. As connectivity among information systems has increased, so has the likelihood of intrusion into the systems, thefts of business information, fraudulent use of information, defacement of organizational Web sites, and other forms of information loss or damage. A worldwide army of hackers, virus writers, and scam artists stands poised to inflict as much damage as possible on the Internet-connected organization. Organizations are always vulnerable to these external security threats to some degree, but industry research by Ernst and Young (2002) suggests that many expensive security breaches in fact result from activity that occurs within organizations: the so-called insider threat posed by employees or contractors who possess trusted access to the company's information and technology. At the low end, losses from security breaches of all types have been estimated at approximately $20 billion per year (counting U.S. organizations only; Security Wire Digest, 2000). Such losses cause organizations to open their wallets: According to a 2002 industry survey by *Information Security* magazine, very large organizations spend an average of $6 million per year on information security measures; smaller ones spend nearly 20 percent of their overall information technology budgets on security.

Among the various security technologies used in organizations, many provide the means to monitor employee behavior. Organizations deploy these complex and expensive monitoring technologies under the belief that secure management of an organization's information assets depends in part upon the behavior of employees. Employees are the "end-users" of much of the organization's information, and that information is very literally at their disposal. When employees are careful to handle information in a secure way, the organization, its customers, and its shareholders benefit from the protection of this key asset. Alternatively, mismanagement of information or the malfeasance of isolated individuals who "go bad" may have devastating effects on the organization's success.

Organizations possess an increasingly powerful technological toolbox for finding out what people are doing on their computers and on the network. For the many employees who use computers, a detailed electronic trail of communications, software utilization, and network activity now fills the log files of company servers. Almost every organization with business processes that connect it to the Internet uses one type of system or another to assess networked computer usage, track network access, warn about inappropriate behavior on the network, or try to ensure that such behavior cannot occur. Software and hardware vendors provide a huge array of options for collecting, storing, analyzing, and generating reports based on telecommunications records, logs of Web usage, addresses of e-mail recipients, and e-mail message content. A plethora of details about employees' work habits, computer usage, and personal demographics, and a wide range of other potentially sensitive information is collected and stored in organizational information systems. Enterprise computing systems contain centralized work records and other information about job-related activities in huge interlinked databases. Camera surveillance has also become increasingly common, particularly in the public spaces of the organization (e.g., lobbies, parking lots, customer areas of retail stores), but additionally in non-public spaces such as employee break rooms. Smart cards and proximity badges help the organization know where employees are located and what facilities they have used. All of these forms of monitoring and surveillance allow organizations to increase the visibility of employee behavior, analyze typical usage patterns, flag unusual or unauthorized activities, and reduce the lag between the discovery of problems and subsequent action or decision making. Monitoring and surveillance technologies seem to provide a panacea of observation, analysis, prediction, and control for those who wish to reduce the uncertainty, unpredictability, and risks related to the behavior of information systems users.

A series of U.S. industry surveys has shown that employee monitoring and surveillance occur to some degree in the majority of U.S. work organizations (9 to 5, 1990; Orthmann, 1998; Society for Human Resource Management, 1991, 1999, 2001). In their 2004 survey on workplace e-mail and instant messaging, the American Management Association and the ePolicy Institute found that 60 percent of organizations they contacted used software to monitor employees' e-mail correspondence with parties outside the firm (American Management Association & ePolicy Institute, 2004). Although regulatory controls on monitoring and surveillance are sometimes stricter in other locales, such as Canada, Western Europe, Japan, and Australia, the use of electronic monitoring and surveillance of workers and workgroups occurs in those places as well (International Labour Office, 1993; Mayer-Schönberger, 1999). Employee monitoring and surveillance in emergent industrial economies such as India and China also appear to be widespread, but definitive figures from these countries are more difficult to obtain.

On the surface, these varied capabilities for observation and tracking of employee behavior seem to open up a Pandora's box of potential privacy violations, but using the emotionally loaded word "violation" clouds the subtleties involved in the control over information assets in the organization. Managers have always sought strategies for controlling the environments surrounding their organizations and reducing the risks to which their organizations are exposed. Haggerty and Ericson (2000) referred to these concerns as based on management's "desires for control, governance, security, [and] profit ..." (p. 609). Among various methods to impose control on unruly environments, technology has often played a substantial role (e.g., Simon, 1965, p. 73). Technology stabilizes business processes and makes them more routine. More pointedly, information technology streamlines and amplifies the collection and analysis of data and its use in decision making. Good managerial decisions, in turn, provide the foundation on which successful and sustainable businesses are built.

In opposition to this view, however, privacy advocates and other critics discuss how monitoring and surveillance violates societal norms, cultural preferences, and fundamental personal rights of workers. These critics suggest that with the tacit or explicit approval of regulatory bodies, organizations routinely overstep their bounds by capturing too much information about employees, too frequently, and with too little control over how the data are used, protected, or maintained. The evidence that critics cite arises from a variety of U.S. legal cases—the majority of which have typically been won or settled in the organization's favor—as well as union grievances and popular reports of notable individual cases. These lawsuits arise from aggrieved employees who have been fired or who feel they have suffered some other injustice in the workplace as a result of inaccurate or inappropriate information that has been gathered about them or as a result of information being used in unfair ways. A related danger lies in potential damage to management-labor relationships: In 1987, the U.S. Congress Office of Technology Assessment (OTA) released a report documenting the opposition of 21 national labor unions to the use of computer technology to monitor worker performance (U.S. Congress OTA, 1987, p. 86). Employee privacy is one of its major concerns; few would disagree that it is highly difficult to make any long-lasting or ironclad guarantees about the privacy of confidential data collected by organizations. All of these issues have been used by critics to argue against the extensive use of surveillance and monitoring technologies.

In the present book, we take neither the side of the technologists nor the side of the privacy advocates. Each of their perspectives may have validity in different contexts, but making this issue either black or white passes over a lot of gray territory by assuming that employees simply accept these technologies as deployed; that information technology professionals administer them exactly according to managerial edicts; that relationships among employees, managers, and technologists are either irrelevant or unchanging; and that organizations either impose monitoring, surveillance, and security technologies in one monolithic, unilateral step or not at all. In reality, we know from research that integrating any type of new technological capability into a firm requires lots of formal and informal negotiations among the different parties involved: managers, employees, information technology professionals, and others (e.g., Davis, 1989). Every group has a different stake in the issues, and we want to ask whether those stakes are ever put down into common ground. It may be that in some organizations a process occurs in which employees, information technology personnel, and managers weigh what valuable information can and should be captured, what the benefits might be for the different parties involved and for the organization as a whole, and what alternative options are available for simultaneously ensuring information security and protecting employees' interests. In other organizations, managers, employees, and information technology people may simply stumble along, reactively implementing technologies in response to one perceived information protection crisis after another, with no clear vision of how the consequences of their decisions about security and privacy will unfold.

With *The Visible Employee*, we take the view that many people in organizations recognize that information is a highly valuable commodity: Thoughtful managers, information technology professionals, and employees function as "intuitive information economists" and work diligently in their own spheres to collect, control, and organize the information at hand. One important kind of information pertains to what people are doing on the network, minute by minute, hour by hour, day by day. Few would disagree that controlling the flow of information about one's own computer activities or those of other people is useful, but how one achieves that control probably depends a lot upon where one stands in the organization. More powerful people have one way of controlling things, while the less powerful have other ways. Personal assets, such as expertise, social relationships, and social exchange, may determine who can learn what, when, and at what cost. Expertise is an increasingly important asset because the sheer complexity of organizational information systems has catapulted information technology professionals upward with respect to the control and influence that they have over organizational processes. Information technologists are therefore taking on a new role in organizations as behavioral observers, analyzers, and even sometimes enforcers. In many organizations, information security specialists and other information technology personnel occupy the driver's seat of employee monitoring and surveillance technologies. This alteration of the traditional organizational hierarchy complicates the standard tug-of-war between labor and management by creating a new three-way relationship among employee end-users, information technology/security professionals, and managers.

Note that we use this three-way classification of job functions throughout the book with the knowledge that it simplifies (and perhaps even oversimplifies) the politics and roles in many organizations. Yet, as you will see when we present our interview and survey data, this three-way classification seems like a workable simplification by virtue of the consistency in attitudes and beliefs among many members within each group. Even though certain individuals in some organizations may simultaneously live all three roles—for instance, an assistant director of information technology may have deep knowledge of technology and limited executive power but may also feel like just another worker in the context of the larger organization—we believe that the bulk of the members of any sizeable organization think and act most of the time in accordance with one of the three roles. In short, managers manage, technologists control technology, and workers get things done. Members of each group may have a different take on security, privacy, and monitoring based on what they each need to do to survive and thrive in their respective jobs.

Given the likelihood of different perspectives among the three groups, we think it is reasonable to wonder whether they can all see eye to eye on the question of how to maintain security within the organization while respecting the rights and preferences of those whose behavior is monitored in fulfillment of this goal. We believe that it may be possible and feasible for organizations to navigate between the Scylla and Charybdis of information insecurity and employee mistrust. Organizations can have success with both information security and labor relations through careful, simultaneous attention to issues of employee privacy and autonomy, clear communication of organizational policies, and a thoughtful, multiparty approach to information system design. Such efforts will likely require an unprecedented degree of cooperation and integration among managers, human resources staff, information systems professionals, and other functions within organizations. Although such cooperation may be difficult to achieve, we hope that *The Visible Employee* will make cooperation both more feasible and more likely by illuminating the separate perspectives for the benefit of the whole organization. By documenting and analyzing the relevant information protection problems from perspectives that encompasses managerial, employee, and technological concerns, we expect to describe a middle road that leads toward secure organizational information while also respecting and protecting fundamental employee rights and expected employee privileges. The data we have collected and that we report in this book can inform both future research and humane practice in organizations.

The development of a perspective that simultaneously considers privacy, social dynamics, and technological capability may also provide a useful starting point for further research in monitoring and surveillance. Privacy, in particular, though extensively studied as a legal and philosophical concept (e.g., Garrett, 1974; Gavison, 1980), is a messy area that social scientists are still trying to figure out (e.g., Newell, 1995). From a practical perspective, we believe that evidence of employee resistance to organizational deployment of information technology systems underscores the point that the introduction of monitoring and/or surveillance into an organization is likely to work best after a set of negotiation processes that bring management, employees, and information technologists to the same table. With recognition of and attention to the social dynamics surrounding new information technology by all involved, it is possible to envision effective and beneficial use of organizational monitoring and surveillance to maintain information security.

We refer to our overall approach to conducting research on employees, security, and monitoring as "behavioral information security." In exploring behavioral information security we are trying to understand the nature and origins of security-related behaviors in organizations and use this understanding as a basis for providing practical and principled approaches for increasing information security while respecting employee rights and preferences. We believe that situational factors in the organization interact with personal characteristics of employees to facilitate or inhibit appropriate information security behaviors. In our view, monitoring and surveillance techniques implemented by organizations are one of the most powerful situational factors, but the deployment of these techniques may not always lead to the outcomes that organizational managers anticipated.

The remainder of the book explores these ideas in three major sections. In the first section, Chapters 2, 3, and 4 provide a context and orientation behind the relevant research work we have conducted in organizations over the past four years. Chapter 2 outlines the array of information security problems faced by organizations and the involvement of employees in both the causation of these problems and the prevention of them. Chapter 3 provides a non-technical introduction and review of the information technology and techniques used in information security in general, as well as more specifically in surveillance and monitoring of employees. Chapter 4 provides a straightforward description of the psychological basis of privacy, along with supporting comments relating privacy to a few of the critical societal and legal issues.

In the middle section, we provide an overview and analysis of the data from our research program. We organize this section based on the perspectives of different groups of people. Chapter 5 describes interviews and other data obtained from managers about monitoring, surveillance, and the role of information security in the organization. Chapter 6 describes data collected by interviewing information security specialists and other information technology professionals with an interest in user behavior. Finally, Chapter 7 describes the employee perspective—including interviews and surveys conducted and observations we have gathered across many different organizations. In each of these chapters, we provide extensive quotes from organizational members with whom we spoke in order to convey the authentic voices of people who have direct concerns and responsibilities for information protection in their organizations. Their thoughts provide a rich picture of the challenges, problems, successes, and failures that contemporary organizations face as they tackle the complex problems of information protection.

In the third and last section, we close by providing reflection, discussion, and recommendations based on our data. In Chapter 8, we provide an integrated perspective on the work we have conducted with one eye on future research directions and perspectives. In Chapter 9, we provide research-based recommendations for managers, human resource professionals, employees, and information security specialists that we hope will lead toward more effective organizational policies and practices in organizations that use information technology. We have also provided a series of appendices, which focus on two separate issues. First, we provide some additional information that shows how we collected our data and what we found. Second, we provide some resources—such as model policies—that we believe may be helpful as organizations move toward more effective structuring of their measures to protect privacy and maintain security. Teachers and students should note that Appendix A lists supplemental readings for major topics we have covered and Appendix B contains discussion questions pertaining to each chapter of the book.

A Note About Terminology

We have attempted to make *The Visible Employee* comprehensible to a non-technical audience, to those with a modest grasp of information technology, to students in technology and social science programs, and to others with an interest in organizations and information but limited exposure to security concepts. We have tried to minimize use of acronyms, jargon, and specific brand or model names of products in an effort to make the book as reader-friendly as possible. As a result of our trying to thread this needle, some hardcore technology people may find our descriptions of security technologies rather simplistic, and some social scientists may consider our descriptions and analyses of data long-winded and pedantic. All we can ask is that you bear with us and feel free to skim over the parts that seem too elementary. In the material that follows, we provide a few explanations of terminology in advance that may save some problems later.

First, as previously discussed, we have made a tripartite division of organizational roles. When we refer to "managers," we mean all of the people from the executive suite down to the middle management level who have the power and discretion to make decisions, set policy, and spend money. In general, we do not include in this category frontline supervisors or professional employees, even though people in these groups may have some limited spending power and some staff under their control. When we refer to information technology people, information security people, technology experts, and technologists, we are including all individuals in the organization who have responsibilities for some aspect of the organization's information technology infrastructure. Finally, everyone who is not a manager or technology person we call an employee or worker. Collectively, we sometime refer to employees who use information systems as the "user community." We acknowledge that managers and technologists themselves have the same legal employee status as other workers and that they, too, use information systems, but we split the organization into these three groups in order to analyze and understand what makes their information protection roles different from one another.

We use the phrase "information protection" as an umbrella term to cover any and all efforts to maintain information security as well as the privacy or confidentiality of sensitive information. We define "information security" as the range of technical and social approaches to keeping information confidential, integral, and available (more on this in Chapter 3). We use the term "privacy" to refer more specifically to the control of sensitive information about people (more on this in Chapter 4). In our estimation, organizations cannot protect privacy of employees, customers, or others without a good information security program. For organizations with solid technical information security protections, however, it is still possible to have problems with privacy that adversely affect people. This is because privacy is a human construction—a personal process of controlling information about the self—and the technical security controls that assure the safe flow and storage of data cannot ensure that someone does not become offended or harmed by the way this data is collected, handled, or distributed. Thus, information protection encompasses both security and privacy. As the rest of this book shows, mastery of both the technical and social dimensions is necessary for effective information protection.

CHAPTER 2

How Employees Affect Information Security

In most organizations, information serves as a driving force behind the organization's so-called value chain. Whatever an organization's main mission may be, whether in the commercial, nonprofit, or governmental sector, it is likely that information is an important resource in fulfilling that mission. Organizations that produce tangible products, such as manufacturers, rely on information to control their supplies of raw materials, their production processes, and their marketing, sales, and logistics activities. For organizations that produce intangible products, like software, information itself is the product. For organizations that create services, information is the organization's memory of what it is doing, what it needs to do, and how it gets the job done. Almost all actions on information require information technology, and that technology comes in many forms: networked personal computers, personal productivity devices, software applications, the Internet, and more. Even before the Internet became part of the fabric of daily life, security of information was a matter of concern to organizations. Marketing plans, product designs, and customer lists were valuable commodities prior to the influx of computing into organizations and remain to the present the favored targets of competitors, industrial spies, and rogue employees. The widespread use of the Internet has simply magnified the size and intensity of the problem by making information resources more interconnected. As a result the security of information and the technology used to manipulate it have become organizational preoccupations of corresponding magnitude in many firms. In this chapter we examine some of the threats to information and information technology as well as how employees are involved in vulnerability to and protection against those threats.

An Information Security Overview

Recent history has revealed an accelerating trend toward inter-connection of computing devices. In 1950 a computer was a big box that stood alone in a big room. In 1980 a computer was a small box that stood alone in a small room. By 1995 a computer became something you could hold in your hand, carry in your briefcase, or leave on your desk, but in any form it was probably interconnected with other computers and devices. At present, computers exist in myriad forms—in objects as diverse as refrigerators and cars—but one thing that many of them have in common is that they are con-nected to a very large network of networks, the Internet. The Internet makes every computer a primitive but powerful little social object, creating relations to its neighbors that collapse the relative importance of space and time as well as the significance of physical barriers that were once the heart of information protection. This collapse provides unprecedented opportunities for unfortunate things to happen to all of our computers: Bad people have always had the ability and tools to do bad things, but now bad people can do bad things to your computer using their computer, regardless of whether they occupy the cubicle next to yours or some dusty base-ment halfway around the globe.

So interconnectedness vastly enhances the usefulness and produc-tivity of a computer but at the price of also making it more vulnerable to attack. The situation is in some senses analogous to communicable diseases: People derive many benefits from interacting in social groups, but at the cost of perhaps catching a cold (or worse) that could have been entirely avoided by becoming a hermit. From an organiza-tional perspective, attacks on computers and the information they contain can come from two main places: from outside the organiza-tion and from inside. Although the distinction between inside and outside is becoming less meaningful because of trends in the forma-tion of business partnerships—including outsourcing—we can use it to broadly classify the information security threats that affect most organizations. On the outside are individuals or institutions that have strictly limited privileges or no intentionally granted access to the organization's information resources. On the inside are employees and others, such as contractors and temps, who are intentionally given privileged access to some parts of the organization's network and data. Not surprisingly, one of the strategies that outsiders may use to attack the organization involves co-opting an insider's more privileged position—either with or without the insider's knowledge and consent—in order to effect a more powerful attack.

With outsiders, insiders, and outsiders who use insiders, the net result is that there are three big sets of information security issues that organizations must master. First, the organization's networks, computers, and data must be protected against a variety of automated and manual attacks that come in from the outside, primarily through the Internet. Second, the organization must guide and regulate employee behaviors that might lead to an enhanced possibility of attacks from the outside. Finally, organizations must protect their information assets from unintentional mistakes or intentional malfeasance of employees working on the inside. We briefly discuss each of these three issues in turn. A more detailed discussion of security technologies and the threats against which they protect is presented in Chapter 3.

Outside Attacks

Connect any computer to the Internet and it immediately becomes the target of a barrage of attacks. These attacks come from a menagerie of automated tools that hackers around the world have activated in order to scan for vulnerable computers. Vulnerabilities in computers come primarily from software. Writing software is a difficult, complicated, and rapidly evolving craft. Only the very simplest and smallest pieces of software can ever be said to be free of defects or what software engineers call "bugs." Application programs, operating systems, drivers, and all the other varieties of software resident on modern computers are usually so complex that they inevitably contain many, many bugs. Most of these bugs are harmless and would require an extremely unlikely combination of circumstances to cause the user any problems. Other bugs can be triggered by the right combination of inputs; unfortunately a host of individuals around the globe is constantly looking for the right combination that will cause these bugs to emerge and provide an opening into your computer. These individuals are referred to by many names—virus writers, script kiddies, crackers, and so forth—but we will refer to them by the most commonly used term for any persons who attempt to conduct an unauthorized attack on a computer: hackers.

The most common type of bug that hackers try to take advantage of is called a buffer overflow exploit. Imagine a one-liter bottle sitting on top of your computer. Holding your funnel firmly, pour water into the bottle; everything is fine as long as you pour less than a liter. Pour more than a liter and the water overflows onto the computer, creating sparks, smoke, and other ruinous results. The metaphor holds in the design and operation of software: Software engineers do their best to make each bottle as large as possible or to prevent an overflow by other means. But inevitably some bottles are left unprotected. These bottles—which in reality contain pieces of information or records of data instead of water—are called "buffers" in software parlance, and when these buffers overflow, the resulting chaos can provide the opportunity for hackers to take control of the program that is using the buffer. Under the right circumstances, taking control of that program may possibly give the hacker nearly complete remote control over the computer.

Once these vulnerabilities in your computer's software have been identified, a worldwide assembly of curious hobbyists and hardened professional miscreants begins to figure out how to take advantage of them. Hackers who possess strong software engineering talents proceed to write a tool—for example, their own software application that uses the Internet to try to locate computers that have a particular vulnerability. Then, to prove their own prowess, they hand the tool over to an army of less talented hackers—sometimes called script kiddies—who proceed to run the tool day in and day out from a hundred or a thousand different networks all over the world. The net result is that the Internet is bristling with hostile information packages that rattle every network address and location at random until they get a response that indicates the presence of vulnerability. If that vulnerability is on your computer, a hacker somewhere in the world may be alerted that you are an available victim.

These exploits, while potentially devastating to their victims, generally pale in comparison to the effect of viruses and worms. The popular press is full of reports about viruses and worms, and it is interesting to note that some of the same dynamics are at work here as with other efforts to exploit your computer's vulnerabilities; it is only the method of delivery that differs. In the case of a mass-mailing worm—the most common type, and often erroneously referred to as a virus in press reports—the exploit is passed from computer to computer by means of an attachment to an e-mail message. Otherwise, however, a lot of the details of how the worm came into being are quite similar. The core mechanism of the worm itself was probably devised by a hacker with expert software engineering skills. That hacker may have written a special worm-generating program that could be used by script kiddies to easily create a multitude of variations on the basic worm. The script kiddies in turn do the work of setting the worm in motion by e-mailing it from bogus accounts all around the world. When activated on a victim's computer, the worm exploits weaknesses in the operating system or in application programs in order to wreak havoc. In the most benign case, the havoc may simply involve the consumption of large amounts of network bandwidth as the worm propagates itself by sending hundreds or thousands of copies by e-mail or other means to additional potential victims. In more dangerous cases, the worm may leave traces of itself on the victim's computer in the form of a spy program that collects sensitive information from the victim's computer, such as passwords and credit card numbers. In the worst case, the worm may delete all of the victim's files or seriously damage the victim's computer in some other way. Some worms do all of these things. The latest not-very-amusing variation on these attacks involves making the malicious software encrypt a computer user's files and leaving the user a ransom note: Pay the hacker this amount of money and you will receive the electronic key that will let you decrypt your files and make them usable again.

Beyond viruses and worms, the latest threat to home and corporate computer systems comes from a phenomenon commonly referred to as spyware but also described as adware, scumware, and a variety of other labels. Generally speaking the purpose of spyware is for an unauthorized outside party to learn what an individual does with his or her computer. In the simplest—and possibly most benign—case, a Web site places a so-called cookie on an individual's computer. A cookie is a small, customized information package that Web sites can use legitimately—for example, to remember how far along an e-commerce customer is with a purchase. The use of cookies as a form of spyware is analogous to having a salesperson follow you around in the store to see what you are interested in buying: annoying, somewhat invasive, but usually not a terribly serious threat. A more severe form of spyware involves the installation and running of an actual program that records Web site visitations or other computer activities and relays this information to an unauthorized outside party without the computer user's permission or knowledge. In the worst case, these more active types of spyware can allow highly sensitive information to leak out of an organization.

Outside Attacks That Use Insiders

Another method of gaining access to organizations' information and technology involves duping employees into providing key pieces of information that can subsequently be used in the commission of a fraud or other crime. Like the more impersonal forms of hacking, this process of duping employees—sometimes called "social engineering"—can be both highly productive and highly damaging. Whole books have been written on the topic of social engineering in an information systems context, most notably by reformed hacker Kevin Mitnick (*The Art of Deception*, 2002) and by corporate security consultant Ira Winkler (*Corporate Espionage*, 1997). Thus we will present only a brief introduction to the topic here.

Social engineering of this kind takes advantage of a basic human impulse toward helping other people, what psychologists and sociologists call prosocial behavior. As communal creatures, humans thrive on helping one another—although it may not always seem that way when commuting to work in your car. Most people want to help others, given the opportunity and the means, particularly when others are in distress. Hackers who devise social engineering gambits develop plausible cover stories in which they seek the assistance of "helpful" employees in the provision of important pieces of information. In the resulting fabricated scenarios, the hacker may pose as another employee from a branch office, as a government official, or as an influential business figure. Then, using the telephone or e-mail, or even occasionally in person, the hacker amasses the pieces of information needed to cause chaos—everything from company directories and organizational charts to usernames and passwords. In many cases, crafty hackers need not break any law, although the employees whom they exploit often break a variety of corporate policies in their efforts to help the wayward poseur.

In fact, poorly learned, poorly enforced, or outright contradictory corporate policies are often at the heart of the vulnerability exploited by the social engineer. Many employees labor under the powerful and oft-repeated corporate mantra of "friendly customer service" and this mantra can create situations in which employees are tacitly or explicitly encouraged to make exceptions or bend the rules in order to please someone of importance to the organization. The classic example is when a help desk attendant—who may not be paid very much and in any event is near the bottom of the corporate power hierarchy—gets a call from someone who claims to be a principal bigwig with a request to reveal a forgotten password. Under threat of job loss by the impostor caller, even the most conscientious and dedicated employee may unwittingly reveal sensitive information to an unauthorized stranger.

In the wake of a successful social engineering exploit, a hacker may possess essentially the same information and access as any highly placed insider. Because many large organizations now provide a variety of tools and methods for remote work, the hacker's insider knowledge may then put him or her in control of the most valuable organizational information assets without ever entering the organization's physical facilities. Exploiting this insider access to steal or destroy organizational information assets then becomes considerably easier and more powerful than the technical exploits that the typical hacker must employ. Using remote access also relieves the computer criminal of the need to be physically present at the victim's facility. In addition, individuals with relatively unsophisticated computer skills can use so-called proxy mechanisms to route their exploits through a chain of intermediary computer systems—some of which may be outside the country—making it extremely difficult to trace the perpetrator. To pour salt in the wound, many writers who have discussed and tested social engineering exploits report that these exploits are usually extremely inexpensive to execute. The cost of a few phone calls and a few hours of time can yield a large amount of insider information that is subsequently either valuable on its own or useful in a more conventional computer intrusion.

A new set of variations on the basic social engineering strategy often takes advantage of different, but equally powerful, human impulses: greed and fear. Criminals of various types broadcast large numbers of e-mails to recipients in a strategy called "phishing." The term signifies the intention of these messages to fish for useful information that the e-mail recipients might be tempted to provide. Tapping into the greed motivation, phishing scammers inform the e-mail recipients that they have won a lottery or become eligible for some other large cash award but that the only method of obtaining the award is to have it directly wired into a bank account. In contrast, the fear strategy usually involves suggesting that the e-mail recipient is facing some kind of important problem with an online account that can be rectified only by reentering key pieces of information onto a Web site. These Web sites are usually constructed to look like legitimate online financial or retailing institutions but are in reality fraudulent replications of their legitimate counterparts that collect information for the scammers. Like other social engineers, the scammers hope to use these strategies to successfully obtain useful information—generally financial or identity information—that can be used for subsequent fraud or extortion attempts. By broadcasting tens or hundreds of thousands of these phishing messages, the scammers are generally thought to succeed in a sufficient number of cases to make the effort worth the risk. In fact, the risks for these criminals are generally quite low because many of them operate in countries with lax laws or ineffective law enforcement.

Although most phishing scams are aimed at the general public rather than employees of a specific organization, it is still likely that employees occasionally get caught in the net—particularly if those employees work with a large variety of online interfaces or accounts. Furthermore, if it is not happening already, it is likely that savvy criminals will soon recognize the value of targeted phishing attacks that attempt to exploit the employees of a particular organization. As with the general public, a successful phishing scam requires only a small set of gullible respondents—even just one employee entering organizational credentials or account information into a bogus Web site could cause a major failure of information protection.

Insider Mistakes and Attacks

So far we have discussed malevolent outside agents who, for one reason and another, want to gain access to an organization's most sensitive information and information technology. In some instances of damage to information resources, however, no outside agent is involved. Although many refer to this situation as the insider threat, our research has suggested that more frequent, though usually less consequential, damage may come from innocent mistakes rather than intentional malfeasance.

In our earlier discussion we mentioned the presence of many defects or bugs in most applications and operating systems. Just as software is usually not good at protecting itself against malicious exploits, it is usually equally unforgiving at fail-safe operation in the face of user mistakes. In one organization where we conducted research, a hapless employee mistakenly deleted some content of a minicomputer that contained important financial information Unfortunately the organization was also in transition between a previous—and somewhat incompetent—information technology specialist and a new one who had not had the time or opportunity to

---

The National White Collar Crime Center

The National White Collar Crime Center (www.nw3c.org) is a federally funded nonprofit corporation that was created to coordinate and assist the efforts of a wide range of law enforcement agencies in their efforts to detect and control white collar crime. One of the activities conducted by the center is the development and publication of various reports on the incidence and nature of white collar crime. In its most recent report on employee theft (2002), the center reported that the cost of employee theft of monetary and tangible assets to U.S. businesses may be as much as $90 billion per year. When intellectual property theft is added to the tally, the annual price tag rises to $240 billion. The report cited a U.S. Chamber of Commerce study suggesting that as many as three-quarters of employees steal something from an employer at least once and half that number steal at least twice, although many of these thefts involve a ream of paper rather than a wad of bills. Employees' use of information technology facilitates more expensive crimes: The average employee embezzlement using information technology reportedly costs a firm more than 17 times as much as traditional misappropriations involving checks or cash. Embezzlements appear to cause at least one out of every three business failures that occur in the U.S. Even if one treats these statistics gingerly and retains one's faith in human nature, the motivations behind organizations' decisions to monitor their employees become more obvious, if not justified, by reports such as these from the National White Collar Crime Center.

recognize that regular backups of the minicomputer were not being made. As a result the files were permanently lost and had to be recreated from original materials. This example represents an extreme case in which the time and energy to reconstruct the lost information was substantial, but most users can probably think of one or more times when a lost file, bad command, unintentional deletion, or other mistake was simply annoying and time-consuming to repair. Probably only a small subset of such mistakes have any meaningful effect on information security—for instance when an employee mistakenly disables virus protection on a computer—but such mistakes can have important ripple effects on the overall information security of the organization.

Of course we do not intend to downplay the importance or potential peril of true insider attacks. Newspapers are rife with reports of employees who embezzle company funds or conduct insider frauds, and some of these crimes are committed through the abuse of information systems privileges. A team of researchers from the U.S. Secret Service and Carnegie-Mellon University has developed an analytical report on 49 of the best known and most expensive insider cases that occurred between 1996 and 2002 (Keeney et al., 2005). Although most organizations suffer damages in the range of $500 to $20,000, this report also showed that some organizations had remediation costs in the millions of dollars. Although the motivations for such acts vary—greed and anger toward the organization are two of the most common motivations—the common thread that runs through them is that the extensive knowledge and access that employees have by virtue of being "insiders" gives them unparalleled access to the organization's information resources. According to some industry surveys (e.g., Ernst & Young, 2002), these insider information security attacks are the most extensive and damaging to organizations as a direct result of the breadth of access that the employee perpetrators possess. Of equal importance, these attacks are the most difficult ones to protect against because employees must be granted access to the organization's information resources in order to get their jobs done. The balancing act between employee access and protection against mistakes and attacks originating inside the organization is the topic of the next section.

Employees' Involvement in Information Security

In Appendix C you will find a listing of close to 100 specific employee behaviors cited by information technology professionals as potentially influencing information security for better or worse. Although this list of behaviors varies across a wide spectrum of situations and security issues, the foregoing discussion suggested that all of these behaviors may fit into three broad areas in which employees in contemporary organizations must play an important role in the effective provision of information security: 1) through assistance in maintaining protections against outside attacks; 2) through resistance to social engineering attacks; and 3) through virtuous treatment of the organization's information resources. Employees are in a critical position to play these roles because they comprise the bulk of the end-user community within the organization. As such, employees make the greatest and most frequent use of information technology to accomplish the work of the organization. Employees collectively have access to most of the organization's information technology files and databases. Employees as a group comprise the most frequent users of information services, such as Web applications. Employees also have control to a greater or lesser extent of the settings and configurations of the information technology devices they use.

Note that we use the term "employee" broadly to include frontline workers as well as supervisory staff and first-line management. Supervisors and managers who do not rank in the highest echelons of an organization often have similar information technology needs and preferences to those of lower ranking employees as well as similar limitations on their routine information technology privileges. Also note that we exclude from our discussion, at least for the moment, the technology uses and needs of information technology staff members, particularly those involved in information security. We discuss these individuals and their work in subsequent chapters.

Although employee roles and job responsibilities differ across the spectrum of job titles, departments, and business units, to one degree or another most employees require similar benefits from information technology. Their needs include safe storage for work in progress, access to shared data and information services of the organization, the use of communications tools such as e-mail, the use of application tools appropriate to their roles, and access to the Internet for research purposes and for accessing business data and processes not available on their intranets. Each of these areas of information technology usage has unique implications for information security, and in the section that follows we discuss each area in greater detail.

Security Implications of Employee Information Technology Usage

Storage for Work in Progress

Employees who use information technology usually work on a combination of shared information resources and personal work products. Examples of shared information include databases of products or part numbers, documentation of business processes, and customer files. In contrast to these shared resources, most employees also have their own files of archived work and work in progress. In medium- and large-size organizations, these files are usually stored on one or more local servers. The use of servers for file storage is preferable because it simplifies the administration and protection of that storage. For example, storing data on a server allows information technology personnel to perform regular back-ups of the data. From a business continuity perspective, this capability is critical because most people neglect to perform regular backups of the data that resides on the hard drives of their own machines. Despite the availability of server space for storing work in progress, many employees still store a subset of their files on the hard drive of their desktop machine. Likewise, employees who use laptops instead of desktops almost inevitably have some files stored on their hard drives because of the challenges of using network or modem connections to access the firm's local servers when on the road.

There are two major security implications related to the storage of work in progress. The first implication is suggested by the foregoing indication that even with access to local servers, some data will inevitably be stored on desktop or laptop hard drives. From a business continuity perspective this puts information at risk. The significance of this risk depends on the job role and work of the individual employee. Those who handle sensitive data or intellectual property put the company at greater risk than other employees when they store files on a desktop or laptop hard drive. The staff of the organization's information technology team often responds to the local storage of files by attempting to impose stricter controls over data storage and configuration. These controls include locking down the employee's computer so that local storage is wiped after each system reboot and so that the employee cannot tamper with the settings that make this possible. A related technique involves permitting remote access to the employee's computer when it is connected to the organization's network so that the contents of the system can be examined, reconfigured, or backed up as information technology staff members see fit.

The second security implication works in the opposite direction. Without the capability of storing files locally, or with that capability curtailed to one degree or another, employees will store *their own personal data* on the organization's servers. Such data can include relatively benign information, such as resumes, personal contacts, and household information. Unfortunately, however, such data can also contain files of grave concern to the organization: illegal materials such as unlicensed copies of copyrighted media (e.g., song or video files), pirated software, intellectual property of other organizations (e.g., customer lists an employee might have brought from a previous employer), or problematic content such as pornography, recipes for making explosive devices, or messages containing hate speech. Although it is relatively uncommon for employees to store such data on the organization's servers, a number of documented cases have occurred (see for example, Panko & Beh, 2002), and the presence of such files on the organization's equipment may open it up to legal liability. Public revelation of inappropriate content stored on an organization's servers may also have adverse effects on its industrial reputation, stock price, desirability as an employer, and standing in its community. Because the organization often owns the equipment that stores the data, it generally bears some responsibility for the contents of those data.

Access to Shared Data

An organization's capability to use its networks to provide employees with access to shared resources is arguably one of the most powerful benefits of computer networking. Through shared access to databases, common documents, business process status indicators, and other resources, employees can divide and coordinate their work in ways that make them more efficient. At the same time, control over shared resources provides one of the most vexing information security problems for information technology staff. The most valuable information an organization possesses for improving organizational productivity is often the most valuable for competitors, regulatory bodies, and industrial spies. Every time an additional employee obtains access to a shared resource, that resource becomes somewhat more vulnerable to theft or attack as a result. While the majority of employees working in organizations are essentially honest individuals who are unlikely to destroy or steal firm resources for their own benefit, the success of a single transgressor in copying a customer list, chemical synthesis process, or patent application for the benefit of a competitor can have devastating effects on an organization. Such events are usually quite unpredictable because they comprise a combination of unusual motivations (such as grudges) with serendipitous circumstances (such as an employment offer from a competitor).

The process of providing access to shared organizational resources and attempting to minimize the vulnerability of those resources is known as access control. Actually, one step prior to access control comes authentication, which is the process employees use to identify themselves to a computer system. This identification process usually involves a username and password, and the creation of secure passwords is itself a complex process with which many employees have difficulties (see, e.g., Sasse, Brostoff, & Weirich, 2001). We discuss authentication techniques in greater detail in Chapter 3. For now, keep in mind that authentication is a prerequisite step that then allows an information system to administer access control according to the rights assigned to a particular user.

Access control is a rapidly developing area in computer and information sciences, but the actual practice of access control in organizations is still more of an art than a science. In fact, most information technology teams are so busy that careful, thoughtful, and timely management of access control is a dream left unfulfilled in favor of more pressing concerns. Several problems can arise as a result. First, employees sometimes request escalation of their privileges in order to complete a task or project whose requirements exceed their usual needs. Afterward, it is probably not uncommon for information technology staff to forget to remove the extra privileges. Indeed, the social dynamic between the employee and the information technology staff is such that a privilege once granted is often difficult to take away. Removal of a granted privilege communicates the idea that the employee might not be trustworthy enough to handle the privilege responsibly, and this is a message that few people enjoy delivering to a co-worker. The employee's supervisor may reinforce this social pressure if the elevated privileges appear to bring increased productivity.

Second, when employees move within the company from one role to another, or when employees leave the firm, their profiles may or may not be updated to reflect the new role. In our research we have encountered organizations that lack any coordination or notification between the human resources and information technology departments. In such cases, information technology staff may be completely unaware when an employee's role has changed, even to the extent of not knowing that an employee has been fired. The tendency in the organization may be to take the path of least resistance: If removal of privileges is warranted by a change in role, it can be a difficult thing for an information technology staff member to accomplish if the employee wishes to retain the privilege.

Finally, the granularity of roles is often too coarse to implement subtle but important differences among employees who work in the same department or have similar job titles. For instance, a temporary worker, hired for a few peak months in an accounting department, may receive the same privileges as a longtime employee in the same department despite the likely differences in organizational commitment and other characteristics of the two employees.

Thus, the basic security implication contained in employees' access to shared resources is that the more people with access to sensitive and valuable resources, the more those resources are at risk. Using access control as a method of helping to ensure the security of organizational information assets and reduce this risk inevitably leads to minor (if not major) mismatches between the needs of employees to access shared resources and the privileges they are actually granted. Usually the mismatch goes in the direction of giving the employee more resources than are strictly needed. As a result, the main purpose of the access control—to prevent adverse use or loss of an information resource—is often defeated by the messy reality of dealing with the pressing everyday productivity needs of employees.

Use of Communication Tools

One of the most powerful and productive uses of information technology is to enable more convenient, faster, or less expensive communication among employees across distances. Some researchers lump generic information technologies, such as computers, together with communications technologies, such as cell phones, under the term *information and communication technologies* (ICTs). The breadth of this term is appropriate given the blurring of the functional boundaries between devices and the convergence in services. A cell phone, for instance, can be a device to send e-mail and text messages while a computer can be used to make phone calls given the right equipment and service subscriptions. As a result, organizations are faced with a variety of challenges related to the fact that many different technologies can send information across organizational boundaries. In effect, ICTs make organizations porous with respect to information, and this porosity represents a risk insofar as employees may communicate inappropriate messages across the boundary.

At least two important issues arise with respect to employee communications across organizational boundaries. First, the organization has a strong interest in maintaining control over its intellectual property. Whenever plans, patents, formulas, engineering data, or research results are sent out of the confines of the organization, the possibility exists that those data will fall into the wrong hands. Second, organizations have liability for information that employees give to clients, customers, regulators, and the general public. Misleading or inappropriate information can provide the grounds for civil or criminal penalties. A particularly salient example comes from the securities industry, in which statements by traders and brokers about the value or characteristics of various financial instruments are scrutinized by the U.S. Securities and Exchange Commission. In addition, particularly when dealing with text communications—for which a permanent record often exists—there is always a possibility that employees may inadvertently enter the organization into a contract with another organization or individual. On some occasions courts have upheld that an employee's e-mail on a business matter can serve as a binding legal contract with significant financial obligations (e.g., *Reese Bros. Plastics Limited v. Hamon-Sobelco Australia Pty Limited*, 1988). On a related note, communications that are internal to the organization can also create a basis for liability. The clearest example of this is when employees circulate e-mail messages or other materials, such as pornography, that create a hostile work environment. An employee who feels threatened or discriminated against as a result of hostile work environment conditions can bring suit against the employer for civil penalties, restitution, back pay, and attorney's fees. Similar penalties can be imposed when e-mail or other internal communications records are used to document quid pro quo harassment (for example, when a supervisor solicits sexual favors from an employee in exchange for a promotion).

In summary, because communication tools facilitate human interactions from person to person or from person to group, a danger always exists that employees will say something that is damaging to the reputation of the company or that puts the company at legal risk. Likewise, because modern Internet-based communication tools also facilitate the transfer and broadcast of digital data, the danger exists that employees will send valuable or inappropriate files to other people inside or outside the organization. In effect, digital communication applications break down the old physical barriers that used to exist around many organizations and make the organization and its environment considerably more interconnected than it was in the pre-Internet era. While this degree of connectedness can be a boon for collaboration, cooperation, and productivity, it can also be a security nightmare if the wrong communications go to the wrong people at the wrong time.

Use of Application Tools

In addition to e-mail and other communications programs that employees use on their computers, many employees also use a variety of application tools. These tools include mundane office productivity applications such as word processors as well as more sophisticated tools used in specialized settings. Examples of specialized applications include the geographical information systems (GISs) used in mapping and surveying, computer aided design (CAD) tools used in research and development, computer aided manufacturing (CAM) tools used in production, and data visualization tools used in the financial industry and elsewhere. Although these tools do not generally create the same kind of security headaches as e-mail and other digital communications programs do, unique security risks do exist with applications and their data.

The primary risk that exists for any application pertains to the destruction of its associated data. The most powerful applications used in organizations often provide access to a common underlying database using a specialized client application. Such databases not only contain content added by employees as a part of their daily work but can also contain a long history of previous work and configuration data crucial to the normal productive use of the application. Using a GIS example, a group of employees may all work simultaneously on the same underlying geographic database. The database may comprise work in progress, data from recently completed work, and data representing years of prior effort on mapping, synthesis, and analysis. One trouble that can arise is that employees who are authorized to use the application may have access to and the ability to overwrite any and all of the data either inadvertently or on purpose. Another concern is that malicious employees with access to such a wide range of data will often possess the capability of copying and stealing that data.

Both of the aforementioned problems occur because of the difficulty in providing highly granular access control to the application's data. Unlike the situation in which shared access to network resources threatens data security, applications such as GIS do not always provide straightforward mechanisms for restricting an employee's access to a broad swath of the underlying data. With files on a network store or tables in a database, one can decree that this employee has access to this file, that employee has access to that table, and so on. With specialized design tools such as GIS, CAD, and CAM, the application and the data may be useless to an employee without the ability to make changes across a wide stripe of data that may reach from one end of the database to the other. The same situation can arise in a variety of cases in which a team of employees collaborates on a project that depends upon a large, interlinked information store.

In short, applications and their data are vulnerable because the employees who have access to them may damage them, either as a result of incompetence or malevolency. Although many organizations conduct regular backups as an essential part of their business continuity activities, using backups to restore damaged application data can take time and energy that in turn means a loss in productivity. In addition, many application environments are not well defended against theft of application data, so individuals with malicious intent who gain access to the application data may have an easy time removing that data from the organization for use by competitors and others.

Unauthorized Equipment on the Organization's Network

For employees who are fortunate enough to work for a company with the necessary resources, it is standard practice for the organization to provide a desktop or laptop computer for shared or exclusive use. A number of firms also provide personal digital assistants (PDAs), wireless e-mail devices, cell phones with messaging and Internet capabilities, tablet computers, and a variety of other devices that may connect with the organization's network. Beyond personal devices, the organization also typically provides the network infrastructure that makes computers so useful—wired networks, wireless networks, servers containing various data and services, and an assorted variety of other data appliances (e.g., switches, routers) that make the whole bundle work.

Unfortunately for the mental health of information technology professionals, however, the same forces that have made corporate computing effective and affordable have also put a wide variety of inexpensive consumer electronics in the hands of many employees. Whether or not the organization supports their use, many employees come to work with their own personal laptops, PDAs, and smartphones. In some cases they may seek authorization to connect these devices to the organization's network, while in other cases they may try a do-it-yourself approach. Depending upon the sophistication and available tools of the organization's information technology professionals, it may take hours, days, or weeks to notice that a do-it-yourselfer has plugged in an unauthorized device. Also in the do-it-yourself vein, some employees may bring a consumer-grade wireless access point to work, or even a Web server, and try to get these things connected with or without the help of the information technology department. Quite a few information technology professionals have been chagrined to learn that anyone can gain open access to the corporate network using a laptop computer in the parking lot. This can happen when some misguided employee sets up a "rogue" wireless access point and connects it to the network for the employee's "convenience," without realizing the opening it creates for unauthorized individuals to connect to the network.

Although setting up a rogue access point does not require a lot of expertise, the bit of intricacy involved in getting it working may make this gaffe relatively uncommon. What is probably much more common is the transfer of organizational information from protected internal storage areas onto the personal devices of employees. Many thousands of laptops are left in taxicabs and airport security lines every year, and a significant proportion of these are likely to contain important or sensitive files transferred from corporate servers. Every time an employee burns a CD to do some work at home or sends some files by e-mail attachment to be stored on a personal laptop, organizational data are leaving the relatively protected confines of the firm and migrating to an uncontrolled environment. The other direction hurts as well: An employee may spend significant time creating some useful work product on a personal machine, only to lose the data because it was never backed up or transferred back into the organization. Well-trained, motivated, and security conscious employees may take special care to back up important files created on their own machines, to destroy files on their personal devices that are no longer in use, and to protect their personal possessions when traveling, but we suspect that there are many well-meaning employees who lack the training, the impetus, or the conscientiousness to take the appropriate level of care.

Access to the Internet

If there is one capability that security experts will point to as the source of many of their woes, it is employees' access to the Internet. Employees with access to the organization's networked computers may use the Internet for a variety of legitimate purposes, personal uses, and a big grey area in between, but all of these uses have in common the potential to make the organization's networks and computers vulnerable to attacks. Employees cause difficulties for their organizations by using the Internet in a variety of adverse ways. At the most basic level, recreational or non-work use of the Internet clogs the organization's network and slows the flow of legitimate work-related traffic. As previously discussed, when employees use the Net to download copyrighted materials such as music, movies, or software, it can open up the organization to liability. Likewise, when employees use the Web to download offensive materials such as pornography or hate speech, they run the risk of creating a hostile work environment for other employees. But by far the worst threat comes from the introduction of malware—"malicious software"—onto the computers, servers, and other devices supported by the organization. Vulnerabilities in Web browsers and other tools that employees use to access the Internet sometimes provide an easy point of entry for malware. It is a sad and unfortunate fact that simply viewing certain "hacked" Web sites using an unpatched Web browser can introduce a Trojan horse or other nasty malware onto one's computer.

Another issue with Internet access arises when employees who are temporarily or permanently located outside the main organizational facility use the Internet as a way of connecting themselves to corporate resources. Many years ago, the normal way of accomplishing this was by using a modem (modulator-demodulator) to connect one's computer directly to a corporate mainframe or server over a public telephone line. Although this technique certainly offers opportunities for unauthorized use, one significant advantage is that the traditional public telephone line provided a single, continuous point-to-point connection between the remote computer (i.e., the user) and the host computer (i.e., the organization's server or mainframe). Although this setup is not perfectly private, it is pretty close. This type of connection has become less and less common, however, as the Internet has grown in popularity. Now, rather than using a slow modem, employees connect themselves to the Internet using services provided at hotels, airports, cafes, or in their own homes. Back in the organization's home facility, the information systems to which the employee wanted to connect are also attached to the Internet. As long as one knows where to find them (e.g., the IP address or URL), and what type of client application to use (e.g., a Web browser), one can gain access to the needed information and services. All in all this represents a great boon for those employees who travel a lot or need to conduct some of their work from home.

The major problem, though, is that the security-conscious information technology professional who provides such excellent support and protection within the four walls of the organization has very little control over the nature of the Internet connection that the employee uses at a remote site. Plugging into the network at any hotel means plugging into a telecommunications infrastructure that is completely unknown and that may be extremely insecure. Any important data that the employee sends or receives can often be intercepted at any of a dozen different points along the way back and forth to the organization's servers. What's more, an increasing number of remote Internet connections occur through wireless networks. When using these networks, every computer is a little radio station, madly transmitting and receiving its data through a set of radio signals that can be picked up by anyone in the area with another appropriately equipped device. Although there are measures available to protect data transmitted over wireless networks (discussed in Chapter 3), their proper use and deployment depend heavily on employees' having the training, knowledge, and habits to work safely in a daunting variety of complex circumstances.

Traffic Jams on the Corporate Network

Bandwidth is a term that refers to either the average or maximum rate of data transfer between pieces of computer equipment. Because bandwidth correlates with the cost of an Internet connection, even the largest companies have limitations on the bandwidth with which they connect to the Internet. Small companies may use a single low-speed connection through a cable modem or DSL line. In either case, it is relatively easy to fill up the available bandwidth if one or more employees are using the Internet for several demanding purposes. Although these purposes may include legitimate business activities, many information technology departments have investigated their organization's bandwidth usage and found that the major consumers of bandwidth come from non-business use of the Internet for the entertainment of employees. For example, many people like to listen to music; one way to use the Internet is to connect to streaming music sources. The streaming music sites send a continuous gush of packets containing audio data that can quickly overload a low-speed Internet connection. Digital video generally uses even more bandwidth than digital audio. Using streaming movie sites, employees may watch trailers or short films that completely clog the available bandwidth for a workgroup or organization.

One interesting aspect of the use of this streaming media is that its popularity within an organization can grow rapidly by word of mouth. When one employee happens to see another employee enjoying music, headline news, or other media on a computer, the relevant

URL is exchanged and yet another streaming-media user begins to consume bandwidth. Through this word-of-mouth process, the number of users can grow rapidly within an organization. As a result, the organization's bandwidth in its connection to the Internet can quickly be eaten up as the popularity of streaming media grows. Other users who are trying to complete legitimate work find a gradual or rapid degradation in their ability to connect to work-related Internet sites and services. The first indication that streaming media are beginning to affect an organization's Internet bandwidth often involves complaints offered to the information technology group that "our computers are too slow" from employees who are trying to get legitimate work done.

Copyrighted Materials

Just as most people love music or movies as streaming media, they also may wish to download files that can be stored permanently on their hard drives or transferred to CD-ROM. Many search engines will provide rapid access to MP3, MPEG, and other formats of entertainment files that individuals may enjoy listening to or viewing multiple times. The problem that arises is that many of these materials are copyrighted, and the methods that employees may use to download them do not provide for an appropriate method of obtaining an authorized license for the use of the materials. Although this difficulty is most closely associated with the use of peer-to-peer systems—some of the more famous of which are Napster, KaZaA, and Morpheus—it is simple enough to download illegal copyrighted materials without the use of peer-to-peer systems. Using policies to prohibit or technology to prevent the use of peer-to-peer systems does not necessarily deal with the problem of copyrighted materials.

Even in a work environment where individuals typically do not download entertainment materials, it is still frequently the case that they will download or use illegal CDs to install copyrighted software on their computers. Hundreds of sites on the Internet provide both downloads of software installers and the necessary keys or passwords to complete the installation. With a little research one can find copies of the most popular office productivity suites, operating systems, and other applications for download at no cost. Although there are relatively few cases in which a company has suffered serious financial consequences because employees have illegally used copyrighted software, it does happen and can be very costly for the firm. In addition, illegal software offers no technical support, may conflict with other software installed, and in the end may create more costs in maintenance than what the original software license would have cost had it been obtained legally. On a related note, software that is downloaded from a site with unknown origins is much more likely to contain malware (more on this shortly) that creates its own problems when installed on the employee's computer.

Content Related to Hostile Workplace Concerns

The U.S. has a variety of applicable laws designed to prevent discrimination against women, minorities, the disabled, and other protected groups. These laws have been interpreted to include prohibition against the creation of what is termed a hostile workplace. A hostile workplace is one in which an individual member of a protected class (e.g., a woman) is made to feel a threat or unreasonable discomfort as a result of treatment by other workers or by environmental conditions. Materials available on the Internet have made hostile workplace conditions extraordinarily easy for unthinking or malicious employees to create. The most common example that has appeared in the human resources literature revolves around the distribution of obscene or pornographic textual material in e-mail messages or attachments. When employees send around rude or off-color jokes and in particular when they aim those jokes at particular classes of people, they run the risk of creating a hostile work environment that may lead to a lawsuit against the organization and the employees involved. The same is true if employees download visual pornographic materials that are displayed on company equipment. The organization may be liable even if it has written policies against such activities, although documented evidence of well-enforced policies can help to mitigate this liability.

On a closely related note, the company's reputation may be soured in the public eye if employees are caught gambling, distributing hate speech, or engaging in any other activity that appears to run counter to the company's mission and values. Although some of these activities seem almost ridiculous—you might ask, "Who in their right mind would do that?"—it is unfortunately the case that across any large group of employees, a few will display poor judgment in a given situation. It is also unfortunately the case that just one well-publicized instance of illegal or unethical behavior on the part of an employee can have devastating consequences for an organization even if everyone else is behaving very well.

Malware

Malware comes in a dizzying variety of forms and can be introduced into organization through any number of "infection" mechanisms. Although the popular press generically refers to the viruses as the most prevalent form of malware, in fact the most common form is the worm. A worm is a stand-alone program that requires no host program or file in order to accomplish its dirty work. Another common type of malware that receives relatively little attention in the popular press is the Trojan horse and its close cousin the "backdoor." A Trojan horse is a program that masquerades as something useful, such as a screensaver, but contains within it something malicious, like a backdoor. A backdoor, when installed and operating, permits malicious outside agents to control the function of the computer remotely and generally without the knowledge of the user. As mentioned at the beginning of this chapter, one of the newest forms of malware is known as spyware (or sometimes scumware). The range of possible forms of malware is wide enough that entire books have been written about the topic (see Skoudis, 2003, for example), so we limit our discussion here to employees' involvement in the introduction of malware into the organization and largely ignore the various types of malware.

Although the most common method of introducing malware onto a computer or network is by opening a malicious e-mail attachment, an increasing number of other mechanisms are used by malware programmers to introduce their malicious code. Perhaps the most pernicious method is through the normal activities involved in Web browsing. Because of security problems in the most common brands of Web browsers, malware authors have found ways of exploiting normal Web browsing activities to introduce malicious software onto the computer that is running the browser. Another closely related mechanism involves the automatic or semiautomatic downloading of helper programs that work with the browser to view certain customized materials. These helper programs are known as ActiveX controls, flash viewers, real players, and more generically as plug-ins. Depending on the current security settings in one's browser program, these helper programs may download automatically or with a brief and inscrutable confirmation requested from the user. Unfortunately, there is no way for the user to verify that the operation of the helper program will be beneficial. In the worst case, such helper programs may contain malware that captures keystrokes or screenshots and sends them to an unknown agent, or they may open up a backdoor that allows a malicious agent to control the computer remotely. Programs that capture keystrokes and other information, commonly referred to as keyloggers, have become an increasingly popular way for hackers to obtain passwords, financial information, and other sensitive data from a victim's computer. Interestingly, keyloggers also have a legitimate use in law enforcement and are one of the forms of employee monitoring used in some organizations (described in greater detail in Chapter 3).

Finally, users may download and install malware onto their computers without knowledge that they are doing so. Fancy screensavers, specialized "search bars" for quick access to Web searching capability, little utility programs, templates for office documents, and other apparently beneficial files often contain various types of malware, including spyware, Trojan horses, keyloggers, and backdoors. When employees have the capability to download such materials and no technical protections exist against the installation of malware, their computers quickly become clogged with useless or deleterious programs.

Employees as Amateur Information Technology Staff

Although most that is written about information security tends to focus on larger organizations with the resources to employ dedicated information technology departments, it is worthwhile to keep in mind that small businesses are big employers: According to the U.S. Bureau of Labor Statistics, the majority of U.S. workers are actually employed in firms with fewer than 100 employees. In organizations this small, business owners may not find it economical or may not believe it necessary to have a dedicated information technology staff. Although these business owners may as a result contract with outside firms for information technology equipment and support, in many small firms those employees with a bit of technology knowledge—but without an information technology job title—take on the de facto role of information technology professional. These "information technology amateurs" often purchase computers, install software, run virus scans, lay network cables, set up wireless access points, do backups, and perform a number of other functions as a sideline to their primary role as office manager, accountant, Webmaster, or supervisor.

Professional information technology magazines and corporate information technology vendors pay little attention to these information technology amateurs—perhaps in part because the advertisers believe that small companies do not have much buying power to acquire professional-grade networking and security equipment. Yet information technology amateurs in these small companies may have substantial influence over the security of the organization's information and the productivity of its employees. When one considers the worldwide problem of Trojan horses and backdoors mentioned in the previous section, information technology amateurs in small firms may also have an important hidden role in the information security community. Hackers quickly recruit any unprotected computer systems at small businesses into their so-called botNets: networks of systems used in distributed denial of service attacks. For these reasons, the "regular" employees who also serve as information technology amateurs may have a disproportionately large influence on an organization's information security relative to other employees. An information technology amateur's training, knowledge, and skill (or lack thereof) may also influence the quality of service obtained from outsource providers that install and maintain the organization's computers and networks, because the amateur serves as a purchasing agent and liaison with the outside firm. Thus, in many small businesses, information technology amateurs provide the first line of defense in information protection. While it is better to have an information technology amateur than no information technology person at all, the amateur's skills and knowledge of information security are often quite limited.

Summary: Employees—Both a Vulnerability and a Resource

The widespread use of the Internet has enabled new forms of communication and collaboration and has sped up the pace of existing methods of work and communication. One major cost associated with these benefits has arisen from the security issues related to interconnectedness of modern computing devices. Most computers, laptops, PDAs, and cell phones would be useless without the capability of connecting to a network and communicating with other devices. All of this interconnecting and communicating has amplified both the number and the power of information security threats, and the unfortunate result is that many organizational resources must be devoted to the provision and maintenance of information security.

Employees are at once one of the primary sources of vulnerabilities and a major potential resource for helping the organization to resist information security threats. Employees are a source of vulnerability largely because they "hold the keys to the kingdom." As a group, employees have access to most or all of the organization's most valuable information assets. Their actions have a profound influence on the safety and protection of those assets, even in situations in which information technology professionals have put monumental efforts into imposing mechanical controls on what users are allowed to do with the company's computers and networks. The high degree of access that employees have makes them a target of social engineering attacks from outsiders. In relatively infrequent circumstances, employees may also "go bad" and misuse the organization's information resources for personal gain or revenge. More commonly, however, it seems likely that employees make innocent or careless mistakes that lead to the destruction or inadvertent exposure of important information assets.

This chapter has focused on understanding the roles that employees play in information security, both good and bad, and the mechanisms through which their actions may impact information security, as well as confidentiality and privacy of an organization's records. In the jargon of information security, we examined the "threat vectors" and "vulnerabilities" associated with employee behavior. In Chapter 3 we turn to protection and mitigation methods: the systems and techniques that information professionals use to help deal with some of these threats and vulnerabilities. In keeping with the theme of the book, we focus most of our attention on those technologies that impact employee rights and privacy—the tools and techniques, including monitoring software and surveillance cameras, that are used to protect information and other resources inside the organization.

CHAPTER 3

Information Security Technologies and Operations

The primary focus and emphasis in the technical areas of information security has historically been to develop solutions for three fundamental information security problems: how to store, transmit, and receive information in a secure manner; how to prevent modifications of information by unauthorized individuals; and how to keep information services available to those who are legitimately allowed to use them. These problems are often referred to as the "CIA" triad: confidentiality, integrity, and availability. To this basic triad, some information security professionals also add a fourth information security issue: non-repudiation. Non-repudiation can be thought of as a record of a transaction (e.g., a receipt from the purchase of a product) that prevents one or both of the parties involved from later saying that they did not conduct or participate in the transaction.

Security Technology Overview

A wide variety of security technologies has been developed to address the security needs of protecting the confidentiality, integrity, availability, and non-repudiation (CIA+NR) of information and information systems. Firewalls are hardware or software products that have been developed to protect the enterprise's perimeter by acting as a gatekeeper on what types of information are allowed to enter and leave the organization's network. The application of mathematics to the development of cryptography—a process for translating data to and from an unintelligible form—has formed the basis of many other types of information security products. For example, virtual private networks (VPNs), based on cryptography, have been developed to prevent eavesdropping while information travels across public networks. Other forms of cryptography, such as the "Secure Sockets

Layer" technology used to encrypt transmissions to and from Web browsers, serve the same purpose. Anti-virus and anti-spyware systems protect the organization's computer equipment against malicious software. Intrusion detection systems function like automated counterintelligence agents that find and locate security breaches that have gotten past other defenses such as the firewall. Password-generating devices, smart cards, and biometric authentication devices (such as fingerprint readers) have been developed to authenticate users based on what they know (password), what they have (a token), or who they are (biometrics). Internet monitoring and filtering software aims at protecting the enterprise against Internet and e-mail abuse. Although we will discuss all of these types of technology briefly, we will focus most closely on Internet monitoring and filtering software in keeping with our emphasis on those aspects of information security that have to do with employee monitoring and surveillance.

In general, most security technologies are concerned with one or two of the four areas of CIA+NR. By far, the greatest number of products on the security market are dedicated to the problem of confidentiality. Confidentiality is an important organizational problem because so much of the information that an organization possesses has high value for the operational success of the organization. Confidentiality of data both in transit and in storage is extremely important. We know from real-life experience that information is sometimes in transit—as when a telephone conversation is passing over telephone wires—and sometimes in storage—as when an audio or video recording of a conversation lies dormant on a cassette. Each of these scenarios presents a different challenge for maintaining confidentiality.

Taking storage first, most of the data that a typical organization possesses exist in paper and/or electronic form at a location within the physical confines of the organization's facilities. In such locations the information is relatively safe unless the building itself were to be burgled or burned down. As discussed in Chapter 2, however, as soon as an organization becomes connected to the Internet, some or many of its electronic data storage areas are potentially exposed to examination, copying, or destruction by individuals or software agents on the outside. To keep the inside information confidential against prying outsiders, devices called firewalls are placed between the Internet and the organization's internal network (often called an *intranet*). A firewall is like a guard at the gate: Certain incoming data are allowed to pass, while all others are rejected. Firewalls can also restrict the kinds of information or requests going in the other direction, that is, trying to leave the inside and go out onto the Internet. This latter capability is important because malicious software programs that do somehow successfully take up residence on one or more of an organization's internal computers sometimes try to smuggle information from the inside to the outside. Firewalls are offered by a wide variety of technology companies, and these companies tailor their products for organizations of various sizes and for networks of varying levels of speed and complexity. The guarding strategies used by firewalls range from a simplistic discarding of prohibited chunks of data all the way up to a complex set of algorithms that can learn what kinds of network traffic is normal and abnormal. All digital network traffic is transmitted in the form of "packets"—small chunks of information that often contain just a small part of a file, data record, or information request. One of the major challenges for developing the more sophisticated varieties of firewalls is knowing when, whether, and how to combine the information that pours into the organizations in these individual packets in order to determine whether the information poses some kind of a threat.

Confidentiality of information in transit from one location to another presents a different technological challenge. Organizations with a significant, ongoing need to transmit information between locations often use *leased lines* to do so. A leased line is a data transmission connection provided by a telecommunications company for the exclusive use of particular client organizations. Leased lines work similarly to a courier service: You buy the service from a trusted company that guarantees the safety of your packages in transit. Such services are expensive, however, and—because transmitting data over the Internet is so much cheaper in comparison—many companies prefer to send their data from place to place over the Internet. The problem with this approach is that data in transit over the Internet are handled by a dizzying array of organizations, none of which guarantee the confidentiality of those data (or their timely delivery, for that matter). The Internet works by breaking data into packets and does not guarantee that the packets will all take the same route to get to their destination. To overcome this lack of protection, organizations use the technique called *encryption* to make the data unreadable to unauthorized parties.

Encryption works by scrambling readable data into unreadable gobbledygook with the help of what is known as a key. A key is nothing more than a longish sort of password, but once the encryption technique has used the key to scramble the original message, it becomes very difficult or nearly impossible to find out what the original message was—unless you possess your own copy of the key. An example of encryption using a key such as "aq4327ca34DzFe89" would be to change the message "Hello, world" (technically known as "cleartext") into an encrypted version, such as "@d&(*$FDdfya87vafs" (technically known as "ciphertext"). Unless you know the key, it is generally extremely difficult and time consuming to figure out the "Hello, world" message based on the encrypted version.

Encryption makes possible two strategies of ensuring confidentiality, one simple and one more complex. The simple one is to use a software tool, such as "PGP" (Pretty Good Privacy), to encrypt every message or file individually. The advantage of this strategy is that you can send your encrypted message to any recipients you like, and as long as they can get a copy of your key, they can read your message at their leisure and without a lot of complicated software on their end. The more complex method is the VPN. Using a VPN, one can create a semi-permanent kind of "tunnel" that uses the Internet as the transmission medium. It is not a real physical tunnel, of course, but by encrypting every bit of information that passes from one end to the other, the VPN makes it extremely difficult for unauthorized individuals to see what is happening inside the "virtual" tunnel. One end of the tunnel can be at one physical location, such as a traveling worker's hotel room or a company's satellite office, while the other end of the tunnel is at a different location, such as the company's home office. Running a VPN requires compatible versions of specialized software running at both ends of the tunnel, so it is hardly worthwhile to open up the tunnel to send a single message. Instead, workers and companies use VPNs to create safe and temporary connections between a firm's internal information resources and some other computer connected to the Internet. For example, a worker could use a VPN in a hotel room to connect a laptop to a "home" network file storage area back at the office. The worker's files, messages, and transactions can go back and forth inside the tunnel, and the VPN takes care of all of the details of encrypting and unencrypting the data, with little if any intervention on the part of the worker.

Interestingly, encryption in its various forms can also help to ensure the integrity of the data—the "I" in the CIA triad. Recall that the goal of integrity is to make sure that nobody makes unauthorized changes to a set of data. Integrity is a particular matter of concern with financial transactions: If someone could make unauthorized modifications to the purchase price of your product as a buyer completed a transaction with you, the actual funds transferred could be changed to be 10 times or one 10th of the actual purchase price. Encryption solves this problem in two ways. First, by obscuring the message contents, it makes it nearly impossible to know what bits and pieces of information need to be modified in order to change $100 into $1,000 or $10. Second, because of the mathematical properties of encryption, changing even the smallest piece of encrypted data usually makes the remainder of the message unreadable by the recipient—and therefore easy to recognize as fraudulent. Additionally, programmers who create secure systems will usually use a cousin of encryption—called *hashing*—to make a unique fingerprint for every message. The receiver of the message recalculates the *hash value* based on the actual message received, and if this does not match the transmitted value that was originally calculated by the sender, the receiver knows there is a problem and can ask the sender to try sending the message again. Hash values themselves can be encrypted so that a snooper cannot easily learn or change the transmitted value.

Encryption has one additional capability of interest: non-repudiation. As with integrity, non-repudiation is an extremely important issue for financial transactions. If Acme Corporation orders 10,000 special widgets from your company's Web site and you go ahead and make them before you get paid, you want to have an ironclad record of the fact that Acme placed that order. To prevent Acme from backing out of the order at a later date, you need to have some token—something as good as the ink signature of Acme's CEO—that could have been provided only by Acme. One new technology that makes this possible is called *digital signatures,* and this technology often uses encryption to ensure that a non-repudiable record of the transaction has been made. Managing all of the peripheral information that needs to be kept around for digital signatures—often referred to as public keys and private keys—is a major challenge itself and often requires complex and expensive software systems.

Next, turning to the security problem of availability, we have a situation kind of analogous to confidentiality. Whereas confidentiality has the goal of ensuring that no one messes with your data, availability pertains to the problem of making sure no one messes with your services. By "services" we mean all of the electronic capabilities that a company provides to its employees, customers, trading partners, and the general public. This encompasses everything from the serving up of Web pages on demand to the accessibility of inquiries into an inventory control system. Availability is a function of many different factors, including such mundane ones as reliable electrical power and regular hardware maintenance, but when security people talk about availability, they are mainly concerned with what they call *denial of service attacks.* For political, financial, or entertainment purposes, a variety of individuals and organizations will attempt to interfere with the availability of a company's Web site and other services. For example, every time the U.S. gets involved in some imbroglio with a foreign country that has widespread Internet access, hackers from that country and from the U.S. get into strikes and counterstrikes using denial of service attacks—often against prominent U.S. Internet companies such as eBay or Amazon. Companies that exist more on the fringes than the mainstream, such as gambling services hosted in small countries with loose regulatory structures, are routinely threatened with denial of service attacks from organized crime groups to extort "protection" money.

These denial of service attacks use a variety of methods to disrupt a company's services, but they all have in common the goal of making the services unavailable to those who need and are authorized to use them. In order to have enough computing power to make denial of service attacks feasible, inventive hackers will often try to subvert a large number of computer systems of campus or home users in order to mobilize an army of "zombies" against the target of their attack (this is known as a distributed denial of service attack, or DDoS). The term *botNet* is sometimes applied to a large collection of such compromised systems; command of the botNet gives the "owner" significant power to inflict damage on Web sites and Internet-based services. The technologies that companies use against denial of service attacks include routers, which can try to verify whether the sender of a request is legitimate; firewalls, which detect and discard certain kinds of malevolent requests from the Internet; intrusion detection systems, which can help to alert system administrators to the occurrence of an attack that successfully enters a company's intranet; and so-called edge servers, which can make it difficult for an attacker to succeed by necessitating the simultaneous attack on many redundant service providers.

Of course, denial of service is not the only threat to the availability of a company's information resources. Another important threat known as malware, which we introduced in Chapter 2, includes familiar types of pests such as viruses and worms as well as more unusual beasts like Trojan horses and backdoors. Malware represents a threat to availability because once it infests a user's computer or one of the company's servers, it can cause, in the least harmful situation, a slowdown of legitimate functions as the malware reproduces itself and, at worst, the corruption or destruction of important information resources on the affected systems. Repairing problems created by malware can be a time-consuming task for the organization's information professionals, and while such repairs are occurring, the service provided by that computer—whether on someone's desk or in the server room—is unavailable to those who need it.

The primary technology used to combat malware is anti-virus protection, and although the name implies protection against only one type of pest, the anti-virus companies have been very successful at preventing infestation by a wide range of malware types. Responsible organizations have anti-virus protection on every single computer they own, as well as specialized anti-virus scanning capabilities attached to the major file transfer services they provide, such as e-mail. Larger firms generally manage the deployment of anti-virus products centrally, so they can ensure that all computers are kept up to date with signatures—the digital profiles that allow the anti-virus software to recognize malware—and that the computers regularly scan their own memories and disk drives looking for malware that evaded detection upon entry. Such systems can also alert administrators to attempts to shut down the virus protection, whether such attempts originate with the actions of a user or are caused by malware itself.

Most of the foregoing examples of security technologies are aimed at preventing problems that arrive from the outside: malevolent individuals and pieces of software that try to use a company's connection to the Internet as a way of creating havoc with the firm's data and electronic services. These security technologies have often achieved notable successes at supporting the goals of confidentiality, integrity, availability, and non-repudiation. The companies that provide them are constantly attempting to improve their products. Protection from outside threats is important and necessary, but from one perspective it can also be considered a relatively well-defined set of problems with clear boundaries around them. For example, in protecting against denial of service attacks, firewalls can detect patterns of incoming information that are simply wrong—not permissible, not within the specification of how things are supposed to work, or not useful for any legitimate purpose. The firewall's "decision" to disallow such traffic—as programmed by the organization's information professionals—is relatively straightforward. In contrast, the problems of confidentiality, integrity, availability, and non-repudiation *inside* the organization are quite a bit more complex because many people inside the organization have a legitimate right to access, modify, and even delete the company's information resources. As a result of this complexity, different strategies and different technologies are used for protection inside the organization, and these are the topic of the next section.

Protection Technologies for Use on the Inside

Just as certain types of information must be protected against exposure to the public, competitors, and other outsiders, some types of information require restricted access with respect to employees and contractors within the company. For example, human resources managers often keep salary information protected so that employees cannot easily learn what other employees are making or change their own salaries to boost their own paychecks. Thus the problems of confidentiality and integrity are highly relevant within organizations: Files, databases, and other stored data must be protected against unauthorized viewing, modification, or deletion by internal users. These concerns apply primarily to stored data because most organizations are not usually highly concerned about the confidentiality and integrity of data in transit *within* the organization. Because the organization usually owns and/or controls all of the transmission equipment and media that are used to move data around within the organization, it is much less likely that an unauthorized snooper will have the opportunity to tap into the wires or fibers that make up the organization's intranet.

The one exception to this rule is the increasingly popular wireless network, which by its nature often allows someone outside the organization's facility to "sniff" information in transit given the right equipment, software tools, and a parking space near the building. Although security measures to protect wireless networks have improved in recent years, vulnerabilities still exist in these systems that allow unauthorized system or data access. Of further concern, the technical administration of wireless networks is often quite complex; as a result it is not impossible for information technology personnel to make mistakes in setup or deployment that can lead to security vulnerabilities.

But setting aside the problem of wireless access within any organization, an important information security goal lies in protecting stored data. In order to restrict access to stored data to those employees authorized to obtain it, organizations begin with authentication technologies that attempt to positively verify the identity of a computer user—what is known in common terms as "logging on." The simplest and most common form of authentication is the username and password pair, and there is a surprisingly large amount of technology behind the scenes even for this simple measure. Software systems often dictate the form and length of password (and occasionally the username as well) in order to ensure that a password is "strong" and they store the password in an encrypted form that helps protect it against theft. A strong password is one that is difficult for an unauthorized person or program to guess. Generally speaking, passwords are strong if they are at least eight characters long, contain a variety of uppercase, lowercase, numeric, and punctuation characters, and are not words from the dictionary or proper names. The reason that such passwords are stronger relates to the difficulty of guessing an unknown password. Freely available programs that generate hundreds or thousands of password guesses per second can often guess a short password or a password based on a dictionary word within a matter of minutes. The problem with strong passwords, of course, is that they are more difficult for people to remember. If a user has many passwords to remember, and the passwords must all be different and must all be strong, it is a foregone conclusion that the user will write down one or more of these passwords, and that is an invitation to have the password stolen. As a result, many organizations have begun to move toward *single sign on* password systems that require only one username and password combination to gain access to many or all of the organization's information resources. Single sign on, in turn, creates its own set of problems.

One important problem with single sign on is that it makes that one username-password combination both very valuable and very vulnerable to theft or other compromise. Imagine if the newly hired chief accountant of a firm happened to leave password on a sticky note that was later thrown in the trash and obtained by a dumpster diver: All of the various accounting and finance programs and records of the company would be available to an attacker with the username-password pair. Because passwords are sometimes relatively easy to guess or steal, particularly when users write them down, companies with high security needs turn to *two factor* or *three factor* authentication systems. The "factors" they are referring to are things that the user must possess or characteristics they must have in order to complete the authentication process. With respect to things a user must possess, the typical object is some type of card or keychain device that contains extra information to be used during the authentication process. For example, one type of keychain device displays a new 8- or 10-digit number every minute. The numbers appear in an unpredictable sequence that is otherwise known only to the computer to which the user is trying to authenticate. The device also contains an accurate clock so that it can remain synchronized with that computer over a long period of time. The user types in the password and also types in the unique number displayed on the keychain device. If one of the two factors is compromised—if the password is stolen but the thief does not possess the device, or if the device is stolen but the thief does not know the password—security is still maintained because the device is useless without the password and vice versa.

The other factor used in authentication comes from an area of research called biometrics. Biometrics is a branch of biology concerned with measuring the distinguishing characteristics of humans and other organisms. The best-known human biometric characteristic is the fingerprint, which has of course been used for decades as an identification tool in law enforcement. Only recently, however, have biologists, computer scientists, and engineers put their heads together to create a device that can reliably change a scan of a human fingerprint into a unique digital identifier that can be used in an authentication process. Because the pattern of a fingerprint is so geometrically complex—not to mention the fact that it can be obscured by cuts, abrasions, dirt, oil, etc.—it is difficult to ensure that a legitimate user will always be positively identified and an unauthorized user always rejected. Two problems—false positives and false negatives—must often be traded off against each other because the system design choices that reduce one type of problem tend to exacerbate the other. If we design a system that almost never erroneously locks out a legitimate user, it is likely that the same system will make fairly common mistakes that allow access to unauthorized users. Similar challenges arise in other areas of biometrics, such as hand geometry, iris patterns, and retinal patterns. All of these technologies have made gradual progress, however, and lower cost and improved reliability have begun to make them practical for large-scale use. Some portable computing devices such as laptop computers are now configured with built-in biometric authentication devices—most commonly, fingerprint readers.

By using a username and password alone, or putting together a password with a physical token of some type and/or a biometric measurement, users can complete the first step in gaining authorized access to the organization's information resources. The next step, access control, happens in a way that is largely invisible to users. As discussed in Chapter 2, system administrators assign a certain set of rights to a particular user by working with the access control technologies present in the operating systems used by their company's computers. Almost all operating systems, such as Windows, Linux, and OS X, contain access control facilities, and although these vary in their particular capabilities and sophistication, they all share the job of mapping a particular username onto a set of privileges. Once a user has authenticated with a particular username (whether it actually belongs to the user or not), the privileges associated with that username become available to that user. Those privileges usually include access to a personal storage area, as well as shared storage areas for collaboration with other people in the company. The state of the art in access control is "role-based" access control (e.g., Sandhu et al., 1996). Using role-based access control, information technology staff members assign rights to employees based on their job roles in the organization. For example, individuals whose work lies in accounting and finance receive access privileges according to a profile that is common to the various individuals with similar roles. The byword in the creation of such profiles is to provide only the access that is needed and no more—what security experts call "the principle of least privilege." Ideally, only the most trusted employees with the most pressing need to know would have access to the organization's most sensitive and valuable resources. An operating system's access control facilities also sometimes contain a kind of logging function that records who first created and who last modified a particular data file. More sophisticated systems even keep a log of every modification made to a file and part of that log is a record of which username made the modification.

Computer Monitoring and Surveillance Systems

The problem with all access control systems, even when the principle of least privilege is religiously applied, is that somebody has to have access to each and every information resource in the firm. As long as just one person can get at that payroll file, those product plans, or the formula for the firm's soft drink, the information is at some risk. As a result, most security professionals consider it inappropriate to authenticate people into systems and then just let them run wild. Instead, due diligence appears to call for keeping track of what everybody is doing, at one level of detail or another. In terms of the primary focus of this book, here is where the fun begins: A whole host of technologies is available for tracking who did what, where, and when, everywhere within the organization's network. At the simplest level, most operating systems running on modern computers contain features that allow system administrators to keep track of every information request that comes and goes on their servers. This begins during the login process, where most systems keep track of failed logins and may even disable a user's account if the password is typed incorrectly more than a few times. Following authentication of a user, access control lists, journaling file systems, and security logs work together to ensure that each time a user retrieves, modifies, or deletes a file, a record is made of the fact. If a user tries to modify or delete a file and the access control list indicates that the user is not authorized to conduct that operation, this fact, too, can be logged. Security logs provide system administrators with the most fundamental kind of information about user behavior, and security-minded systems administrators periodically analyze their log data looking for breaches and violations of correct behavior by users.

A more sophisticated technology that some organizations use to protect the data in files is known as *versioning*, or *version control*. Version control provides a method of layering new modifications to the contents of a file on top of old ones. If a problem ever arises with the newer data, the changes can be "backed out" or "rolled back" to reveal the earlier versions of the work. Version control helps address the problem of an employee inadvertently or purposefully overwriting good older information with bogus new information. Version control can also provide a bit of a boost in tracking possible thefts of information. Most version control systems include a method of "checking out" certain data, the way one checks out a library book. Checking out data makes it unavailable for modification by others until the data and any included modifications are returned. The checkout system and any related tools for viewing data prior to modification can provide a trail of crumbs leading to anyone who has used the data for legitimate or illegitimate purposes. On a related note, version control can provide supervisors with a fairly effective method of tracking employee productivity. Logs of activity in the version control system can show who worked on what files, how long was spent working on them, and the extent of the changes made before the files were checked back in.

Using either the built-in access control facilities of an operating system or the more sophisticated capabilities of a version control system, there is usually a self-limiting aspect to intentional corruption or destruction of file contents, in part because these methods typically ensure that users cannot even "see" the presence of files for which they do not have permission. In other words, because users typically cannot even know of the existence of a file that is off-limits to them, their ability to do anything bad to it is restricted.

A more complex problem arises from shared resources such as databases. Because a database is a specific kind of structured file that may contain a mixture of information that is accessible to a particular user and information to which the user should not have access, additional facilities are needed to ensure database security. Like file systems, most large database systems have a facility, known as a subschema, analogous to an access control list, which provides a user with access to just a portion of the database's stored information. Large database systems also contain "auditing" capabilities that provide database administrators with a running record of who has done what to the database. When unauthorized viewing requests, unexpected modifications, or inappropriate deletions are detected, a system administrator can often track the problem back to a particular user account.

So far, then, we've seen that system administrators can track access to file systems and databases on a user-by-user basis. Next we turn to uses of the company's network facilities to gain access to the company's intranet and the Internet. The two major activities that workers conduct on networks and the Internet are communication and information access. In communication, the most common applications in use are e-mail and to an increasing extent instant messaging programs. Although small companies frequently rely on an external vendor for these capabilities, larger companies generally host e-mail, messaging, or both on their own computers. In this case hosting refers to the relay services and temporary storage functions that make it possible to send and receive mail. When a company hosts its own e-mail or messaging, it has substantial control over the flow of messages. At the most basic level, companies often keep a record of who sent messages to whom—sender and recipient addresses. At the next level, companies sometimes keep complete records of the contents of messages because these records are sometimes needed for legal or regulatory purposes. For instance, messages sent from securities analysts to their clients may provide an important record of a firm's compliance with relevant industry regulations and practices. Both the tracking of senders and recipients and the long-term archiving of message contents mean that records may exist for messages that employees did not intend for company representatives to see (for example, e-mail of a personal nature to a family member). Such situations are a driving force behind many firms' acceptable use policies: Many firms consider it important to make sure that employees are aware of message archiving practices so that they can at least make an informed judgment about whether they would want a particular message to be "discoverable" either by a manager or in the legal sense during a lawsuit against the organization. The famous corruption scandal of the Enron Corporation was marked by the public dissemination of a huge e-mail archive, with concomitant embarrassment of the many employees who communicated sensitive personal information to friends, family members, and each other.

Web Tracking and Filtering

Web tracking and filtering programs stand as a gateway between each employee's computer and the Internet at large. Many, although not all, organizations use a technique called network address translation (NAT), which makes it technically impossible to reach the Internet *directly* from the desktop because the employee's computer has what is termed a "private" network address. Those private network addresses must be translated—in effect, brokered into an address that can be used on the Internet at large—in order to provide the employee with Internet access. Another device, called a router, generally serves as an intermediary between the employee's machine and all outside network activities. While network address translation provides a measure of security in and of itself, it also provides the opportunity for examining and recording every single Web-based activity of a given user. The log files generated by this process are often voluminous, and few system administrators have the time to look at them entry by entry unless they are investigating a specific problem. Instead, some system administrators recruit the assistance of automated systems that compile reports of the places that employees have visited. One network security consultant we spoke with in the course of our research said that when he installs one of these tracking programs at a small- to medium-size company, he routinely finds that three-quarters or more of the company's Internet, bandwidth is taken up with nonbusiness uses of the Internet such as shopping, reading the news, downloading music, and viewing pornography.

When the bosses learn that employees have been using the company's Internet connection for a lot of nonbusiness purposes, the next move is often to begin restricting access. Technically this is a relatively small and straightforward step. It is often the case that the same system used to generate the reports about which Web sites employees have been visiting can also be engaged to place restrictions on their access. The two most common methods of restricting access are time based and site based. Time-based restrictions put an upper limit on the amount of time that an employee can spend on nonbusiness sites or may allow access to those sites only at specific hours of the day, for example during lunch hours. Site-based restrictions can work in one of two ways: by denying access to a specific list of Web sites or by permitting access only to a specific list. Both strategies can create some administrative headaches for the information technology people, in the former case because of ongoing requests to unblock a particular site and in the latter case because of the continuing need to add legitimate sites to the permitted sites list.

On balance, the "deny list" strategy is often more workable because the vendors who sell the Web-filtering software often maintain master lists of "bad" sites that include exhaustive inventories of pornography, gambling, gaming, chat, software download, hate speech, weapons/violence, substance abuse, and other undesirable sites. For a subscription fee, the Web-filtering firm will frequently and automatically update an organization's local copy of the list. This largely eliminates the need for the organization's system administrator to decide which sites to block. Some filtering vendors even maintain different lists for different types of clients, with more aggressive filtering used for, say, a school library, and less aggressive filtering for a business. Further, it is possible to combine the time-based and site-based strategies: One company in which we did research restricted access to nonbusiness sites at all times except between 12 P.M. and 12:30 P.M., when employees could browse any Web site they pleased except for pornography sites.

A more surreptitious strategy used at some firms involves no overt filtering—that is, nothing that is obvious to the user in the behavior of his or her browser—but instead creates tallies of visits to prohibited sites and raises a flag to a system administrator if a particular user goes over a preset limit. Using a system with this capability, information technology people might ignore the occasional hit on a pornography domain—after all, any user might make an errant click during a search process or might experience a pop-up ad from an undesirable source while viewing a legitimate site—but would alert the user's supervisor if evidence appeared that the person was spending a significant amount of time retrieving data from such a site. As with filtering, the sites that the organization considers undesirable are organized into a variety of categories, such as gambling or hate speech. This provides the information technology administrators with the capability to create customized reports for each user showing the number of hits on specific categories of sites over a particular period of time. Often these reports show their data interactively, with the capacity to drill down to finer and finer levels of details, such as the URLs of particular sites the offending user has visited, the amount of data downloaded from each site, and the period of time spent browsing them.

Keyloggers, Screen Capture Programs, and Application Usage Trackers

In the preceding sections we reviewed a variety of systems that companies may use to discover legitimate and prohibited patterns of use for particular activities such as e-mail and Web browsing. It is also possible to use a more general strategy to discover what is happening on a particular individual's computer at all times and regardless of the particular application or activity involved. Roughly three strategies exist: Recording or tracking the user's inputs; capturing the computer's outputs; and logging what programs are in use and when. These three such strategies can be used in combination or separately.

Programs that track user inputs are often referred to as *keyloggers*, mentioned briefly in Chapter 2. Keyloggers infiltrate parts of the computer's operating system related to capturing the information that users provide from the keyboard and with pointing devices such as mice or touch-pads. The keylogger "listens in" on the conversation between the input device (e.g., the keyboard) and the operating system and quietly records everything that happens. Some keyloggers have built-in screen capture technology that converts the image appearing on the screen into a graphics file and stores a new version of this file every few seconds (see the following section). Keyloggers are a favorite tool in law enforcement, industrial espionage, and criminal activity because they yield a rich stream of information such as usernames, passwords, and other sensitive information. Companies may use them for straightforward purposes of assessing productivity—appropriate, for example, in assessing the performance of data entry clerks—or in more contentious situations, such as when an employee is suspected of fraud or another crime. The most sophisticated keylogging programs on the market can be installed in such a manner as to be extremely difficult for the computer user to detect. In some cases only a computer expert armed with a set of forensic tools would be able to determine definitively that a keylogger was present or absent from a particular system. Because the user is generally unaware of the use of a keylogger on a system, the potential for abuse of this kind of technology—in essence a kind of unauthorized "wiretap"—is significant.

Screen capture programs take a different approach to finding out what users are doing on their computers. Because the contents of any computer screen are represented internally simply as a large collection of digital data, it is relatively simple to copy this information and store it on a hard disk or to transmit it over a network. Screen capture programs generally work on a timer: At intervals set by the person installing it, the screen capture program copies the entire contents of the computer's screen and stores it for later transmission or use. Given the wide range of information that usually appears on-screen in computers that are running contemporary graphical user interfaces, much can be learned over time about a user's activities. This technique yields different information from keylogging—for example, it would usually be impossible to learn passwords with screen capture alone—but nonetheless, the same groups tend to use the programs: law enforcement, corporate investigators, spies, and criminals. Screen capture provides one of the most reliable methods of assessing exactly what a user is doing over short periods of time. Because the screen shots generally must be individually examined by a human analyst, this method is relatively inefficient for recording user behavior over a long period of time. Likewise, the amount of data generated by screen capture tends to be large, and so storing it locally or transmitting it continuously over long periods can exert a substantial burden on computers and networks. As previously noted, it is quite common for screen capture programs and keyloggers to be integrated into the same surveillance application; the individual conducting the surveillance then has a choice of whether and when to use keylogging, screen capture, or both. Literally hundreds of vendors sell these surveillance programs, which vary in scalability and capabilities such that almost any organization, no matter how small, can easily afford to establish substantial surveillance over all of its computer-using employees.

To get a better picture of what users do over the long haul, *application usage tracking* systems keep comprehensive records of which software applications employees use, how long they work on these applications, the filenames and file types of the documents they create or modify, when documents are printed, and so forth. Depending upon the specifics of the organization's computing environment, the tracking may apply only to applications that are accessed from company servers—such as financial or database applications—or may apply to each and every program that a user runs both from the local hard drive and from the server. The latter type of application tracking typically requires installation of a program on the employee's computer, much as would be the case for keyloggers and screen capture programs.

Application trackers can provide the organization with comprehensive statistics on patterns of computer usage, a detailed information profile related to the productivity of a single individual or a work group, and information useful for tuning up the allocation of network and server bandwidth for particular purposes. While application tracking can be used for forensic purposes—for instance, to provide evidence of whether an employee may be committing a financial fraud—it is not as effective as other surveillance methods. Depending upon the level of detail provided by the application tracking system, it can be difficult to determine if an employee is using an application for a legitimate or an illegitimate purpose. As a final note, it has become more and more common for monitoring and surveillance systems to include a wide range of monitoring options in the same basic package—keylogging, screen capture, application usage, e-mail monitoring, Web tracking, and a variety of other, even more detailed data collection techniques. Many of these comprehensive monitoring and surveillance systems allow for centralized administration and give information technology staff members the capability of turning on or turning off the various features and data collection techniques as well as generating group- and individual-level reports of computer-related behavior.

Where the Surveillance Data Goes

In all cases—keyloggers, screen capture, application usage track-ers, and other data collection techniques—the surveillance results in a substantial stream of data that must be delivered by some method to the individual or institution that installed the surveillance mecha-nism. The most clandestine method of obtaining this data is to keep it stored temporarily on the target system until someone can manu-ally copy it to removable media. Obviously this requires physical access to the system under surveillance and cannot be overtly accomplished if the targeted user is to remain unaware of the sur-veillance. For organizations of any substantial size, this kind of clan-destine work would also be too costly to be practical except in unique cases of cooperating with law enforcement on the investigation of a fraud or other crime.

Thus, in most cases the surveillance data that are captured by these systems are packaged up and sent over the organization's intranet, or even over the Internet. (Likewise, the surveillance appli-cations themselves are often delivered to the user's computer and configured remotely over the organization's intranet.) Unlike the aforementioned clandestine methods, sending the monitoring and surveillance data over a network connection is fairly easily detectable by the intended target, even for those individuals who lack substantial computer expertise. Computer users can install a variety of free utilities to "sniff" the network traffic that is sent to and from their systems. Using one of these network sniffers on a system that is running monitoring and surveillance software quickly makes it obvious that records of computer activity are being broadcast. On a related note, these monitoring and surveillance systems can sometimes eat up a substantial amount of a computer's processing horsepower and network bandwidth, so computer users who detect the presence of monitoring and surveillance programs on their computers may be tempted on several counts to disable them if they can figure out how.

Surveillance Cameras, Smart Cards, and Proximity Systems

So far we have discussed employee monitoring and surveillance systems that focus only on the employee's use of a computer. The same economic forces that have made computers cheaper and more readily available have also worked their magic on other devices, however, so many new possibilities exist for automated monitoring and surveillance of employees' noncomputer behavior. Even the oldest and most widely used of these technologies—the surveillance camera—has been bestowed with some remarkable new capabilities. Years ago most surveillance cameras created an analog electrical signal representing the picture (and less typically the sound) captured in bank lobbies, convenience stores, and other places where theft or violent crime was likely to occur. To provide a reasonably economical solution to the surveillance problem, these analog signals were transmitted along cables and viewed by human security guards or recorded for later review on a low-speed video recorder. Only the government and some very large corporations could afford wireless transmission of video signals from remote locations or automated analysis of the video data.

By contrast, today many small companies can afford to deploy wireless security cameras at any location where a supply of electricity exists. These cameras broadcast their video signals in digital form over short or not-so-short ranges, and they can be picked up and viewed or stored on any ordinary computer with wireless networking capabilities. Some of these cameras have pan, tilt, and zoom capabilities, some are available in weatherproof packages, and some are even solar powered—all for less than the cost of a night in a good metropolitan hotel. In fact, hotels themselves are extensive users of surveillance camera technologies because of their need to ensure the safety of a large number of guests and extensive physical property without a large cadre of security guards. Moreover, new digital video processing capabilities have begun to enhance the effectiveness of surveillance cameras at providing useful data. Two in particular, motion tracking and biometric identification, have enhanced the capability of cameras to collect data on what people are doing. Motion tracking overcomes a basic limitation of cameras with pan, tilt, and zoom capability—the need for a human operator to move the camera to follow a target. Biometric identification addresses a parallel issue: In the past a human would have to review a surveillance tape or actually see someone on camera to identify a person; the latest software algorithms for facial and gait recognition have ever-improving capabilities for automatically identifying a target.

Organizations often see these camera surveillance techniques as a cost-effective way to simultaneously guard the physical security of employees and to prevent loss or theft of material goods. Camera surveillance has another application, however, that may become more widespread as concerns about "insider threats" continue to afflict organizations. Using inexpensive digital video technology, it is possible to provide surveillance of locations where computers or network connections are positioned. As we have already pointed out, it is possible to automatically analyze the digital video stream to detect the physical presence of a user or even that user's specific identity. Thus, surveillance cameras may soon have a new role as a form of biometric authentication. Unlike other forms of biometric authentication, such as fingerprint scanners, however, digital camera surveillance can continue throughout the user's whole computer session. This provides information technology personnel with a method of ensuring that no one other than an authorized user makes use of a particular set of authentication credentials and to ensure that the user logs off at the completion of a work period. Finally, digital camera surveillance also makes possible correlated analysis of certain activities such as sending a sensitive document to a network printer, which can then be tracked both as a set of network transactions and as physical activity. These capabilities are not likely to become common in smaller organizations, except at companies in which secrecy of intellectual property is an important concern. We note, however, that one company we visited had correlated camera and computer surveillance in a sensitive security monitoring facility.

In comparison with these sophisticated capabilities of digital camera surveillance, smart cards and proximity detection systems are sort of the dumber cousins. The term *smart card* refers to a family of technologies for putting information and processing power on credit card–size devices. The archaic magnetic stripe on the typical consumer credit card is increasingly being enhanced to hold a much larger amount of information and to provide onboard processing, such as cryptographic tasks. Proximity systems take this capability one step further by providing an information source that can be queried at a distance rather than having to be swiped through a reader. Anyone who has used a windshield-mounted toll-paying device in an automobile has used a proximity device. One particular proximity technology, the radio frequency identifier device, or RFID, has received considerable attention recently as major retailers have integrated the devices into logistics operations such as warehousing and delivery. A highly controversial area of current RFID application involves the insertion of such devices under the skin of pets and, in a few isolated cases, even people.

Smart cards of various types have been in use as a means of physical access control for a number of years. Only recently, however, have the card readers become easily and fully integrated into a company's overall network. Now it is routine for the card readers to record the identifier on each card as it is swiped and relay this information to a server on the company's intranet, where it is logged into a large database. In this way, the firm creates a semi-permanent record of who has passed through which doors at what time across the whole facility. Proximity devices make these same processes somewhat more pervasive because the proximity reader can be located anywhere and does not require an action by the employee—such as a swipe—in order for the system to record the presence of the device.

In addition to the many non-computer-related applications of smart cards and proximity devices, such as in hospitals, where the devices can assist in locating a doctor who is urgently needed, the devices can be used as part of the authentication and access control processes used to obtain admission to the company's information resources. For example, a smart card reader may be plugged into a computer such that, with appropriate programming, a set of user credentials can be used only if that user's smart card is also swiped at the workstation. The use of a proximity device instead of a smart card may make the process more convenient from the user's standpoint but also provides the capability of ongoing monitoring of the user's presence at or near the workstation.

Summary: Two Pitfalls of Employee Monitoring

Reflecting over this chapter, you may have a variety of reactions. One of them may be to think that we as authors have painted a paranoid picture with respect to the ways that technology is being used or possibly misused in the name of information security (or physical security). Although we acknowledge that it is easy to fall into this mindset, we believe there are many legitimate uses of technology in supporting an organization's mission and goals, as well as with respect to important aspects of diligence and care for employees. For example, the use of surveillance cameras to protect employees from crimes and the use of access control mechanisms to prevent unauthorized tampering with employees' work products clearly represent reasonable and appropriate applications, as does the use of electronic performance monitoring to ensure that employees are rewarded fairly for their efforts on the job.

By showing the capabilities and power of these technologies, however, we also highlight the potential for two pitfalls. The first, known in defense circles as mission creep, refers to the process of adapting a technology or capability to some new purpose for which it was not originally intended. Mission creep can gradually or abruptly turn a legitimate performance-monitoring method into a powerful and possibly gratuitous surveillance technique. The other pitfall pertains to the responsibilities that these technologies put on information technology staff members for meticulous care and control of monitoring and surveillance data. Mishandling and misuse of monitoring and surveillance data are inevitabilities unless information technology staff members receive the training, support, and supervision they are due when entrusted with these masses of sensitive data. Even the most diligent employee can make mistakes, and many widely publicized cases of corporate privacy breaches have made it evident that mistakes with sensitive data can be costly in both financial and human terms. Further, without careful and extensive checks and balances in the procedures that organizations use to process and protect sensitive data, it is always possible that malicious insiders will attempt to use their extensive access to such data for some inappropriate purpose.

It is critically important for all managers and staff members involved in the collection, processing, and storage of monitoring and surveillance data to have a clear and accurate understanding of what information privacy means to people in general, to employees in particular, and to the organization as a whole. Armed with such an understanding, managers and staff members will be able to make more intelligent and thoughtful decisions about monitoring and surveillance. While the intent of this chapter has been to highlight the available and developing technologies, the discussion of workplace privacy that follows is designed to put their usage into relevant human context.

CHAPTER 4

Employee Monitoring, Surveillance, and Privacy

As we have seen, one way in which networked information technology has affected the workplace is by enabling a variety of new ways that organizations can collect information about their employees. Although these data collection technologies certainly have benefits, they also collect and store a vast amount and variety of information about the behaviors of employees and the outcomes associated with those behaviors. Capturing and storing information about human behavior connects intimately with the concept of privacy. Privacy has become a prominent issue for the general public in the U.S. ever since the Internet began to connect all of us to each other, to corporations, to the government, and most important, to a new breed of cybercriminals (Agre, 1997; Harris and Associates & Westin, 1981; Kahin & Nesson, 1997, p. x; Newell, 1995). Widely publicized problems such as identity theft have sensitized many people to the fact that information about them is valuable and that when their personal information is misused, major trouble can ensue. In our previous research on privacy in organizations, we have found that these general concerns for privacy have translated into a greater awareness by employees about privacy issues in the workplace (Stanton, 2002; Stanton & Weiss, 2000, 2003).

Both employers and employees often wonder what degree of privacy is appropriate in the workplace, what kinds of privacy protection mechanisms are mandated, and what the effects of too little—or too much—privacy may be. These confusions have caused plenty of problems at work, with some employees suing their employers for breaches of privacy (*Dallas v. England*, 1993; *Shahar v. Bowers*, 1993; *Soroka v. Dayton-Hudson Corp.*, 1991; *Thorne v. El Segundo*, 1983). Not all employees immediately call their lawyers when they have a problem, but perceived violations of privacy can lead to more subtle problems, such as job dissatisfaction, turnover, and retaliation (Eddy,

Stone, & Stone, 1999; Sipior, Ward, & Rainone, 1998; Stanton & Weiss, 2000; Stone & Stone, 1990).

Organizational researchers began examining the privacy of workers in earnest during the 1960s and 1970s (e.g., Barrett, 1964; Kirchner, 1966; Schein, 1977). Unfortunately, the many different threads of organizational privacy research—research on work spaces, equipment design, information privacy, and protected communications—provide no common account of the affected individuals' feelings about privacy or their behavior when privacy is threatened. Nor does the legal landscape of privacy provide much in the way of signposts. Modern legal discussion of privacy traces back to the famous American jurors Samuel Warren and Louis Brandeis (1890), who expressed some major concerns about how the press was prying into the private lives of the wealthy and well known. Warren and Brandeis asserted that a right of privacy was implicit in the U.S. Constitution, which gave U.S. citizens the "right to be left alone." Other legal experts, however, have argued with this interpretation of privacy as a distinctive right, separate from other constitutional rights (e.g., Kalven, 1966; Prosser, 1984; Rehnquist, 1974; Thomson, 1975). When it comes to workers and the workplace, though, much of this arguing is moot because in the U.S., private-sector employees possess few legal protections for their personal information and effects in workplace settings (Pincus & Trotter, 1995). Ironically, as the next section will show, in some ways government employees have more protection than private sector employees do because they work for the government: Laws and constitutional protections that restrain the government's powers in relation to its citizens also restrain the government when it acts as an employer (Baird, Kadue, & Sulzer, 1995).

Laws Affecting Security and Privacy

Despite the lack of comprehensive privacy law in the U.S., or perhaps because of the lack, a complex assortment of laws does affect organizations' responsibilities for information protection. Very little of that legislation has a direct effect on employee surveillance and monitoring, however. In fact, a side effect of several recent pieces of legislation has been to create a need for more monitoring of employees' computer-related activities.

For example, the Sarbanes-Oxley Act was legislated by the U.S. government in 2002 in response to a number of accounting scandals that occurred in companies such as Enron, WorldCom, and the Arthur Andersen accounting firm. Sarbanes-Oxley, or more formally the Public Company Accounting Reform and Investor Protection Act of 2002, has had major impacts on the practices of information security in public corporations. One of the major requirements imposed by the act pertains to the development of "internal controls" meant to detect and prevent fraud. Although the act does not specify this, such controls may include both technical security measures and non-technical governance type controls. As a result, Sarbanes-Oxley has become a driving force behind the deployment of a variety of new measures that effectively constitute employee monitoring—for example, e-mail filtering and archiving. The act has probably spurred many public corporations to increase investments in monitoring technologies in order to establish compliance with the law's requirements for internal controls. Sarbanes-Oxley is not privacy legislation per se, however, and it does not speak to the rights of employees or organizations with respect to the deployment of monitoring. Rather, the act is focused on protecting the rights of shareholders and their desires to have organizations report accurate information on the financial status and health of the organizations in which they invest. In Appendix A we refer to several books that focus on compliance with the Sarbanes-Oxley Act as well as some of the other laws mentioned in this chapter.

In a similar vein, the Gramm-Leach-Bliley Financial Services Modernization Act of 1999 was passed not primarily as a privacy law, but rather in response to changing industry conditions in the financial services industries. Protections for the personal and financial information of customers of financial institutions were introduced almost as an afterthought and were in fact opposed by the financial services companies that had originally pressed for passage of the bill (see Hoofnagle & Honig, 2005). An unlikely coalition between Republican and Democratic legislators helped to facilitate the passage of the amendments containing the privacy provisions after one representative began to receive unwanted junk mail from a lingerie retailer: The representative's contact information had ended up on a marketing list after his bank sold his personal information to a third-party marketing firm.

As this story suggests, the privacy protections in the Gramm-Leach-Bliley Act pertain to the protection of consumer information possessed by financial institutions. The act affects only a limited range of firms: banks, insurance companies, securities traders, financial advisers, and the like. Among other things, the privacy provisions require the financial institution to notify customers of its privacy practices, to allow customers to opt out of sharing of data with non-affiliated firms, and to impose internal controls to ensure the protection of customer records. This latter obligation has an effect on financial institutions (both privately owned and publicly traded) similar to the effects of the Sarbanes-Oxley Act on public companies. In effect, the banks and other financial service providers have to design, deploy, and monitor administrative and technical controls that help to ensure customer privacy. As a result, although the law does not directly affect employees of financial institutions, an indirect effect that is likely to occur in a variety of financial services companies is the imposition of new or more extensive employee monitoring strategies to ensure that employees are not mishandling customer data.

Completing the triad of contemporary legislation that affects information protection is the Health Insurance Portability and Accountability Act (HIPAA) of 1996. As the name suggests, the legislation contains two separate areas of regulation, one pertaining to portability and one pertaining to accountability. The portability provisions improve workers' capabilities for maintaining continuous healthcare coverage when moving from one job to another. The accountability provisions—ironically, known as the administrative simplification measures—mobilize the healthcare industry's drive toward fully electronic healthcare records and simultaneously provide for the protection of the confidentiality, integrity, and availability of those records.

Unfortunately, rather than set the framework for such protections itself, the U.S. Congress passed the responsibility for rule making under the act to the U.S. Department of Health and Human Services. The necessity for extensive public and industry input into this rule making and the technical challenges of establishing a nationwide set of standards for electronic healthcare records caused a series of delays; almost a decade later, that law is still not fully in effect. In addition, the maze of rules that has emerged from this rule-making process has spurred healthcare organizations to examine and adopt a wide range of changes to their everyday work practices. For example, the government's definition of "protected healthcare information" is broad enough that it seems to cover verbal disclosures of patient information in addition to disclosures of electronic records. As a result, hospitals and other providers have made substantial changes to work rules that affect what staff members can say to one another on the job. Thus, as our results in Chapter 7 will show, the HIPAA act has had a more *direct* impact on the attitudes and everyday behaviors of workers in affected industries than either the Gramm-Leach-Bliley or the Sarbanes-Oxley acts. Like those two acts, however, the increased necessity to protect patient privacy has also led to indirect effects on employees, such as the increased use of employee monitoring to ascertain who is accessing patient records.

These three pieces of recent legislation receive the most coverage in the general news and the trade press; they have also spawned a new sub-industry of consulting firms that seek to assist affected organizations with the complicated range of measures needed to attain compliance. Yet as our review has shown, their influence on employee monitoring is indirect and usually manifests itself in the form of increased pressure on organizations to implement new or more extensive monitoring techniques. The few regulations that push in the opposite direction arise from a patchwork of constitutional, federal, and state protections. U.S. constitutional protections under the First, Fourth, Fifth, and 14th amendments are often extended to the government employment context and are interpreted as giving limited expectations of privacy for the personal information of governmental employees. Title III of the Omnibus Crime Control and Safe Streets Act of 1968, as amended by the Electronic Communication Privacy Act of 1986 (and again in 1994 to cover cordless telephones), prohibits illegal interception of any wire, electronic, or oral communications by any means. Under this act employers have occasionally lost court cases and had to pay fines as a result of overzealous attempts to monitor employee communications (e.g., *Deal v. Spears*, 1992; *Sanders v. Robert Bosch Corp.*, 1994). Exceptions are permitted, however, when consent has been granted for such interceptions or when business necessity dictates that private businesses intercept the business-related conversations of their employees. This consent rule probably serves as one of the driving legal forces behind the common organizational practice of having employees sign a statement upon hire acknowledging their acceptance of the monitoring techniques their organization uses.

The National Labor Relations Act of 1935 allows labor unions to set work conditions that may limit or prohibit certain kinds of monitoring of employees who are union members. Exempt employees, generally meaning anyone who is paid on a salary rather than hourly, cannot join unions and as a result never obtain protections under these union rules. Connecticut enacted a state law in 1998 that helps to ensure that employers provide written notice of most types of monitoring to employees, but the law does not restrict the kinds of monitoring that can occur. Delaware enacted a similar law in 2001. Alaska, Arkansas, California, Kansas, Massachusetts, and Minnesota have all considered bills with language similar to the Connecticut law's but at the time of this writing had not passed them.

Analyzing Privacy at Work

The foregoing discussion suggests the absence of a comprehensive set of laws governing monitoring and surveillance of private sector employees in the U.S. Although we are not lawyers—and you *should* ask an attorney to provide guidance about laws affecting your organization—our analysis suggests that most employers have broad discretion in the methods they can use to gather information about employees, particularly if they obtain consent beforehand. This discretion is not a blank check, because employees still have a well-founded expectation of privacy in some workplace settings, such as bathrooms and locker rooms, but in most other business settings, there are few legal constraints on what information employers can collect or the methods they can use to collect it. Because organizations usually own much of the equipment on which employees perform their work, this situation gives them a substantial degree of control over how, when, and where that equipment is used. This control is particularly notable with respect to information technology: Because employers own their information technology (or have effective ownership through leasing agreements), they also "own" the information that is stored, transmitted, and processed on that technology. Only enlightened self-interest—and virtuous business ethics (see, e.g., Clement, 1996; Kling, 1996b)—poses any constraints on the type and amount of monitoring and surveillance conducted by employers.

As a result of this wide discretion, employers fall victim to the temptation to set quite draconian policies pertaining to the collection and use of information about employees. As previously noted, however, the effect of such policies on the employees who are governed by them may create worse problems than the ones employers are trying to solve. Most people would agree that it would be a mistake to spend thousands of dollars on hiring and training professional employees only to have them leave as a result of the lack of autonomy that managers have inadvertently caused with restrictive monitoring policies. For this reason, understanding the thoughts and feelings of people who are affected by monitoring and surveillance policies in the workplace can be beneficial for predicting the likely effects of a new piece of technology or of new technology policies, even if no law prevents or tempers their deployment. Putting this a bit differently, the legal perspective informs as to what can be done to avoid going to court, but not how to avoid angering employees.

Figuring out how people think about privacy can thus help us understand what to expect in response to new monitoring and surveillance technologies or policies. Organizational leaders make decisions about the implementation, features, and day-to-day uses of these technologies. Those leaders also charge information technology professionals with deploying, maintaining, and generating reports from these monitoring technologies. Employees are affected by the new monitoring and surveillance and may react by altering their work behavior and attitudes toward their jobs and organizations. As always, individuals respond and act based upon their beliefs, thoughts, and values about personal and performance information. Our previous research has also documented the sensible idea that managers try to anticipate employees' reactions to monitoring policies and technology and that this anticipation shapes managers' choices (Stanton & Weiss, 2003). All of these considerations suggest that a social analysis of privacy in the workplace can help to illuminate what happens with monitoring and surveillance. This analysis will help us think about what types of information are appropriate for organizations to collect about employees, the proper tools and contexts for such data collection, and the ethical use of the information collected. Most importantly, although privacy is an important keyword in this discussion, our research suggests that we need to account for a broader range of concerns related to personal control, trust, and fairness.

To begin analyzing privacy in the workplace, one can turn to perspectives from social psychology, sociology, and anthropology. Alan Westin wrote an important book, entitled *Privacy and Freedom* (1967), which drew on each of these fields. Westin's definition of privacy provides a nice starting point for our discussion: "Privacy is the claim of individuals, groups, or institutions to determine for themselves when, how, and to what extent information about them is communicated to others" (Westin, 1967, p. 7). Although he articulated this definition well before the Internet was even a twinkle in any computer scientist's eye, its focus on information is highly apropos today. Westin also proposed four psychological functions of privacy—personal autonomy, emotional release, self-evaluation, and limited and protected communication—and these, too, seem relevant to our contemporary networked world. Westin's book was successful in generating new research on a variety of topics, such as the value and effects of solitude (Hammitt, 1982; Hammitt & Brown, 1984; Hammitt & Madden, 1989; Priest & Bugg, 1991) as well as on a matter of substantial relevance to today's cubicle dwellers: the effects of the physical office environment on job satisfaction (Duvall-Early & Benedict, 1992).

Westin's book also set the stage for public interest in the topic of privacy, and over the following decades, researchers readily picked up the yoke. Irwin Altman's 1975 book, *The Environment and Social Behavior*, as well as some of his later work (e.g., Altman, Vinsel, & Brown, 1981) led to a theory that addressed privacy in environmental contexts (Proshansky, Ittelson, & Rivlin, 1970; Proshansky & Altman, 1979). Altman's work continues to spawn studies in architecture (Somerville, 1997), environmental design (Kupritz, 1998), urban planning (Chang, 1997), communications research (LePoire, Burgoon, & Parrott, 1992; Lombard, 1995), privacy invasions in physical space (e.g., Cangelosi & Lemoine, 1988), and of social space (e.g., LePoire, Burgoon, & Parrott, 1992) and other fields. Beginning in the late '70s, organizational researchers also began tackling the topic of employee privacy in earnest (e.g., Schein, 1977). Fusilier and Hoyer (1980) examined privacy in personnel selection; Tolchinsky, et al. (1981), compared perceptions of privacy invasion for different personnel data-handling policies; Cangelosi and Lemoine (1988) examined privacy in office space; Duvall-Early and Benedict (1992) connected privacy and job satisfaction; and Woodman, et al. (1982), explored employee beliefs about stored personnel information. Dianna Stone (1986; Stone & Stone, 1987; Stone & Vine, 1989) and Eugene Stone (1980; Stone,

Guetal, Gardner, & McClure, 1983; Stone, Stone, & Hyatt, 1989) also researched privacy as it related to workplace drug testing programs.

Privacy as Control over Personal Information

Part of the appeal of Altman's approach to privacy was that he approached it as a process, rather than as an event or state of being. In this view privacy is a necessary and ongoing balancing act of, on the one hand, wanting to shelter and protect the self from others and, on the other hand, having the sociable instinct toward wanting to open up and share the self with others. In this view, privacy reflects a personal process of controlling the flow of information about the self: one's personal history, activities, state of mind, and communications. One of Altman's protégés, Carl Johnson (1974, 1976), first articulated this idea of privacy as personal control (also see Hoylman, 1975). Later, Patricia Newell's review (1995) showed that a majority of scholarly definitions of privacy included some type of control component.

For example, contemporary philosopher Julie Inness (1992) focuses on three relevant concepts: intimacy, control, and social access. Inness defined intimacy as the concern for social access into the highly personal aspects of the self—the home, the family, sexuality, one's own mental and physical health or infirmity, etc. The second part of Inness's definition (1992) pertains to control. Control is a concept with clear relevance to the workplace (see for example, Deci & Ryan, 1991; Greenberger & Strasser, 1986; Perlmuter & Monty, 1979). Research has shown that the maintenance of a psychological sense of control in the workplace (as well as in other aspects of life) is critically important for ensuring productivity and well-being (Greenberger, Strasser, Cummings, & Dunham, 1989; Martinko & Gardner, 1982; Stanton & Barnes-Farrell, 1996). Inness said that a loss of control over intimate aspects of the self is at the heart of privacy and its invasions. This part of her definition is important because it distinguishes between information freely given—for example, to a trusted co-worker—and information given under duress or involuntarily. Both situations can signify the release of intimate information, but the former does not entail a perceived loss of control because the trust in the co-worker washes away the anticipation of negative effects. By this reasoning, concerns for privacy arise when control over either decision making or information concerning intimate aspects of the self is threatened. It is important to underscore that from a psychological perspective it is *perceived* control and *perceived* threats to control that are important. These perceptions may or may not be accurate. In one of our studies, we examined the effects of electronic monitoring on performance and satisfaction (Stanton & Barnes-Farrell, 1996). We found that when workers had a switch that they could use to prevent monitoring of their work, they felt a stronger sense of control and performed the task better. These benefits occurred even when the switch *was not actually used*, signifying to us that the mere knowledge that one has power over one's own privacy is beneficial, even when that power is not used.

Implicit in this discussion of control is Inness's third concept, that of social access (1992). The term *access* is important because it encompasses several component concepts that have tripped up previous efforts to define privacy. Prior definitions of privacy have considered the flow of personal data (e.g., knowledge of a person's sexual orientation), as others have focused on sensory perception (e.g., a peeping tom who actually sees someone undressing), while still others have centered on personal decision making and regulation of personal conduct (e.g., legal barriers to the use of contraceptives). Each of these ideas is incomplete by itself because it captures just one facet of what people consider relevant to privacy. Social access encompasses all these facets: An external social agent (individual or institutional) gains, or tries to gain, admittance to the domain of the intimate and personal. When this admittance is unwanted, a breach of privacy has occurred. A common workplace example ties all this together: An organization develops a plan to place video cameras in employee break rooms to discourage a recent outbreak of merchandise theft. Word of the plan gets out to employees, and employees become upset about three issues. First, the video cameras, if installed, might obtain intimate information insofar as activities that occur in break rooms include personal functions like changing clothes. Second, the use of the video cameras would entail a loss of control over this domain because the range of choices for behaviors suitable in this space would be reduced. Finally, unwanted social access occurs because managers, who don't normally mix intimately with employees because of social barriers rooted in the power hierarchy, will now be able to circumvent those social barriers without employee consent as a result of their ability to view the camera images on demand.

The reasons that control is such an important issue arise from the human organism's most primitive and essential needs to master the environment (deCharms, 1968). Averill (1973) reviewed relationships between personal control and stress reactions to aversive events and found that rats, dogs, monkeys, and numerous other creatures experience stress when put into situations where they lack control. Perceptions of control also play a central role in motivation (Deci & Ryan, 1991). Enhancing perceptions of control improves learning and task performance whereas decreasing feelings of control has the opposite effect (e.g., Brigham, 1979; Perlmuter, Scharff, Karsh, & Monty, 1980; Seligman, 1975). Organizations sometimes cause motivation and performance problems by implementing policies and practices that reduce workers' sense of personal control (Greenberger, Strasser, Cummings, & Dunham, 1989; Martinko & Gardner, 1982). For example, Smith, et al. (1992), found that installing electronic monitoring systems caused lower feelings of control among telephone operators who were subject to monitoring. Their research also showed that electronically monitored employees had more job boredom, greater perceptions of fatigue, and more mental and physical health complaints, all of which are linked to lower performance. Other research has consistently found linkages between privacy and perceptions of control (Bowers, 1979; Hoylman, 1975; Iwata, 1980; Stone, Guetal, Gardner, & McClure, 1983). In short, if an organization implements monitoring and surveillance technologies that adversely influence its employees' sense of personal control, problems may arise with job satisfaction, job performance, job stress, and turnover.

It is important to note that enhancing feelings of personal control, or preventing the erosion of these feelings where they exist, may in fact require little effort or expense. Anyone who has ever fretted about the location of a parking space at work knows that a relatively minor issue—as expressed in physical terms such as the distance from car to office—can have enormous symbolic import. The opportunity to provide input on monitoring and surveillance systems, to have safe spaces that remain unmonitored, and to have the benefits and necessity of monitoring explained are all potentially good techniques for enhancing the sense of personal control. A consultative management style does more than provide additional brainstorming ideas—it also makes a strong statement to those who are consulted that their input matters and has been considered.

Privacy and Trust

In an earlier example, we described how a person would be more likely to reveal intimate information to another person if that other person was trusted. In that example, trust was based on the anticipation of whether harm would result from the revelation. Trusting a person is similar to saying that you expect the potential for harm to be low should you put something at stake with that person (Boon & Holmes, 1991; Lewicki, McAllister, & Bies, 1998). With respect to privacy, you trust another person with a piece of information about yourself if you feel confident that the person will avoid revealing that information under the wrong circumstances or to the wrong people.

Research on trust captures this idea of anticipated harm by examining the idea of social or economic exchanges between people (cf. Rousseau, Sitkin, Burt, & Camerer, 1998). Economists, for example, talk about trust as anticipated benefits or harms in a "principal-agent" relationship (Eisenhardt, 1989; Frey, 1993). The principal-agent perspective proposes that when a manager can directly track and control an employee's behavior, the employee acts in the manager's interests, but otherwise the manager must have trust in the employee in order for a productive relationship to exist. In this view, trust becomes a substitute for rigid contractual agreements that would otherwise be needed to govern the behavior of another party (Macaulay, 1963). Trust becomes, in effect, a "psychological contract" between two parties that each will avoid harming the other. Denise Rousseau's work on psychological contracts (Robinson & Rousseau, 1994; Rousseau, 1989) documents the idea that when an organization breaks a psychological contract with workers by causing some perceived harm, those workers' feelings of trust toward the organization drop precipitously. Psychological contracts have the interesting property of usually remaining unstated until they are broken. Workers we interviewed in our previous research said that they construed the use of surveillance and monitoring (e.g., use of video cameras) as a breach of the psychological contracts they felt they previously had with their employers (Stanton & Weiss, 2000); in these cases it was the change from the old methods of supervision to the new methods that had the impact, not the methods themselves. Thus, the concept of trust as a kind of psychological contract is useful for explaining workers' reactions to monitoring and surveillance: Employees are likely to object whenever the introduction of a new monitoring and surveillance technology obviously (to them) runs counter to their *usual expectation* of how they are treated by the organization. Precipitous changes in the organization's monitoring and surveillance policies and practices are the ones most likely to raise eyebrows and erode the trust that employees have in their organization.

In contrast to the contractual/economic perspective, other researchers have examined trust as a basic aspect of how people see each other in interpersonal relationships (Boon & Holmes, 1991; Lewicki, McAllister, & Bies, 1998; Rempel, Holmes, & Zanna, 1985). For example, using social psychological ideas originating with Fritz Heider (1944), Strickland (1958) found that surveillance increased *supervisors'* mistrust of monitored employees. That is, the mere fact that they were using surveillance on employees decreased supervisors' level of trust in employees even though the employees' behavior was no different from before. Whitener, Brodt, Korsgaard, and Werner (1998) provided a trust model oriented to understanding trust between managers and employees (also see Lewicki, McAllister, & Bies, 1998). This model emphasizes the idea that trust is a critical component in the smooth operation of the interpersonal relationships that make the workplace function efficiently. The ways that monitoring and surveillance allow managers to watch—and by extension possibly control—employees' behaviors make unsubtle statements about the status of trust between these groups. Secretive monitoring, reviewed invisibly in closed backrooms and acted upon without the general knowledge or participation of the community, is likely to engender the strongest feelings of mistrust among all of the parties involved.

In the earlier discussion, we saw that trust represented a kind of psychological contract between employees and organizations and that it was possible to break that contract by unexpectedly introducing new types of monitoring and fairness. In this latter analysis, we also see that trust is a basic part of the human relationship between people—in the workplace, between managers and employees. Surveillance technology can make the other party seem less trusting in the same way that a uniform can make someone appear more authoritative. By merging these two ideas, we can see that "behavioral transparency" is the issue that must remain carefully balanced. Monitoring and surveillance make employee behavior more transparent to managers, while providing protected and private space makes behavior less transparent. In any organization, there probably has to be an equilibrium point, where enough employee behavior is visible to provide managers with the information they need to manage the firm, but where employees also have some protected virtual or physical space for Westin's four functions—personal autonomy, emotional release, self-evaluation, and limited and protected communication. Trust provides the fulcrum for this balancing act: When managers have justifiable trust in employees, that protected space can be enlarged without creating unacceptable risk; a loss of trust in employees corresponds to a need to make behavior more visible (and thereby reduce risk) by using monitoring and surveillance. For their part, employees maintain their positive feelings of trust in the organization until that balancing point is moved, and particularly if it is moved without sufficient advance notification and appropriate justification.

Privacy and Fairness

The importance of justification arises from principles of justice and fairness that researchers have uncovered over recent decades, an area of inquiry that some people term *organizational justice*. Recent research on information privacy of human resource information systems has indicated that merging privacy concerns with ideas from organizational justice provides a useful strategy for constructing organizational privacy policies (Eddy, Stone, & Stone, 1999). Additionally, some of our earlier research (Stanton, 2000; Stanton & Weiss, 2000) revealed that justification, which has been examined within an organizational justice framework (Shapiro, Buttner, & Barry, 1994), may be a key factor in workers' beliefs about monitoring and surveillance.

Organizational justice is a set of ideas that arose from an earlier kind of tit-for-tat view of fairness and justice called "equity theory." The basic idea of equity theory was that all people are happy in a venture if they get something out of it in equal measure to what they put into it. Equity theory also contains the idea of social comparisons to other people. So if you make $100 for 10 hours' work, and I make $50 for five hours' work, we're both happy because the ratio of inputs to rewards is the same for both of us. Leventhal (1980) and others criticized equity theory as being too simplistic. Sometimes we don't get everything we want out of a situation, but we can still feel satisfied if we believe that the way the business was conducted was fair. In other words, it may cost more than you expected or hoped it would to fix your car, but as long as the additional amount was the result of a fair and appropriate valuation of necessary repairs, you can live with the higher price tag. In contrast, you would be justifiably angry if the mechanic used an arbitrary or inconsistent method for calculating what you owed for the repairs. So the contrast between equity theory—which only weighs the inputs and outputs—and organizational justice is that the latter also takes into account the *processes* by which the decisions were made about your repair bill, your salary increase, or your promotion. Research has consistently supported the power of organizational justice to help us understand when a situation will be seen as fair or unfair by employees (for example, Greenberg 1986a, 1986b, 1986c, 1987; Kanfer, Sawyer, Earley, & Lind, 1987; Landy, Barnes, & Murphy, 1978).

From a somewhat different perspective, John Thibaut and Laurens Walker (1975) approached organizational justice in the context of how disputes are resolved between one party and another party. In their work, they were able to explain what they learned using two principles: decision control and process control. Decision control, or "choice," predicts circumstances under which disputants turn over control of a decision to a third party, such as a judge or an arbitrator, and, while important in areas such as union relations, is relevant to our discussion only insofar as arbitration or judiciary procedures are used to deal with employee infractions detected by monitoring. Process control, or "voice," describes the degree to which disputants influence the processes of evidence collection and presentation: in essence, what voices can be heard during the process of resolving the dispute. Research has repeatedly demonstrated the importance of voice in determining people's beliefs about the fairness of procedures and outcomes. For example, Tyler and Caine (1981) and Tyler, Rasinski, and Spodick (1985) found that people saw their leaders as more effective when the leaders gave them an opportunity to voice their opinions and concerns, even if those opinions and concerns did not affect the final outcome of the situation. Cropanzano and Konovsky (1995) used similar ideas in their study of how organizations handle drug-testing results. They found, among other things, that employees were more satisfied with a drug-testing program when they had the opportunity to voice concerns about the program and have input into its procedures and operation. What these findings suggest is that the successful implementation of monitoring and surveillance technologies or policies may require giving employees the opportunity to voice their concerns and make suggestions about how the technologies and policies will operate.

Robert Bies and John Moag (1986) developed a somewhat different take on organizational justice. They realized that the interpersonal treatment that individuals receive in the context of decision making or allocation procedures influences fairness judgments. Bies (1985) provided empirical evidence for the importance of a decision maker's behavior in several dimensions: honesty, courtesy, and concern for the rights of those affected by the decision. Bies and Moag (1986) dubbed this area of inquiry interactional justice. The focus on the interactional aspects of fairness provided a fruitful basis for research. Studies by Bies (1987), Bies, Shapiro, and Cummings (1988), and Shapiro, Buttner, and Barry (1994) converged on the importance of providing an adequate justification— either in person or through written memos—for organizational processes and outcomes. In our research on electronic monitoring of employees, we found that employees found monitoring more acceptable if the organization had provided a meaningful rationale for monitoring (Perrault, Stanton, & Barnes-Farrell, 1998a, 1998b). Additionally, we have found that it is easier to make the case with employees for the necessity of collecting information about their job performance—as opposed to information about non-performance issues such as health status or financial standing. Interviews we conducted with employees in our previous research indicated that employees' need for justification of an organizational information-gathering policy depended most strongly on the perceived job relevance of the information (Stanton & Weiss, 2000). In more detail, workers judged whether a request seemed fair and appropriate based on whether they saw a direct connection to information that they believed the organization had a right to know or control. If a request failed this fairness test, then the worker experienced a much stronger need to have an organizational representative explain a suitable rationale.

The Zone of Acceptance

Drawing upon many studies on organizational justice such as those we have described here, psychology researcher G. Stoney Alder proposed what he called a "zone of acceptance" in which employees would not scrutinize the fairness of organizational monitoring practices (Alder, 1998; Alder & Tompkins, 1997; also see Zweig & Webster, 2002). In discussing the zone of acceptance, Alder made the important point that not every organizational practice, information request, or policy change triggers a lengthy deliberation in the mind of the employee on the topics of control, fairness, and trust. Most of us are far too busy to worry too much about apparently routine matters at work, and we give careful consideration to our privacy concerns only when we feel suddenly threatened by some novel and significant change. Routine information requests at work (e.g., for timesheets) fall within the zone of acceptance; these requests, too ordinary to arouse a feeling of threat, would not cause the careful evaluation of control, fairness, and trust implied by the foregoing discussion.

In our previous research on organizational information requests (Stanton, 2002), we discovered three pieces of evidence supporting Alder's ideas about the zone of acceptance. Employees reported to us that when they thought of a policy as "common practice" among most organizations, they did not carefully scrutinize the information request that the policy mandated. In effect, they had apparently learned from others or through previous employment experiences that some personal information was typically requested by organizations (e.g., age, marital status) and was therefore, by custom, not sensitive. Confirming this idea, another piece of evidence suggested that if employees had previous experience with an information request, they were less likely to find it problematic. Finally, if the request made by the organization was for information that was available elsewhere anyway—for example, from a resume, Web page, or the phone book—then the request was not seen as problematic. These ideas seem to accord with Alder's idea of a zone of acceptance. The implication for monitoring in the workplace is that abrupt, severe, and/or unusual changes to monitoring policies are the ones that are most likely to evoke careful consideration by employees on the status of their relationship with the organization.

Information Privacy in the Workplace: Three Factors and the Zone

The foregoing review examined the history and relevance of three factors that surround privacy concerns associated with monitoring and surveillance. The key mental state associated with privacy may be the sense of control over personal information or social access. For workers, loss of such personal control trades against the organization's needs to manage and control them. The right balance point depends upon the level of trust between workers and organizations: High trust facilitates relinquishing control, low trust inhibits it. In low trust situations, or when unexpected demands for access or information occur, careful justification of the organization's rationale is required. Of course trust works in both directions: Workers trust or distrust management and management trusts or distrusts workers. Fairness mechanisms, such as justifications for worker data collection, also influence trust, leading to interplay between trust and fairness. We have pulled all of these concepts together under an umbrella we call "information boundary management." We borrowed the term *boundary management* from communications researcher Sandra Petronio (1991), whose work in the area of privacy has successfully explained interpersonal privacy regulation in marital, family, and other interpersonal contexts.

In an echo of Irwin Altman's work, Petronio (1991) argued that all human relationships contain an intrinsic tension between sharing of oneself and maintaining one's autonomy from others. Petronio argued that this tension is intrinsic in all human relationships, including those in the workplace (Petronio & Chayer, 1988). Indeed, in our research we have found that employees view monitoring, surveillance, and other organizational means of personal data collection as ways in which they become "revealed" to the organization (Stanton, 2002; Stanton & Weiss, 2000). Having one's workplace activities electronically monitored provides a conduit through which a supervisor or manager can receive detailed information about one's productive or unproductive behavior. Likewise, working in an environment with video surveillance cameras makes one's conscious and unconscious behaviors while on company premises available for scrutiny. Finally, collection of personal data (e.g., lifestyle information for insurance purposes) also communicates intimate aspects of the self to others within the work environment. All of these methods of monitoring and surveillance constitute communicative activities in the workplace by which the self (the employee) becomes known to the other (supervisors, managers, or human resources professionals). Most importantly, employees feel that it is necessary and right for them to influence the deployment of these forms of monitoring and surveillance, or what we call "regulating information boundaries."

As we have already discussed, employees have well-documented needs for autonomy and control (cf. Deci & Ryan, 1991; Greenberger & Strasser, 1986; Spector, 1981). Most employees want to control their immediate work environment, their choice of tasks, their rate of working, and the impressions that other individuals have of them (particularly powerful others such as managers). Many research studies on the topic of impression management (Giacalone & Rosenfeld, 1991; Morrison & Bies, 1991) and socially desirable responding (Moorman & Podsakoff, 1992) attest that individuals have consistent and sometimes strong motivations to control how others see them. Electronic monitoring and surveillance generally reduce the control that employees have over what is seen and unseen. By using these technologies, managers take charge of the information boundaries and in doing so try to exert more control over the amount, nature, and circumstances of gathering information about employees.

But employees will not lightly give up such control if they have means at their disposal to resist surveillance or influence its deployment. If monitoring and surveillance are deployed in a manner that seems unfair to employees, or if managers have not established a sufficient climate of trust within the organization, it is possible that employees will find ways of subverting the technologies. In an adverse environment, where trust has broken down between management and employees, workers can be extremely creative about subverting monitoring and surveillance. When video monitoring is used, employees can use another spot to congregate; if e-mail is monitored, employees may use third-party e-mail services. If these direct methods fail, employees may resort to work slow-downs, absenteeism, sabotage, theft, and other subtle or not-so-subtle forms of resistance. We believe that perceived control, trust, and fairness are the keys to avoiding such unfortunate results.

Employees open their information boundaries—and are therefore amenable to revealing information through electronic monitoring and other organizational data collection methods—when they perceive reciprocity and trust in their relationship with the organization.

This trust can occur when there is a sense of interdependence between employee and employer, when the employee does not perceive an undesirable level of vulnerability to negative consequences of being monitored, and when the organization communicates clearly to employees the benefits—both individual and collective—that might be realized from judicious and legitimate use of monitoring and surveillance. One way that organizations can avoid triggering difficulties related to employees' perceived control, trust, and fairness is to keep policy and procedural changes within the zone of acceptance. As long as employees see the organization's monitoring techniques as customary and expected, and as long as these techniques are not subject to large, abrupt changes, employees are not likely to expend time and energy on vigilant and painstaking appraisals of trust and fairness.

These issues make up some of the subject matter of the next few chapters: We have interviewed and surveyed many managers, information technology professionals, and regular employees to find out their perspectives on information security and electronic monitoring of employees' computer-related behavior. While reading quotes from our interviews and when interpreting our survey results, keep watch for how respondents think about monitoring as revealed in what they say about each other, their organizations, and the technologies their organizations use. We expect that you will see personal control, trust, and fairness emerge implicitly and explicitly as underlying impulses that influence beliefs and actions about security, privacy, and monitoring in the workplace.

CHAPTER 5

Managerial Perspectives

Beginning in this chapter, we present and analyze the data we have collected on information security and workplace privacy over a four-year period. Our research program has primarily involved two kinds of work: field research in existing organizations, mainly in the form of one-on-one interviews, and surveys of large groups of employees and managers from various organizations all around the country. Using these techniques we have collected information from thousands of individuals working in hundreds of different organizations within several sectors: for profit, nonprofit, educational, and governmental. It should be noted that some sectors are not strongly represented in our data, specifically military and non-governmental organizations (commonly referred to as NGOs). Likewise, not all types of workers are well represented here: Almost all our respondents were white-collar workers with substantial access to information technology in the workplace. These limitations notwithstanding, we believe that the findings presented in this and the following two chapters repre-sent a broad cross section of the concerns of managers (Chapter 5), information technology professionals (Chapter 6), and workers (Chapter 7) in contemporary organizations.

In Chapters 5, 6, and 7, we make extensive use of verbatim quota-tions from individuals who participated in our studies. The resulting text is more raw and personal than what you have encountered in the book so far. We chose to present the material in this manner because we think it may help the reader more fully appreciate the attitudes and beliefs of those whose organizations and livelihoods are affected by successes and failures of information protection. We believe that the concerns, fears, and frustrations (as well as the occasional bouts of apathy and ignorance) of the individuals we surveyed resonate more strongly in this format than if their comments were simply predigested and summarized.

In this first of the three "data" chapters we, focus on the perspectives of managers—those individuals with leadership and decision-making responsibilities within their respective organizations. The interviewees included a wide variety of men and women at various levels in the formal hierarchies of their organizations. All of the respondents reported in this chapter were non-technical personnel; that is, they had no hands-on responsibility for information technology. Thus, while these individuals often had broad strategic goals in mind—for example, concerning employee or customer privacy—in general they were not personally responsible for the daily activities that would cast those goals into action. Thus, the material that we report here tends to highlight an arms-length relationship with information technology in the organization by reflecting employees' appreciation of the importance of information technology as well as a range of beliefs about maintaining control over the information necessary for their jobs. Note that in about half of the interviews, our research team obtained access to the respondents' organizations in order to study the organizations' adjustment to *new* software and/or computer systems that were about to be deployed or had been recently deployed. As a result, a number of the interviewers' queries, as reported here and in the next two chapters, begin with questions about a "new system."

We developed the interview questions used in these studies as part of four different funded research projects. An example interview protocol for managers appears in Appendix D; similar protocols were used with most managers. Two of these projects were funded by the National Science Foundation, one was funded by the research foundation of the Society for Industrial and Organizational Psychology, and one was funded by the CASE Center at Syracuse University with monies from the New York State Office of Science, Technology and Academic Research. In all instances we conducted our research in accordance with contemporary ethical standards for the treatment of human subjects and with the approval of Syracuse University's Institutional Review Board. These ethical standards require protecting the identities of the individuals and organizations involved in the research and ensuring that no individual suffers psychological risks greater than those encountered in everyday life as a result of participation. To ensure these protections, all of the interviewee responses have been edited as necessary to mask the identities of respondents and their organizations. The job titles of respondents and the specific industry or sector of their organizations have also been kept confidential wherever we deemed it would not affect interpretation of the response. In all cases we made a concerted effort to preserve the original meaning and tone of respondents' comments.

The authors conducted many of the interviews; graduate students trained and prepared by the authors conducted the rest. In the quotations from one-on-one interviews that follow, we designate the interviewers' questions in boldface type with the respondents' answers following in plain type. In addition, interviewers' questions are preceded by an "I" whereas respondents' answers are preceded by an "R". In cases where we have represented more than one respondent's answer to the same question, we designate the different respondents by R1, R2, R3, etc., for the sake of clarity. In general, we tried to quote each respondent only once or twice in order to offer a wide range of perspectives, but at the same time we selected quotes that we believed were representative of the responses of many of the managers with whom we spoke.

We have structured the balance of the chapter to describe the managerial "story" as we saw it unfolding across our many interviews. This story begins with the managers' relationship to—and dependence on—information technology, proceeds to a description of managers' security concerns, and concludes with an analysis of electronic monitoring and surveillance from the managerial perspective. The end of this chapter also presents a description of some survey data we collected that compares managers and non-managers on security-related issues.

Managers' Attitudes Toward Information Technology

Managers have diverse responsibilities for different functional areas of their organizations; this implies that they also vary substantially with respect to skills, knowledge, and outlook. Managers in some functional areas—sales, customer service, and human resources come to mind as examples—have not historically had a deep reliance on information technology, although it is also the case that in many companies that reliance has grown substantially over recent decades. In contrast, other areas of the business, such as finance, logistics, and engineering, have often provided the foremost impetus for the development of information technology applications since the earliest commercial availability of computers. Echoing this historical division, we essentially found two prototypical types of managers in our research: "tech-dependent" and "tech-savvy." By choosing these two terms, we don't mean to deny the existence of lots of middle ground—managers who know a moderate amount about technology—rather, we adopt these contrasting terms to draw attention to some distinctions in attitude and outlook that we believe are relevant to our discussion of information protection. We describe our use of these terms further as we extract some of these key characteristics that seem to differentiate the two clusters.

The tech-dependent managers generally recognized the importance of information technology in the proper operation of the business but were either reluctant or apparently not well suited to engage in the learning processes involved in gaining mastery over the technology upon which they depended. To use a household analogy, they recognized the importance of wrenches and screwdrivers but would always prefer to call in a plumber to repair a leaky faucet or clogged drain. Here is a representative exchange with a department manager at a manufacturing firm:

> **I: To what extent do you depend on the information technology department's expertise?**
>
> **R1:** I depend on them a lot to keep things going. I don't have the expertise to do that myself. When the system is down, we have 30-plus people staring at each other, and that's just in my area, not the whole [organization].

This quote indicates that the respondent had a kind of helpless feeling about the malfunctioning of the technology and the need for experts to repair it. The following quote from the leader of an organizational unit suggests a similar level of dependency on the information technology staff:

> **I: What are your concerns in relation to security?**
>
> **R2:** Are you talking about access to confidential information?
>
> **I: Yes, and information security within the organization in general.**

R2: I have to say, it's an area of neglect on my part. I know that [my information technology director] and his crew try to protect us from getting hacked. And that's their charge and responsibility.

These managers appeared to recognize the centrality of information technology to the productivity and effective functioning of the organization. Yet there was also a feeling of passive dependency—that when problems arose related to information technology, there was no other course of action but to bring in experts. On many occasions we heard these sentiments: The prototypical tech-dependent manager seemed both deeply reliant on the technology itself and highly dependent upon those individuals with the expertise to keep the technology running.

This tendency to be dependent on others in the organization for the administration and operation of information technology was particularly pronounced at the executive level. We found that individuals high up in the organizational hierarchy had resources available to them that allowed them to compensate for deficits of user skills and knowledge about information technology. In effect, if an executive employed one or more administrative assistants who handled technology competently, this tended to retard the executive's development of personal skills and knowledge related to information technology. Although the modern stereotype of the corporate executive conjures pictures of someone running through an airport with a personal digital assistant in one hand and a laptop computer in the other, we repeatedly found that the higher up in the hierarchy, the less likely a manager was to be tech-savvy. The following conversation with a chief executive officer (CEO) captures this dynamic:

I: Can we start by talking a little bit about your experience with computers?

R: I remember the first time one of my vice presidents used e-mail, and then my assistant would take it off and photocopy it for me, which was not a hardship for me. And that spring we had a committee of about 40 people, and we were continually sharing drafts. I was trying to be as efficient as I could, and I said, what we're going to do is, you all get your drafts written, and you all have fax numbers, and those who don't, we'll hand deliver so you'll get it right away. And somebody said, "Well, how many of us have e-mail accounts?" And the hands went up, and mine didn't. And it was just about everybody. ... So that summer, it wasn't that hard, I learned how to use e-mail and how to do the simple things. That would have been, like, 10 years ago.

I: How did you learn?

R: My assistant taught me. She sort of gave me the basics and then she left the room, so that she wouldn't have to listen to me (laughs). And so I sort of, then, went through it.

I: And what would she have heard if she had stayed?

R: Oh, I'd call her a lot. I'd yell at her, "Come in, I have some problem. I can't do this. I can't do that." And once I kind of learned, it's not the language; it's the way it thinks. At first I wouldn't know what to do when there was a problem.

Although this last response suggests a desire to learn more about the technology and "catch up" as it were, this desire was apparently not universally shared. Managers whose positions put them in charge of strategic decision making apparently sometimes felt that too much intimacy with information technology might cloud their vision of how to steer the organizational ship. The following exchange with a chief information officer (CIO) first described a predecessor in the position but then segued into a position statement on the proper relationship of a decision maker to the technology:

I: What did you think of [the former CIO]?

R: [The former CIO] was very effective as a spokesperson for information technology, a member of the leadership team, but she was uncomfortable with technology. If you asked her what the operating systems were, she wouldn't be able to tell you, wouldn't know the initials. And so whenever there was a conversation that got to that level, she just didn't want to be there. When vendors or other people wanted to talk to her about the advantages of technology, she just didn't want to be in the conversation. I am a little bit closer to it than that. I am not as close as some people. There are two or three different models of where CIOs come from. One model is that they rise up through the organization, and those people tend to be more technical than the people who come from other parts of the organization. [Those who do come from other parts of the organization] have the advantage that they understand the business a little bit better; they have the disadvantage that they don't have the technological expertise. I think it is dangerous to have a technology expertise.

I: Do you?

R: (Sighs) Yeah. If you are a Novell person, you see all solutions in terms of Novell solutions. And if you are a UNIX person, you see it as a UNIX. If you are an information systems person, you tend to think about things that way. If you came from the support side, you are always thinking about what are individual users going to think about this. There are some advantages to not coming out of any of that. And sort of learning from each of them, OK, what's important about what you do. Trying to understand and get my own opinion of the impact of what they do.

Although this respondent tended to discount the importance of technical expertise for managers in charge of decision making, the comment also made evident that the respondent possessed at least some surface knowledge of the underlying details of networks and operating systems. Such knowledge characterized the tech-savvy managers that we encountered. In contrast to tech-dependent managers, we found that tech-savvy managers were not just willing to engage with the technology but also believed that doing so was an essential part of their job. As the previous comment about a former CIO attests, however, even those in technology-related leadership positions may not always have authoritative knowledge of the technology. The quote also suggests the mechanism by which non-tech-savvy managers end up in charge of the technical strategy in some organizations: Because managers are often rewarded for their successes by promotion up the organizational ladder, those who bubble up to the top may arrive from a variety of functional areas of the organization. One key distinction between the two categories of managers, however, may lie in their level of motivation to acquire new knowledge and skills in the area of information technology. The following quote from a high-level manager suggests this kind of willingness:

I: How much does information technology fit into your daily life? In what ways do you use it?

R: Well, I'm not a power user. I am probably no different from anybody else in my position. I am not an expert, even as a personal user. I am competent but I am not an expert. … So I don't bring a lot of technological expertise, I am just savvy about, it's easy for me to learn about technology, when I need to learn about things. So, one of the things I am not, in the organization, is the technological guru. If you were going to ask, "What is the next operating system?" I probably have a pretty good idea about that but it's not based on my own evaluation. It's based upon the opinions of other people, and often when they look at the technical issues, it comes down to a value judgment. That is, is this more important than that, and these are the things that they don't want to be involved in. So, that's sort of where I pick up. It's when they tell me that, "Well, this would mean this for users, and this one can't, and there would be this much more security," or whatever, those are the kinds of evaluations that I have to make.

The previous quote suggests an additional important distinction between the tech-savvy and tech-dependent manager. Both kinds of managers rely upon the advice and assistance of technical experts in order to make managerial decisions. In contrast to the tech-dependent manager, however, who must simply put blind faith in the advice and actions of the experts, the tech-savvy manager knows enough to evaluate and balance the differing perspectives of his or her resident experts. A willingness of the manager to ask questions and self-educate without concern for looking foolish or uninformed seems to open up the possibility of making better decisions about technology by gathering and evaluating opinions from multiple sources. The following quote captures this dynamic:

I: You're not afraid to admit [a lack of information technology knowledge]?

R: Absolutely. (laughs) I am always amused when I say, "Geez. I don't know what those letters stand for." Two other people in the room who are supposed to be experts say, "Neither do I." And they weren't saying it! (laughs) You know, they wouldn't say it because they are afraid to admit it. You have to be really careful about pretending to understand things—pretending to be an expert about something just because you learned a little bit of the jargon. It just doesn't work.

I: Yeah.

R: It's easy to do but it's also easy to spot. You know, we have a few people around here who do that. We know their names. (laughs) You know, the totally uninitiated can't tell the difference, so they tend to believe some of these sort of pseudo-experts. Everybody knows, I mean, everybody. Professionals know that these people are just sort of learning the jargon and making it sound like, you know, you read [a technology magazine] and they'll know the names of things, but they haven't made any kind of reasoned analysis of what we're doing.

The preceding quote suggests one way in which technical jargon can interfere with honest and straightforward communication between technical staff and non-technical managers. In our interviews with organizational members in all different types of positions, we always asked about communication with people in other job functions. When managers communicate successfully with technical staff members and vice versa, the likelihood of enhanced self-education and, consequently, sound strategic decisions about technology seems to rise. The following quotes from two department managers show a willingness to insist on clear communication between technical and non-technical people:

I: When the information technology staff is talking to you, do you usually understand what they are saying?

R1: Generally, we do. If we don't, if they go on with their big words and total topics, they are talking in their own language and when the lay person they are talking to doesn't, you can usually speak up and say, "What are you talking about? Take it back down to our level," and they generally do.

I: Why do they do that?

R1: I think … it's just part of it. It's their world. It's their language.

I: Do you feel that it presents a problem for you in your job?

R1: Well, if they do talk above me, I am very open to saying, "Hey, c'mon back down here." This is the way I see it in my world. And sometimes they need to come back, regroup, and see it differently, and look at the problem as I am looking at it, or whoever, and we come to some common ground and to where we are getting somewhere.

I: How do you think communication could be improved generally?

R1: I think they just need to remember that whatever they are thinking, to know that they can talk to managers. Sometimes it's good to brainstorm and not to think they have all of the solutions. Tell me the issue and I'll let people work it out together.

I: So you have a lot of contact with [your lead programmer]?

R2: Yes, every day. We have a meeting every morning.

I: You clearly have a good working relationship with him. Do you rely on his expertise?

R2: Oh, yeah. Because I don't have it.

I: How easy is it to communicate with him?

R2: Very easy. He's a very professional guy, intelligent, but yet he has drawn pictures for me. If I am not getting it, he'll put a diagram together for me. He has a way of making analogies to non-technical stuff to help you understand the technical nature. I think he's done an excellent job, but you know, as much of a challenge as I am, our CEO is probably 10 times worse than me. He doesn't have a computer in his office. We've gotten the CEO to the point of agreeing to have a computer in his office, and that's really [the CIO's] doing. [The lead programmer is] a very good communicator. I think he has an excellent way of presenting an argument, bullet-pointing the benefits, you know, here's why we've got to do it.

It is interesting in this quote to see the theme emerge again about executives with limited computer skills. Nonetheless, the "professional and intelligent" programmer referred to by the manager apparently had sufficiently well-developed communication skills to be able to make cogent arguments even to an executive who did not have a computer on his desk. This point underscores the two-way nature of communicating about technology issues: For their part, managers must be willing to ask questions at the risk of seeming uninformed, while in turn technical staff must be willing to translate from their unique terminology and must possess sufficient patience and willingness to serve the tutorial role when necessary. One of the most successful organizations we examined, in terms of effective adaptation to new information technology, was a firm in the health-care sector with about 250 employees. This firm had just hired a new director of information systems (IS) who possessed excellent communication skills and a unique knack for getting managers involved in the information technology decisions that would affect their areas. The following quote is from one of those managers:

I: And my last question is how do you work with the IS department?

R: The IS department has changed. Originally, when I got here, it was [the former director of IS]. Since that time, [a new director] has come and he's the IS director, and [the new assistant director], they are both great guys, I mean they really help you. … They are pretty responsive. … I

> hope this never changes. It's a very friendly atmosphere, and because of that we don't have the confidentiality and the corporate compliance problems. There are not many walls.

This quote nicely illustrates the positive effect on information technology operations when the individuals with technical expertise are able to work and communicate effectively with members of the organization's management team. This quote also reiterates the three major points that have emerged from this first section. First, managers appear to differ along a continuum with respect to how much skill and knowledge about information technology they bring to their jobs. We characterized those managers at the high end who work to keep themselves up to date on information technology as tech-savvy managers. In contrast, we labeled those managers at the low end who are highly reliant on others for basic technology activities and support as tech-dependent. For managers all through this continuum, the information technology professional plays an important role in the functioning of the organization, but we believe that the tech-dependent manager has a substantially higher degree of dependency on the expertise of information technology professionals.

Next, one notable difference between these two "types" of managers appears to be that the tech-savvy manager is in a position to develop a better understanding of what the technical experts know and do for the organization. In contrast, the tech-dependent manager may tend to see technology issues and the people who talk about them as largely incomprehensible. Although one manager gave the opinion that getting too close to the technology might blind one to the full range of options, it seems reasonable that a manager with a *broad* understanding of available technologies should be able to make more effective decisions than one who is largely ignorant of the possibilities.

Finally, our data suggest that effective communication between managers and technical personnel serves as one of the key mechanisms by which tech-savvy managers figure out what is going on with new and emerging technologies. Facilitating this communication appears to require at least two ingredients: managers who are not afraid to ask (dumb) questions of technical personnel and technical personnel who are willing and capable of bringing the technical conversation to non-technical people through metaphor, analogy, diagrams, and other communication tools. As we continue this chapter with a look at information security, privacy, and employee monitoring, we will see these same three issues emerge as the substrate upon which managers make good or poor decisions about how to use technology inside the organization.

Managers' Beliefs About Information Security

In this section we examine the range of responses we received when we asked managers about their biggest security concerns. Other than managers who ran business units involved in information technology or information security, none of our respondents expressed concerns about particular security technologies or specific security mechanisms. Instead, managers noted a clear need for protecting information from leaking outside of the company. On this topic, managers frequently expressed concerns about the confidentiality of customer, client, and/or patient data. This finding probably reflects the events that were occurring around the time of our data collection, which included a number of highly publicized breaches of confidentiality of customer data as well as extensive publicity focusing on federal legislation (e.g., the Gramm-Leach-Bliley Act, the Sarbanes-Oxley Act, and the Health Insurance Portability and Accountability Act [HIPAA]) that had notable impacts on data security. The following quote, from a departmental manager in a for-profit firm, reflects this emphasis:

> **I: What would happen if some information did get in the wrong hands?**
>
> **R:** I fear the breach of confidentiality, if it did get in the wrong hands.
>
> **I: What might happen?**
>
> **R:** It depends on the people I guess. I don't know. They could use it for sharing with other people. Somebody's neighbor could find out about someone else. (Pause) And there are legal issues. There might be unhappy customers. And we don't want that. Not at all.

Although some of the managers with whom we spoke seemed to have a well-developed intuitive sense of the relative value of different kinds of information, few of our respondents mentioned anything about the value or sensitivity of employee data. The next quote, from an executive team member in a manufacturing firm, makes reference to the one exception that some managers mentioned—that an employee should not be able to gain access to or information about other employees' salary data:

> **I: What concerns do you have for the privacy of data in this new system?**
>
> **R:** Now, if there is a department, you could look at the general ledger and get that, but there would be five or six people within that range so you couldn't tell what any one person is making. Payroll is not going to be on the new system, other than we might have some data collection on the floor, but I am sure that those people could get in to find what the other people are making. But since I am administration, I won't be on there, my salary won't be on there. … The only thing really is salaries, and everybody in the administration will just have the [data from their] department, and that's the one I really want to be restricted, only a small number of people will have access to that.

Although we did not extensively explore these concerns behind secrecy of salary data, other researchers have found that managers seek to protect employees' salary information out of a desire to control employee motivation, morale, and performance (e.g., Futrell & Jenkins, 1978). Thus, the two rationales that seem to lie behind managers' main concerns about information security connect intimately to two of their main concerns for the business itself: keeping customers happy and keeping employees motivated. These concerns are certainly legitimate—in particular in for-profit organizations—but we wondered to what degree managers looked beyond their narrow concerns for salary secrecy and confidentiality of customer data to a broader strategic vision of security and privacy in their organizations.

At the time when we were conducting these interviews, we did not have many preconceptions about how managers would respond, the extent to which they would see security as an important priority, or how technically sophisticated their responses would be. In light of the analysis presented in the previous section of this chapter, however, we realized in retrospect a clear division between those managers who had given security some degree of thought and consideration vs. those who saw security as an arcane topic best left handled by information technology experts. We found that the tech-savvy managers had given security some careful consideration and were aware of some of the trade-offs involved, whereas tech-dependent managers had a disengaged approach to security, even when it would affect their department's operations quite substantially. This latter position, tech-dependency, is exemplified by the following quotes from two departmental managers whom we queried about the installation of new software systems in their respective organizations:

I: Is the planning for the new system sufficient to deal with sensitive information?

R1: From what I saw it's sufficient. But depending on what system they choose, I am sure they will sit down and figure it out. The system I saw the demo on certainly has those capabilities; you can have security wherever you want it. That's not up to me, that's up to [the information technology people]. (laughs) I am assuming that there will be. Our [current] system is archaic, (laughs) so I am sure they are going to work it out. I mean, accounting does not want us to access accounting and all that, so I am sure that will be put in place. How easily that will be done, I don't know. Maybe password. I don't know how they do it now.

I: Is the current system sensitive, for example, does it contain information that requires some level of security?

R2: Yes.

I: Do you think that the new system will allow for that same level of security?

R2: I don't know if it's in but I'm going to say that we have the people who were certainly aware of that and took those precautions and yes, there would have to be security in some parts of the system.

These two managers were in charge of departments that planned to use the new systems to organize most of their daily operations; those operations dealt with sensitive patient data (respondent 1) and customer data (respondent 2) on a regular basis. The following quote from a manager of human resources in a manufacturing and retailing company exemplifies a similar attitude:

> **I: Is everything [in the security area] covered, as far as you think?**
>
> **R:** I'm pretty happy with it. I can't think of anything we, the company, really needs. We're pretty basic here and we really don't need any fancy programs or anything, I don't believe in any of that. We try to keep everyone on the same communication plank, that's the important thing. As we grow, this company's been growing, so we're fairly new to this whole Web site, Internet, probably in the last three or four years.
>
> **I: So how do you handle all of those new things? Do you offer training sessions for the employees?**
>
> **R:** What new programs are you talking about?
>
> **I: Well, you said it's pretty new for you to be using the Internet and the company is growing. It makes me think that more people are working here and you have to adapt to giving them access or restricting their access to the Internet.**
>
> **R:** [Our information technology people] could probably answer that better than I can because I don't do any of that. The information technology department provides any computer training, any programs training to any of our employees. I'm not really involved in that at all ...

The previous response and the sentiments of several others among the tech-dependent managers with whom we spoke seem to evidence a distinctly hands-off attitude: An information technology expert is taking care of the security issues, so managers really don't need to worry about them. We found more interesting, however, the responses of managers who appeared to have an erroneous or mis-placed sense of their company's priorities with respect to information security. The next respondent, who was the manager of a small non-profit organization, seemed to focus narrowly on the security of her own computer and files and to not have a strategic view of her organization's security issues:

> **I: I am wondering if any of the information you work with is sensitive. Are there any concerns you have about confidentiality or security?**
>
> **R:** Just, like, in Word documents and so forth?
>
> **I: Or in any of the information you work with.**
>
> **R:** Yes, there are some things like that.
>
> **I: And what concerns do you have about them?**
>
> **R:** None in particular. (laughs) If someone should get on my computer, well, I don't think they would. I have never been tempted to go into anyone else's documents. At this point I am not that concerned. And if it were super, super, super confidential, well, then I might be concerned. I mean, right now all of that financial information is kept [on another server]. (laughs) I wouldn't know how to get into it myself. (laughs)

This comment is interesting on a number of counts. First, we found that many managers transferred their feelings about their own honesty generically to everyone else in their workgroup or business unit. This director said that she has "not been tempted to go into anyone else's documents," and thus seemed to imply that the rest of her staff would automatically reciprocate by not going into her documents. This sentiment seemed particularly naïve to us given that this particular nonprofit organization employed a number of temporary and student employees as well as having a large cadre of volunteer workers who had frequent physical access to the organization's facilities. Second, this director appeared to believe that none of her information was "super sensitive." We also found many other examples of employees at all levels in their organizations tending to discount the value of the proprietary data that was their own responsibility, unless that data fell into an obviously sensitive category (e.g., customer financial records). Finally, the manager quoted here seemed to believe in the myth of "security by obscurity" with respect to her financial data server: "If it is too complicated for me to figure out how to get into it, it must be secure." All three of these points suggest that this particular manager had not taken the time to educate herself about the likely security threats that her organization may face; knowing about these threats was simply not a priority for her.

The next quote indicates a similar lack of knowledge and perspective. The small-business owner quoted here was apparently fixated on "hackers" because of stories he had heard reported in the popular press:

> **I: So now, I am going to ask you a couple of questions with regard to information security. So, what would you say are your biggest concerns with information security?**
>
> **R:** Hackers!
>
> **I: Hackers?**
>
> **R:** There are two things, first of all, I had hackers coming in and going through the computer system; also, electronic eavesdropping of communications, telephone communications. That also occurred to me as a problem. I have sensed that this was taking place using prior equipment. These aren't government concerns, these are industrial concerns and the industry's problems, it's either one person trying to spy on somebody else is having problems or just people who are just curious and want to know what's going on and so it's a casual, you know, a casual villain or vandal or hacker or e-chopper that I'm worried about.

Based on our subsequent conversations with a technical staff member at this small business, we learned that hackers had never targeted the firm's computers to her knowledge, but that instead the firm's equipment had become infected by viruses and worms on a number of prior occasions, primarily due to the fact that the company had not planned sufficient expenditures to keep all of the firm's computers up to date on anti-virus subscriptions. For some non-technical personnel, it is evident that the distinctions between viruses, worms, hackers, vandals, and other potentially malicious agents are unclear. As a result in this particular case, the choices of whether and how to spend money on countermeasures were probably ill informed.

Fortunately, not all of the managers whom we interviewed exhibited such a "hands-off" approach to information security in their firms. As a general pattern we noticed that the larger companies we investigated tended to each have at least one managerial employee who demonstrated knowledge and thoughtful consideration of security and privacy issues. The following response from a manager of a business unit within a larger organization discusses her view of information security vulnerabilities:

> **I: So in your opinion, what is the biggest security concern that you might have?**
>
> **R:** We are to some extent vulnerable like everyone else. Vulnerable to all sorts of malicious kinds of attacks. But we do our best to stay out ahead of those things. We have some people here that are very, very good in keeping what we do secure from those kinds of things. There are—you know, we are dealing with humans. That is where some of the flaws, if you want to say, exist in what we deliver …
>
> **I: So what do you mean, would it be that the major concern is about the human component?**
>
> **R:** I think so. I think all of this is, I mean. Today I bet you, there is probably more than, at least 25 percent of what you manage every day has to deal with keeping things secure. Keeping on top of access, who gets access, and access to what. We produce lots of paper. We produce lots of information on that paper, lots of information that is available through computer access. We always have to be conscious of how this information is portrayed and who has access to it. It is a big part of our job. Especially since the databases that we are dealing with are, everyone is sharing and using the database. We have 50 [remote locations] and 40 of them are sharing the database …

The closing comment, concerning how many of this organization's remote locations were sharing one large database, was a key source of complexity with respect to the information security challenges experienced by this organization. This manager went on to describe the many headaches associated with ensuring that each of the different locations had the access that it needed, but no more than that. A number of anecdotes about mishaps and near misses illustrated the intricacy involved in achieving this balance. Interestingly, the human component of security was a topic that arose in a number of our conversations with managers. Some managers recognized the potential of human behavior to influence information security for better or worse. The following quote came from a manager who was a vice president in a medium-size organization (more than 1,000 employees). His observations about password-related behaviors resonated strongly with some of the survey results we report at the end of this chapter.

I: So in your opinion, what are the biggest problems that you face here?

R: One of the problems that we have with staff members in the functional offices … There are some staff members who, you wouldn't recognize them as being very high on the chain, but they have very high levels of clearance. They have access to very sensitive information and they can go in and change it. … And you know, you still find people who write their password on a sticky tape and put it on their monitor. It's easy to figure out what their user ID is, so you see something like this and it sends chills down your spine. Password protection is very important. For people who come in, log in in the morning at 8:30, log out at 5:00, and they are gone from their computers for hours at a time. Anybody who wants, this includes me, (laughs) could sneak in here and send e-mail, you know, it came from X. So that, I think what we see with staff is sort of casual, careless behavior because they are just not conscious of how serious the risks are. And then there are always intruders. There are people in California who are trying to hack into our systems every day.

Why this respondent chose to single out Californians as computer intruders is unclear, but the theme of casual neglect of information security by staff members in organizations arose frequently, particularly among tech-savvy managers. Apparently those organizational leaders who had been primed by their technical staff to be sensitive to user behavior problems (e.g., poor password management) began to see many examples of unintentionally insecure behaviors. By unintentionally insecure we mean to suggest that the employees who were neglectful of positive security practices were not being neglectful out of maliciousness but rather as a result of a lack of training and/or motivation. The following quote came from the CEO of a medium-size organization who observed the pitfalls created by easy and universal access to e-mail by staff members:

I: Do you have any concerns about that sensitive information?

R: Yes. My concern is that I don't think people understand. [When] I grew up most of my work was in state institutions. In one institution, any ingoing or outgoing mail was a matter of public record. So I grew up administratively believing that you never put anything on paper that you didn't want the world to know about. I think there are people using e-mail and the Internet and they don't understand that. They are the same people who probably put things in writing in letters that they probably shouldn't have. But this is such an attractive thing, but you know, that requires a certain amount of self-policing. It's not an institutional policing kind of thing. It's really in effect saying that if it's really something you don't want anybody to know about, you should probably have a face-to-face [meeting]. That's not different than it was 20 years ago but the frequency is so much more, because you can communicate more rapidly. And I find myself reminding people that things they send on e-mail, you know, just by a simple mistake, you have now sent it to 300 people. ... So, it's only a concern if you are putting things in writing you don't want people to know about, which you shouldn't be doing anyway. I always assume that things I put in writing will eventually be seen by the world.

When the respondent mentioned working at "state institutions," the underlying concern was on the impact of "sunshine" or freedom of information laws. The U.S. Freedom of Information Act obligates federal agencies to release non-classified information to members of the press or public following a formal request. Most states have similar laws that obligate state agencies to do the same. As a result, thoughtful government workers usually realize that any information they commit to paper (or computer records) can potentially become publicized as the result of a freedom of information request. Even though this respondent was not working for a state agency at the time of the interview, the concern is also valid for private organizations, but for a different reason. If an organization becomes embroiled in a lawsuit, paper and computer records can be obtained by the opposing party's attorneys during the discovery phase of the legal process. As a result, employees at both private and public institutions must take care to avoid committing to paper or computer records any comment or information that should be kept secret from the outside world.

We found that records management is a concern at many organizations, but nowhere more intensely than in the healthcare industry. Although organizations in many sectors are moving toward electronic record keeping, the number of paper versions of many records is still high. Following are responses from a healthcare manager who expresses concern about needing specialized staff to manage patient records:

> **I: Why do you think that [problems with records management have come up]?**
>
> **R:** This unit is the only one that I manage that does not have a coordinator for medical records. So we are relying on the staff, myself, and the secretary to manage all of that information in this unit, and there is no one really to oversee that particular process besides myself. So when [a care provider] needs a patient record for whatever reason, I can't be sure that that record has been returned. I don't know where he or she has put it. I'm not sure how long they have had it, what they are using it for. I'm not sure and that's what we are trying to correct now.

I: So, it seems as if there are some procedural problems that need some attention.

R: Yes, I find that the staff is not overly informed about these particular procedures. It's only now that I am becoming more active in day-to-day. I originally had a coordinator here. That's what we are waiting to, for that position to come back. I think that the staff has not been educated to the extent that the other units have.

This comment also makes evident the manager's concern that the staff in this unit does not have sufficient training to maintain the level of information protection she would prefer. After hearing a number of comments such as those of the two previous respondents, we began to ask for more details with respect to employees' involvement in information security. We found that managers frequently believed that employees were "part of the problem" with information security, and to a lesser extent that they could also be part of the solution. We found that it was not uncommon for managers to express some lack of trust in employees' capabilities for keeping sensitive information secure. In the next two quotes, the chief financial officer (CFO) and the CEO of a hospital expressed concerns about employees' use of a new e-mail system that was being installed. The CFO expressed general concerns about casual misuse of the facility. The CEO described his reasoning for not putting physicians on a new e-mail system for fear that they would not abide by the policy of avoiding the transmission of confidential patient information over e-mail. Privacy-related legislation, such as the Health Insurance Portability and Accountability Act (HIPAA), has apparently also had the effect of sensitizing managers to some of the information security pitfalls associated with giving employees unlimited access to electronic communication tools:

I: What kinds of concerns do you have about the new system?

R1: My concerns are rather unusual in that I think my biggest concern is that people use it. I hope that people will buy into it and use it ... I have some secondary concerns, um, that you face with any kind of electronic communication. ... I do have a little bit of concern over misuse. That people will use e-mail to ask, "What time are you going to lunch?" And jokes, chain letters. And all of the things that go along with that.

I: How should access to this sensitive data be controlled, or how do you see it being controlled?

R2: Well, the way I understand it now, our system isn't secure enough to be sending any true confidential information over the e-mail. But the intent is in the long term, to get whatever it takes, and that's about as much as I know, (laughs) to allow it to be secure, whether it is encryption, or signature required on the other side, to make sure you are sending it to the appropriate person and only that person is seeing it. You know, those kinds of things, we want to make sure we are working into the project. I know [the information technology director] and his staff are working very hard at making sure, because clearly, at least half of the communications that are going to take place are going to have some sort of confidential information, patient or financial, here. There is a lot of general stuff. We have really kind of held off on getting the physicians involved because we know it's not confidential right now, or it's not secure right now. We don't know that they will abide by our guidance to not send confidential information by e-mail. (laughs) You know, so we have really held back on the doctors. But the doctors we would love to get up on e-mail so they could communicate better with nurse managers on patient information, how the patients are doing, things of that nature.

In addition to the expression of concerns about electronic communication of sensitive information, it is interesting to note in this latter quote the hands-off attitude toward the implementation issues. The phrases "that's about all I know," "those kinds of things," and "general stuff" indicate an almost apologetic attitude about being unable to provide the interviewer with a greater level of detail about the implementation of the project. This particular individual expressed a degree of confidence in his technology experts ("[the information technology director] and his staff are working very hard"), that they would eventually solve the technical hurdles involved in giving physicians access to the communication tools they want.

Despite the hands-off attitudes of some, we found that many managers were willing to become engaged in at least one area related to information security, namely the formation of security-related policies. The most important and central security-related policy pertaining to employees is the so-called acceptable use policy (AUP). The phrase acceptable use pertains to employees' legitimate uses of company-owned and operated computers for business and non-business purposes. Often, these policies focus primarily on prohibitions—a litany of computer-related behaviors that are considered a violation of the organization's rules—so the term unacceptable use policy might be more frank. In other cases, however, acceptable use policies do give employees specific rights and freedoms. A common example would be permitting limited and reasonable use of company e-mail to contact family members. Many other types of security policies are often implemented in large organizations because of the need for uniform regulation of the wide range of employee roles and responsibilities. The following quote from a vice president (for whom one responsibility was the organization's information technology services group) suggests some of the struggles that managers face in guiding the formation of security policies:

I: What are your [security] concerns?

R: We have a heightened concern about information security for a number of reasons. And part of it is, about two or three years ago an audit committee took a look at the issue of computing security and asked, in a friendly way, if it would be OK to bring in independent auditors to take a look. And they did that, and we had our auditor's report, which was pretty superficial, but it got us thinking about, the more you think about it, the more there is to think about. And we, one of things we did, the committee that works on computing security, was sort of an independent group but they didn't have any formal roles in the structure of the organization. So now I've got that group reporting directly to me. I meet with them whenever they ask me to, and I try to review their work. They are just learning how. I think they need to do more to get used to their role. They were before too involved in implementation details and project determination, whereas what they really ought to be looking at are, "Where are our vulnerabilities?" And "Do we have omissions in policy?" Sometimes somebody can do something that threatens security and you don't even have a rule against it, so you'd better think about that. And we are beginning to do those two things. Think at a higher level. You know, when they first wrote a policy, it was like six pages of all there is to know about wireless networks. And I read this and said, "This is not a policy. This is a document about implementation of wireless networks. It's a nice document, but it's not policy." So they have gotten back to a simpler issue, and the new policy is, whenever you dispose of a computer, you must take the data off. That's the policy. It's a contribution. We never had a rule on that. And so we are getting used to the notion of here's what we are supposed to be doing.

These comments suggested a tension that we encountered in a number of organizations. Managers have a strong interest in regulating employee behavior, but when it comes to computer-related behavior, only the most tech-savvy managers have a clear sense of what the relevant behaviors are, what behaviors should be encouraged by policies, what other behaviors should be strictly against the rules, and which among those can be regulated by purely technical methods. Those managers who are more tech-dependent must rely more heavily upon information security experts and other information technology personnel for information about these behaviors and how to deal with them. Unfortunately, information technology personnel as a group probably have less experience and knowledge of the topic of regulation of general employee behavior, so, at least in managers' views, many of the policies that are created by information technology people have too much focus on the technology and technical details of the policy area and too little focus on what specific tasks and outcomes employees should accomplish. The following quote from an executive-level manager suggests the need to ensure the involvement of both managers and information technology personnel in the policy formation process:

I: How are your information technology people involved in security policies? Do they have any input?

R: We have a variety of policies that cover, you know, acceptable use, Internet use, all that kind of stuff. Those probably need to be reviewed. Those have been developed over time and put in book or you know, put on a shelf or filed. I think there needs to be a review process, at least annually. Just to make sure they are up-to-date. Just like anything else. I think the need there is more frequent review to make sure we've got all the i's dotted because in this business things change rapidly and you could lay down a policy that is already obsolete so we've got to keep on it. You've got to establish a way back and forth to be reviewed or input to be supplied. And that mechanism is in place but it is just not formalized. It needs to be formalized. The whole organization needs to be involved.

This quote also raises an important issue about the maintenance of policies. We fundamentally agree with this respondent that the rapidly changing nature of information technology in business settings ensures that policies written today will be obsolete within a few years. As a result, when a cooperative effort between managers and information technology people leads to the authoring of focused and effective policy, only the first bridge has been crossed in the regulation of employee behavior. Policies must be revisited, at least annually, to make sure that the guidelines are still relevant and appropriate. In addition, policies that are written and placed on a shelf are useless unless they are also clearly communicated to employees. In the following quote, a manager refers to the use of staff meetings and smaller groupings to keep security procedures fresh in employees' minds:

I: Do you feel that most of your employees buy into your ideas about information security on an everyday basis?

R: Yes.

I: They do not find the security procedures onerous?

R: Not the way we approach it. The way we approach it is: This is information for [clients], this is going to help [clients], but it is confidential. It is your job … your job is to make sure all those things that have to do with that

information are kept secure. Yes. I can't say that there are
not employees that don't think about that or deal with that.
I think they are just honest and genuine ...

**I: Is there something that can be done additionally to
make things more secure?**

R: Probably yes, there are always ways to make them more
secure. I've done this in a couple of ways. One is through
talking one-on-one to them and also talking to them in
groups. Meetings that we have, we have frequent staff
meetings. So typically whenever, the topic does not come
up in every step, but it does come up.

The two main themes voiced by this respondent appear to be
motivation and communication. This manager's use of the phrases
"this is going to help clients" and "it is your job" are attempts to
appeal to employees' sense of duty as a basis for helping to keep the
organization's data secure. Next, the respondent emphasizes the idea
of frequent communication with employees as a method for ensuring
that these ideas of helping and duty remain foremost in the employees' minds.

We close this section with a brief conversation with a high-level
executive that, for us, captured the essential management perspectives on information technology, information security, and employee
behavior:

I: Do you do anything else to keep your computer safe?

R: I log off, and [the information technology people] told
us they like us to log off every night, so people when they
come in and log on to their computer, the program will
take care of it. But even a lot of those programs, [workers]
need a password to get into that, so we try to remind people to make sure they log off.

I: How do you remind them?

R: They have training, that's one of the things that they
teach about basic computer behavior. There are programs
out there now that back up automatically. I can't remember

where it is, not at the top of my screen, I back it up. The only person who is in my office in the middle of the day is [my administrative assistant]. She would be the only one who could get to my computer, and she has access to all of that information anyway. (laughs) There is nothing that I have that she doesn't have really. So ...

Looking back over these comments and others presented in this section, we believe that the interviewed managers told the following typical story: The conscientious manager recognizes the importance of confidentiality of information such as customer, financial, and salary data and tries to follow the security guidelines and advice offered by the information technology personnel to safeguard these data. The typical manager also expresses the hope that employees are learning to do the same by taking training that teaches them to abide by company security policies. Although some managers are quite tech-savvy, the higher up the ladder you go, the more likely it is to find a manager who "can't remember where it is, not at the top of my screen." Perhaps out of necessity, those managers with some administrative responsibility for an information technology group or for information technology personnel claimed better know-how and more accurate information about information security and privacy issues than managers whose groups simply use information technology as a business tool. Managers are busy people, so they frequently work closely with others who have "access to all of that information anyway." As a result, managers sometimes reported that their personal security habits stretched the very policies they had a hand in developing (e.g., sharing their passwords or file access with an administrative assistant). Nonetheless, the development, maintenance, and enforcement of security-related policies were reported as important areas of involvement by most managers in information security.

Managerial Perspectives on Employee Monitoring

To conclude our presentation of the managerial interview data, we turn now to the topic of electronic monitoring and surveillance. Although the managers we interviewed described a range of approaches for justifying, developing, and communicating policies related to monitoring, there was an almost unanimous belief in the necessity for monitoring. As highlighted in previous chapters, organizations face a variety of liabilities arising from any misbehavior of their employees, and as a result of these liabilities, managers seemed to feel a strong interest in tracking and regulating employee behavior. In this first quote, the CEO refers to the difficulties one of his colleagues encountered with users who wrote hate speech and used the organization's computers to broadcast it anonymously over the Internet:

I: Has [hate speech] happened here?

R: Not here, but it's happened in other places and I have seen that. [A colleague] has had that [kind of problem at another organization]. It takes one, or somebody here, it takes one, who anonymously writes all kinds of stuff, and then it sort of gets into, what's wrong with a place that would have somebody do that and why is the [organization] not taking a stand, and the [organization] can't find the person, and the [organization] has already taken a stand, and there is nothing wrong with the place, it's just that every society has idiots and bigots and so on. There is a small percentage, but the Internet gives them access to an audience where they don't have to accept responsibility for it.

This idea of the "small percentage" of individuals who abuse their computer privileges came up frequently as a managerial justification for conducting electronic monitoring of information technology and resources. Managers generally espoused the belief that the majority of employees were honest and hardworking, but that the inevitable presence of a few bad apples made it necessary to routinely use monitoring techniques to track the computer and network activities of employees. It was never entirely clear to us whether managers actually believed that only a tiny minority of employees ever caused problems, or whether this was a kind of public relations ploy to suggest how virtuous their organizations were overall. When we dug for details, we frequently found that the available data contradicted the original cheery attitude about the one bad apple. The following respondent, a department manager in a hospital, referred to an earlier practice that employees had of using repeated login attempts as a strategy to try to figure out another employee's password:

I: We talked in our last interview about the ability of the system to monitor the activities of employees. I was wondering how confident you feel about the [new] system being able to handle the security.

R: It's very good. Because we do that. (sigh) Where I was employed before, they had [the same software]. When you go to log on to the terminal, if it takes more than three times, it locks the terminal, if you don't get the right password, and it generates a report. Someone screens those reports. We found out that people were doing that to find out passwords, because they were locking them up all the time. So the flags are available in the system to check for turnaround times, there's flags on the system for everything. It's nice. I mean, I don't want to be big brother on them, but there's benefit to it. It doesn't have to be that it's an employee trying to break the password. We could find out that it's a [customer]. Or we can find out that turnaround times are slow at certain parts of the day and we can get more staff in. So it's beneficial. It's not just red flags. There are lots of benefits there.

Other respondents in this same organization let us know that the reports generated by this new system also showed a number of other interesting behaviors that were occurring. For example, some employees were using the system to try to look up the medical records of individuals in whose care they were not involved. This type of behavior became particularly notable when a local celebrity had checked in or when an employee's neighbor or former spouse was being treated. Although it still may be the case that the great majority of employees are honest and scrupulous, we found that data collected from monitoring and surveillance systems sometimes seemed to contradict the "one bad apple" theory offered by managers. Curiosity and other fairly benign motivations may prompt employees to extend the boundaries of acceptable use further than managers may have originally believed likely. The situation becomes even more complicated, however, when one takes into account the intricacy of the informal lines of communication and control within the typical large organization. In the following quote, the same hospital manager expands on the problem of knowing who has a legitimate right of access to a set of records and who does not:

> **I: What are your thoughts on changes in the system and effects on sensitive information?**
>
> **R:** We need a system that if you don't have any activity, it should go to a screen like this so no one can tap into your information. And, for compliance, there are more HIPAA regulations, it's kind of strange and everyone seems to interpret it differently, I don't know, but I do think that interpretation of HIPAA has gone out of whack. I think, confidentiality in some way that you can measure it, you know, but how do I know? OK, you're a [laboratory technician], you're in the lab, and I call up the report to see where you should be. But how do I know where you shouldn't be? Did a doctor call and ask you about Mrs. Smith's reports, and how would I necessarily know that you didn't need to be there? So that's hard. And we need a way to measure or observe whether confidentiality is being breached. We are trying to see where you've been that you shouldn't necessarily be. So I don't know if it's necessarily accurate.

In this quote, the manager clearly wants to give the laboratory technicians the benefit of the doubt with respect to the possibility of inappropriate access to patients' healthcare records. The reference to needing "a way to measure or observe whether confidentiality is being breached" was clearly intended as a justification of having a monitoring tool available, even if the interpretation of records produced by the tool would try to give the employee the benefit of the doubt. A certain feeling of "trust but verify" seems to lie behind this respondent's words.

This respondent also made mention of HIPAA. At the time of our data collection, many hospitals were struggling to interpret the rules provided by the federal government in order to put into effect a set of policies that protect various kinds of confidential patient health care information. Although non-healthcare organizations do not, at this writing, have a parallel piece of legislation that governs the privacy of employee or customer records, a patchwork of state and federal legislation still exerts a substantial influence on the maintenance of confidentiality in most organizations. Compliance with these many laws also serves as a major motivator and justification of the use of monitoring and surveillance within organizations. The following respondent expresses the belief that a signature on an employee confidentiality agreement is not sufficient to ensure such compliance and that a monitoring function is needed to "track" the compliance of employees' actual behaviors:

> **I: Are there policies related to [confidentiality]?**
>
> **R:** Yes, we have written policies, and there's confidentiality, and we have compliance, that's the buzzword now, corporate compliance, so they yearly have to sign this thing about confidentiality and corporate compliance, and everything else. Words on paper, you know. Hey, I'll sell you some [data] for five dollars, and if I get caught, I'll go somewhere else. I mean, they don't do that, but that possibility is there for anybody to do it. Just signing a statement isn't a big thing. You don't have to be big brother, but you have to have a means of tracking who was in what, when, where, and then you can figure out why.

Despite this respondent's apparent cynicism about the value of signed confidentiality statements, we found it quite common for organizations to require employees to sign such agreements. A component of some such statements is an explicit notice to employees explaining how they will be monitored, as well as explicit acceptance on the part of the employee of such monitoring as a condition of employment. The following quote was representative of the practice of having employees sign such agreements as they came on board into the organization:

> **I: When you say you screen your own employees, do you go back and check logins or something like that?**
>
> **R:** No, part of the process that we use to hire people is to verify former employers, things like that. I ask my staff to sign a confidentiality statement saying that they will never reveal any, anything having the information that they are dealing with on a daily basis with anyone but designated staff.

One final justification offered by managers for conducting electronic monitoring and surveillance was based on the legally correct argument that the organization owned all of the computer and network equipment that the employees were using to do their jobs, and so the organization had both a right and an interest in policing the use of those facilities. The following respondent's use of the phrase "our right" was echoed almost universally by managers we asked about the use of electronic monitoring and surveillance in the organization:

I: How will you handle monitoring of e-mails?

R: [We can] develop some policies and standards of practice on how you use it, what's acceptable and what's not. People would have the understanding that it's our right, it's our property, and it's our e-mail. It's on our system. We technically have the right to go in and look at it anytime we wanted. As long as they understand that. (laughs) And we do have two unions, so this becomes an issue.

I: Have you done any communication with the unions about this?

R: We haven't done any formal communication with the union representatives. We actually are kind of in a situation where we have some very limited messaging within our [existing mainframe] environment, and just found out recently that some people are using that messaging, and it hasn't been for work purposes, "Did you see what Jane is wearing today?" But it is an issue we have to tackle with our [workers]. It isn't a function we can turn off. We have to come up with a policy about it.

The connection between monitoring policies and unions was one that arose in every organization we visited that had unionized workers. Unions have generally been staunch advocates of restricting or limiting electronic monitoring and surveillance in organizations. Union representatives have frequently taken the position that electronic monitoring and surveillance constitute both an invasion of worker privacy and a goad toward unreasonable standards for productivity (e.g., Bain & Taylor, 2000; Westin, 1992). Managers with whom we spoke typically reported an awareness of this position held by unions but also cited the "it's our right" justification as a factor that trumped the union's concerns.

To summarize, then, managers noted a number of examples of problematic user behavior that illustrated the organization's interest in monitoring electronic communications, data access, and other computer-related behaviors. These respondents typically offered compliance with appropriate laws and regulations as a significant driver for the use of monitoring, and often justified to employees the execution of confidentiality agreements—frequently containing built-in clauses accepting the organization's monitoring practices—on the basis of such compliance. When pressed on the rights issues involved in electronic monitoring and surveillance, most managers cited the organization's ownership of the computer and equipment networks as the primary rationale for giving organizational representatives unfettered access to records that trace employees' computer-related behavior. In Chapters 6 and 7, we hear both similar and contrasting perspectives from two other groups: information technology professionals and rank-and-file employees.

Statistical Studies of Managers and Security

To conclude this chapter, we show and describe some data displays from survey studies we conducted that included samples of managers. While the many quotes provided and interpreted in this chapter provide rich insights into the thinking of a relatively small number of managers from a relatively small number of organizations, the data that follow attempt to show a representative sample of managers from a variety of U.S. firms. One advantage of these statistical data is that they are more likely to provide a view of security and privacy issues that is unbiased by the unique personal partiality of one-on-one interviews. In the interview situation, some respondents talk less and some talk more, but in all cases what they say bears the stamp of their own idiosyncratic professional and personal history. The excerpts taken from these interviews describe a wide range of issues in the distinctive vocabulary and style of the respondent; the meaning of what the respondents say, while undoubtedly valid to them, may or may not be widely applicable to the problems of other managers in other organizations. In contrast, the survey data that follow provide insight into just a narrow slice of the many issues related to security and privacy, but they do so in a very standardized way. When we combine this standardization with a good process for selecting survey respondents, the result is a set of numbers that gives us the capability, within certain limits, to say what is happening within a bigger sphere of the population from which the survey respondents were drawn (i.e., solely U.S. firms).

In Table 5.1, we provide a comparison of managers and non-managers on six behaviors and three organizational issues related to information security and privacy. These data were collected in 2004 with the assistance of an organizational surveying firm, Genesee Survey Services, based in Rochester, New York. Each year, Genesee conducts the National Work Opinion Survey. It uses a professionally developed sampling frame to create a representative list of employees—managerial, non-managerial, professional, craft, administrative, and so forth—from all of the major sectors in the U.S. These sectors include a wide variety of for-profit industries; local, state, and federal government; and nonprofits and nongovernmental organizations. The sampled employees occupy a variety of job titles, span the range of pay grades, classify themselves into a variety of ethnicities, and report ages from under 19 to over 65. In short, responses reported in Table 5.1 are likely to represent the opinions of a broad cross section of U.S. workers.

To interpret the data in Table 5.1, make note of two important issues. To start, the first six items on this survey comprised self-reports of the important security-related behaviors involved in password management. Password management is an important issue for virtually all computer users because passwords are the single most widely used form of authentication. The last three items represent opinions about three organizational issues—training, acceptable use policies, and notification about monitoring—that our research has found to be important for the effective maintenance of security and privacy within organizations. Respondents answered all items on a six-point frequency scale ranging from "never" to "one to five times per day." To make the data display more readily interpretable, we collapsed these six categories down to three: "never" (did not occur in the last six months), "sometimes" (at least a few times in the last six months), and "often" (at least once a week).

The second issue to note pertains to differences in the pattern of responses between managers and non-managers. The percentages rarely match exactly, but small differences in the patterns do not necessarily reflect real differences in the greater population because of the "margin of error." Think of each percentage as an estimate that is likely to be off by as much as one or two percentage points. Those items marked with an asterisk reached what statisticians call "statistical significance"—that is, a difference in the patterns that is likely to manifest in the population in a similar configuration.

Taking these two issues into account, let's compare password behavior across managers and non-managers. Managers were more likely to change their passwords and more likely to choose a password that was difficult to guess (that is, at least 8 characters long and containing numbers and punctuation marks). For both managers (68 percent) and non-managers (73 percent), it was striking that more than two-thirds never create a difficult-to-guess password. More bad news

Table 5.1   Comparison of Managers and Non-Managers from U.S. Firms on a Variety of Security-Related Behaviors and Issues

Security Issue	Employee Type	Never	Sometimes	Often
Frequency of changing password(s) for computer access at work*	Non-Manager	51%	48%	2%
	Manager	39%	59%	2%
Choosing a password that is difficult to guess*	Non-Manager	73%	25%	2%
	Manager	68%	32%	1%
Sharing passwords within work group	Non-Manager	85%	12%	4%
	Manager	81%	13%	6%
Sharing passwords within company*	Non-Manager	94%	5%	1%
	Manager	91%	5%	4%
Sharing passwords outside of company*	Non-Manager	98%	2%	0%
	Manager	97%	1%	2%
Writing down passwords	Non-Manager	81%	18%	1%
	Manager	78%	20%	2%
Provision of training to help employees improve awareness of computer/information security*	Non-Manager	62%	35%	3%
	Manager	52%	44%	4%
Enforcement of acceptable use policies governing employee computer use	Non-Manager	46%	43%	11%
	Manager	43%	50%	8%
Communication to employees concerning how their computer activities are monitored	Non-Manager	63%	30%	7%
	Manager	59%	34%	7%

Note: N=1512, with n=1242 non-managers and n=270 managers. Percentages on each line may not add to 100% due to rounding.
*Indicates statistical significance (p<.05), suggesting that similar differences between managers and non-managers are likely to be found in the population of U.S. workers.

appeared in the sharing of passwords. Most security professionals rec-ommend never sharing a password with anyone, ever. Our data showed, however, that 12 to 13 percent of managers and non-managers share passwords within their workgroup, 5 percent share passwords outside their workgroup but within their company, and 1 or 2 percent share passwords with individuals *outside* their company—a truly egregious failure of security. For sharing outside their workgroup or outside their company, managers were more than twice as likely than non-managers to do this "often." We suspect that this relates to the suggestion we heard from tech-dependent man-agers that they frequently need help with their computer usage. Managers who frequently need assistance from technical support personnel, application providers, or even their own children are probably more likely to reveal their passwords in the course of obtaining that assistance.

Looking now at the organizational security and privacy issues, what is striking is the high percentage of respondents who report that their companies never offered training related to information secu-rity, never enforced acceptable use policies, and never let employees know how they were being monitored. More than half of managers and non-managers reported that their companies never offered training. Almost two-thirds also reported that their companies never let employees know how they were being monitored. This finding is particularly problematic because legal experts generally recommend that all employees should be informed about how their computer behavior is monitored if companies expect to have the capability of using the resulting data in policy enforcement and/or investigation of malfeasance. Differences in the pattern of frequencies between managers and non-managers only appeared in the training category: 62 percent of employees reported that their companies never pro-vided training, while only 52 percent of managers reported this.

To recapitulate these findings, we believe these numbers gener-ally reflect a very poor level of attention in U.S. companies to behav-iors related to information security. While there are undoubtedly exceptions, and in other research we have reported notable differ-ences between sectors (see Stanton et al., 2005), in general these people reported that their companies are doing poorly with organi-zation-wide issues and they themselves are not doing their best with respect to personal behaviors related to security. Further, we noted that in at least one category, managers seem to have a view of what their companies are doing that is somewhat more optimistic than the perspective of employees, and that in their own security-related behaviors, managers are not consistently setting a good example for employees.

In Table 5.2, we provide a comparison of managers' and employees' perceptions on 10 different topics related to information security. These data were collected during spring and summer 2004 from approximately 14 different organizations in urban, suburban, and rural areas of upstate New York. These organizations ranged in size from about 10 to more than 1,000 employees. In the larger firms, we obtained data from several different business units within the organization; we had data from a total of 39 such units with anywhere between five and several hundred respondents per unit. Smaller organizations were treated as single business units. More than half of the organizations were commercial, for-profit firms, while a few were nonprofits in the healthcare and educational sectors. Within each organization we collected information from a convenience sample of employees and managers using a brief, Web-based survey. We kept track of which organization and business unit each employee or manager came from, and we aggregated data down to the business unit level in order to compare apples with apples (i.e., to compare managers with employees from the same firm). This is an important point that bears repeating: We intentionally ignored any differences between organizations and focused just on comparing managers and employees within each organization (technically speaking, a comparison procedure called a "paired-samples t-test").

The first column in Table 5.2 shows the item to which the employees and managers responded. For each item, respondents indicated their level of agreement on a one-to-five scale that ranged from "strongly disagree" to "strongly agree" (commonly known as a Likert scale). The middle two columns show the average for managers and employees, respectively, on this scale. Because all of the questions were worded in the same way—with agreement expressing more optimism or satisfaction with the security issue—responses with averages between four and five can be interpreted as reflecting a high degree of optimism about the issue. In contrast, averages closer to three suggest more of a balance between those who were pessimistic about the issue and those who were not. The items are presented in order according to the managerial averages, from most optimistic to least optimistic.

Table 5.2 Comparisons of Employee and Manager Perceptions

Item	Managers	Employees	Who was more optimistic?
I feel empowered to follow my company's security policies and/or procedures.	4.52	4.02	Managers***
The culture of my company encourages care and attention to information security issues.	4.37	3.94	Managers***
There's a lot I can do to keep the information I work with on my computer secure.	4.18	3.59	Managers**
My company consistently enforces an acceptable use policy that governs what employees can and cannot do with their work computers.	4.11	3.52	Managers***
My company will probably successfully avoid future problems due to information security breaches.	4.04	3.48	Managers***
I feel confident that I know how to choose secure passwords for my computer accounts.	3.70	4.38	Neither
My company provides useful training to help employees improve their awareness of computer and information security issues.	3.57	2.94	Managers***
My company seems well defended against problems related to information security.	3.46	3.95	Employees***
The technology people at my company communicate clearly on how to prevent information security problems.	3.14	3.71	Employees***
My company lets workers know about how their computer activities are monitored.	3.13	2.57	Managers***

***p<.001, **p<.01.
Note: All items had a response scale ranging from 1 (Strongly disagree) to 5 (Strongly agree). All comparisons were conducted with a paired samples t-test comparing managers and employees within the same business units (N=39). All comparisons were statistically significant except for the item concerning secure passwords.

One notable finding is that in seven out of 10 cases, managers were more optimistic than employees about security issues. For example, managers felt empowered to follow policies and felt that their company's culture encouraged security, that their firm judiciously enforced acceptable use policies, and that their company provided useful information security training—all to a greater extent than employees within their own business units. For one item, the formation of secure passwords, there was no statistically discernible difference between managers and employees. Even though the averages on this item are quite far apart, the statistical procedure we used indicated that it would be unsafe to assume that the same direction or size of difference would occur in the population. When we looked closely at the data, we found the reason for this: Substantial disagreement about passwords existed within many organizations such that what managers thought about this issue and what employees thought about it were not related. For the remaining two items—communicating with information technology people and feelings about being well defended against information security problems—employees expressed more optimistic opinions than their managers. Both of these items seemed to represent a referendum on confidence in the information technology department, and in both cases managers thought less of the information technology people than employees did.

On a related note, the three issues about which managers were most pessimistic were the revelation of monitoring to employees, communication with information technology people, and the extent to which the company was well defended. On all three of these issues, the average response from managers suggested that slightly fewer than half of the firms had managers expressing a pessimistic view (i.e., a response below the midpoint of the scale). We were disappointed, though not particularly surprised, to find that the worst item for both managers and employees pertained to letting employees know how their computer activities were monitored.

We conducted one follow-up analysis that was illuminating, although a bit unorthodox: We compared managers' average responses on the "well defended" item to their responses on the "avoid future problems" item. We found that the difference was statistically significant, suggesting that managers held somewhat contradictory views: a distinct optimism about avoiding future information security problems combined with pessimism about how well the organization was currently prepared to defend against such problems. Naturally, this led us to wonder how an organization would avoid future information security problems if even the managers, with privileged access to the inside story, believed that it was not well defended against them.

CHAPTER 6

Information Technology Professionals' Perspectives

In this chapter we report the highlights of nearly 50 interviews with information technology professionals as well as a survey of 460 information technology professionals conducted with the assistance of *Network Computing* magazine. This group included a wide variety of people—men and women, technical and managerial, experienced and new to the job—as well as a variety of settings—large companies and small; government, private, and nonprofit sectors; high-tech, manufacturing, financial, educational, and a variety of other organizational missions. What binds together all of the information technology professionals quoted in this chapter is their concern for information security. Whether they were the CIO of their organization or a frontline system administrator, each of them had responsibilities with respect to making sure that the organization's information was protected. Further, their responses often evinced a level of dedication to the organization's security goals that underscored their commitment to both the security of the organization's information systems and the privacy of the individuals whose data were stored on those systems.

As with the previous chapter, we have designated the interviewers' questions in boldface type with the respondents' answers following in plain type. Interviewers' questions are also prefaced by an "I" whereas respondents' answers are prefaced by an "R" designation. In the cases where we have represented more than one respondent's answer to the same question, we designate the different respondents by R1, R2, R3, etc., for the sake of clarity. In general, we tried to quote each respondent no more than once or twice to give a wide range of perspectives, but at the same time we selected quotes that we believed were representative of the responses of several of the information technology professionals from our group. All of the responses have been edited where necessary to maintain the confidentiality of the respondents and their organizations. In all cases we have worked hard to preserve the original meaning and tone of the respondents' comments. An example interview protocol for information technology professionals appears in Appendix E; similar protocols were used with most of our technical respondents.

Despite the variety of the respondents' backgrounds, we found a remarkable coherence in their perspectives, as well as a few important areas of disagreement. With minimal prompting, many respondents made points and told stories that highlighted the importance of the human side of information security—their concerns about attitudes, knowledge, skills, and behaviors of people in the organization who use information systems. For example, when asked about their biggest security concerns for the organization, a number of information technology professionals highlighted their concerns about very specific issues, from the management of passwords to generalized fears of unnamed security breaches. The following responses were representative of respondents from sizeable organizations with very large user communities (greater than 1,000 users):

I: What are your biggest security concerns for your organization? What do you spend the most time thinking or worrying about?

R1: The things that you don't see; the [users] who are smart enough to not get caught are what I am most concerned about.

R2: My biggest concern would be employee negligence. I worry that employees have not sought to educate themselves on the concerns of the company, or have not paid attention to the company training on information security.

I: Which [security issues] are the most worrisome for you?

R: Um, the [problems] that we don't know about ... Those are the most frightening I would say ... malicious behavior that truly looks like [the users] are trying to get at [unauthorized] information ... So there's some steps that are proactive steps that we're taking rather than the reactive we've had to in the past. But like I said, as soon as we get this taken care of, there is going to be something else.

I: So what do users do to compromise security? What have you come across?

R: They go looking for … it's called scanning ports, looking for a port that is open. … If you're in a parking lot and you just went to check to see if any of the car doors were unlocked, that is not illegal, but what is the reason for that? What is the purpose for checking if you don't have some sort of other kind of intention? If they can get into one person's computer, then they can start getting other access, depending on what kind of access levels they get. And then they can get into another level, and it can just kind of infiltrate that way into the system.

The preceding responses suggest that the size and diverse nature of user communities in these large organizations made the incidence of inquisitive, potentially harmful behavior frequent enough to create major headaches for information technology personnel. In contrast to this situation, we found that information professionals in smaller firms had considerably fewer concerns about malicious insiders. In the smallest firms (fewer than 50 people), where every worker typically knows every other person in the firm, we found that most of our respondents reported that they "prefer to do things on a trust basis." We took this phrase to mean that the respondent rarely if ever suspected an internal information technology user of intentional malfeasance, instead attributing any security breaches either to outside agents or to unintentional problems caused by insiders: accidents and mistakes that may have led to a security problem. In fact, while the preceding quotes pertained to negligent or malicious activities that might be done by users, we found that it was much more common for information security people to express concerns about innocent mistakes or unintentional problems created by employees. These problems ran the gamut from the installation of unauthorized wireless networks—committed by an overzealous team of engineers—to unavoidable equipment loss (usually a laptop stolen on a business trip), but all of them had in common the theme that employees sometimes caused problems with security out of ignorance rather than malfeasance. In general, information technology professionals seemed more likely to give employees the benefit of the doubt on problems the employees caused rather than routinely assuming malicious motivations. The following comments showed a range of concerns about unintentional or accidental employee behaviors:

I: My last set of questions is about information security. What are your concerns about information security in general?

R1: One of the new projects that we are initiating is wireless ... but as with most things, as with most big projects it's a very slow process. ... We are not going to put it in that conference room over there yet—well the people in that conference room need that wireless in that conference room [immediately], so they are going to set it up themselves, and the problem that we run into then is that they ... go to lunch, and somebody sits down and does something, and they can do that because there is absolutely no security in that wireless network that they set up. ... Trust me! You need to wait until [we] can do it right. ... Things go wrong, and people's accounts get hacked into, and servers are brought down because of people causing trouble, and sometimes the trouble is unintentional, and you can't track it back to the individual. ... So that is one kind of security problem that we have.

R2: The biggest concern is loss of information from the inside. You can do a lot to protect from unauthorized access from the outside, but keeping employees aware of the policies and the need to protect information is a constant task. Most time is spent worrying about traveling or remote employees. They carry significant information on their laptops and are constantly vulnerable in hotel rooms, etc.

I: So can you think of any other things that people do that make it hard to maintain security?

R: Well, you know it is interesting how people say don't write down your password, you know, there's two factions, one says make your password easy to remember so that you don't have to write it down, but if you make it easy for you to remember, chances are that someone can figure it out, and if you make it so difficult that you have to write it down, at least put it someplace that is secure. ... We would rather have you write it down and put it someplace secure than have a password that a [password cracking] system can guess. ... Go back into the training mode, you know, so pick a good password that you are going to have to write it down, and put it somewhere secure.

I: What are some of the things that people do in their everyday work life that compromise security?

R: Signing up for tip of the month or signing up for things like joke of the week. You know it may look very innocent, but really all they are doing is collecting information and feeding it out to other services. I see stuff going past on the screen on our servers—things from magazines, you know, just a lot of other stuff, a lot of unrelated information passing through our servers. Allowing other people to sit down and use their machine—it's a major compromise; it's a local compromise of our security system. Passing along their username and password to others. ... I don't know if it happens frequently. I do know that people from the outside that come in, maybe they are related to the individuals that allowed them to do it. [The outsiders] will sit down and use [the employees'] computers.

I: What do they do [with their passwords]?

R: Put it on the bottom of your keyboard or tell everybody what it is because you're going on vacation. You know here if you're not working with sensitive data, maybe it's not so big of a deal. When you are talking about security for information systems, it's hard to create in an environment like this. Maybe I'm overly sensitive from my days of banking ... whatever. It was a big deal if your password was compromised. You could lose your job if you were sharing log on or password. Here it is not ...

This individual mentioned his "days of banking" and contrasted that former work environment with his current employer to make the point that the security cultures of the two organizations were markedly different. We heard experienced information security professionals mention such contrasts quite frequently, often with a sense of frustration if the new employer placed less emphasis on information protection than the old one. In almost all cases, however, we found that information security professionals expressed an astute sensitivity to how the nature and mission of the organization affected its overall approach toward information protection. The following quote from a security professional at a financial institution highlights some of these issues in that type of firm:

I: What are some of the big challenges of information security management?

R1: The biggest challenge of information security management is to control the users in terms of how they use the system and what they can access. The problem about [large financial institutions] is there are thousands of people on system who need to have access to the information they need. With everybody wanting immediate access whenever they require it, it is hard to track all of them and to give the appropriate access rights because usually you will end up giving them what they requested instead of what they really deserve. Another hard part is that [our users] are hard to deal with at certain times. Information security management's difficulty gets worse when [users] need what they want but under the information security, you cannot give it to them. This will cause problems within the departments and conflicts break loose. Perhaps this occurs in different firms but this is definitely maximized in [large financial institutions].

R2: We have three separate companies here, and I know others [have] raised concerns about other people getting in and seeing their inventory, or seeing what they have, we sometimes have diverse and conflicting interests between the three companies. We have to balance that. Probably my only current concern is balancing that, the access that each person has in relation to the three different companies, what each person has and what they can see.

The previous two answers were particularly illuminating on the topic of access privileges. Many of the information technology professionals we spoke with outlined the problems with balancing too little or too much access for employees (as described in Chapter 2). Too little access creates social conflicts between information technology staff and users and puts pressures on information technology staff to increase access. Too much access creates security headaches. Even among highly ethical, well-trained employees, it is easy for a simple mistake to cause a lot of difficulties. The following comments highlight a few more of the simple things that employees do that can cause security problems:

I: What are some of the other things that people do that compromises security?

R1: The only thing is that people leave their workstations. With the system we have now, once you are signed on [and a screensaver appears] ... you still have to use a user ID. But we would like them to sign all the way out to the sign-out screen.

R2: The traditional stuff, like the password under your keyboard, and having too much going on a personal machine that they may take back and forth from home to work, and then that machine physically gets stolen, and all those traditional concerns still occur certainly. I was in the [military], as I mentioned, for 10 years. It's not like it's national security type stuff. It'll be just like any corporation. It's corporate sensitive things that are on a lot of people's personal computer especially like [the personal computer of] the director. I don't know who could make use of it, but I know that any information is usable to somebody. You know what I mean, I just could stretch my imagination, and think of the damage that having that laptop fully loaded with the stuff it has got on it, the whole damage that could really do. But as I said, any information is going to be useful to somebody. So you've got information walking out the door that way—whether it's payroll or credit card number, or purchasing card numbers, or whatever— I could probably imagine there is going to be personal data. There's going to be things like purchasing authority.

Not all of the information technology professionals we talked to put their concerns about employees first, of course. Some mentioned their bigger picture concerns or focused on some of the more technical aspects of security. Here are a few representative comments about those kinds of concerns:

I: What are your biggest security concerns for your organization? What do you spend the most time thinking/worrying about?

R1: Threats to the business operations of the [organization], privacy of individuals, information security on the network, physical security.

R2: Probably the biggest security concern in our organization is that the corporate network will become hacked and corporate data will be compromised. I probably spend time thinking and worrying about if our network will hold up to any internal or external attack. Another security concern of mine is if some massive Internet worm or virus gets inside our corporate network and has a negative impact on every server and user computer.

R3: My biggest security concern is to have the security necessary to maintain a stable network throughout the plant. Since we are a production facility, we have become extremely reliant on the production software to do estimates, write job tickets, schedule the workload of the plant, and record employee data collection. Any security breach that affects the stability of the network or production software has a ripple effect that slows or brings production to a stop. Most security concerns come from the Internet access, which is required to do Web-based data collection and scheduling. Disconnection from the Internet to solve a security problem is not an option due to the number of users who use remote access or Web-based data collection.

I: What are your major concerns about protecting information here?

R1: Well, we are obviously servicing people out there confidentially. But as the information technology department has been [doing], we do periodic checks once a month, that all of the work stations are signed on or signed off, that they are not visible to people from outside, that's pretty much what we do ... and the audit reports. You know, periodic checks on the users, that they don't have the password taped to the bottom of the keyboard ...

R2: The most sensitive information is the human resource system and some of the accounting work, which would be partnership distributions. In the human resource system, there is the payroll information, but then there is all of this other information that comes out of the accounting system, depending on the agreement that the individual has made. The human resource system is pretty tightly shut down, based on user. [In] the accounting information, there are different levels of security that are set. Instead of focusing on an organization as a whole, to block or put a brick wall up to protect you from the outside, you pick and choose the areas you are going to be targeting to provide the most security to. So, our most secure areas from outside threats would be really on the virus level, so we have the various levels of virus protection on our servers and on our gateways, things like that, but, [for] internal data, each of the users have shares that only they have access to ...

I: Is there anything troublesome about that for you?

R2: The only thing that has happened, not out of vindictiveness but by accident, is when someone sees something on the general share and they find that they don't need it, and it turns out that they deleted a number of other people's stuff. So there is an education that has happened there. Fortunately, the turnover here is not that great. And when it is, it's not of a vindictive nature.

As the last two sets of comments suggest, even the technical protection goals of information security tend to become intimately interwoven with the human frailties and oversights that affect information protection. On the whole, these responses showed that a wide range of employee behaviors may adversely affect information security. It is clear from the specific examples given by the information technology professionals we interviewed that even with a restricted range of privileges, the typical user can cause problems as a result of thoughtless or inappropriate behavior. Although many of the cited problems pertained to authentication and access control (e.g., the issues related to passwords), the next most important set of issues related to the use of e-mail and the Internet.

Influencing User Behavior

Our data collection efforts generally focused on getting the perspectives of information security managers rather than those of technical personnel, but our group of respondents also included frontline systems administrators and other technical people whose concerns one might expect to focus exclusively on the bits and bytes of firewalls and intrusion detection. Regardless of their specific responsibilities, however, we found that the majority of information technology professionals were both cognizant of the role that user behaviors played in security and interested in shaping those behaviors. Even among the highly technically oriented respondents, there was generally a strong sense that the users were "out there on the network," and that it was important to get those users to work for security rather than against it:

> **I: So when you do the technical background of incident response, how far do you follow through? Where do your responsibilities go from there?**

> **R:** So when we see things, it's trying like, kind of like holding spaghetti through your fingers: As soon as you pick up one, it starts sliding through the other. It's trying to contain it all [that] is [a] continuous [challenge]. As soon as you think you have one part of the system secured, then the network or that part figures out another way. It's like a cat-and-mouse game constantly. It's just continuous: Everybody is trying to outsmart each other and see what they can do.

> **I: The [users], you mean?**

R: Well, yeah I do. … They're smart. They're so smart. And sometimes, um, the little bit of knowledge can be dangerous—where they don't realize the ramifications of what they do. And so it's also a teaching, learning process. So you have to take each case individually that way. Just by attitude and behavior.

The question of how to accomplish the task of getting members of the user community to serve the goals of information security was not as easy for our respondents to answer, however. Perhaps because of their technical and engineering backgrounds or perhaps as a result of a kind of corporate isolation from the strategies and philosophies of top managers and human resources people, information technology professionals speculated about some approaches to influencing human behavior that some might consider simplistic or even naïve. For example, many of our respondents expressed a kind of blind faith in the efficacy of deterrents and punishments. While a few respondents admitted that they felt unqualified to answer the question of how to influence user behavior, others made comments like these:

I: What do you think motivates employees to do the right thing with respect to information security practices?

R1: More of a negative reinforcement, consequences of not doing it.

R2: Seeing the repercussions on not practicing good security …

R3: A combination of being a good person with morals and a commitment to their workplace combined with the fear of crossing the line and losing their job.

R4: Basically, people are good, people want to do the right thing. Sometimes there are legitimate [users] that might not be using technology in the proper manner, but they are not doing it intentionally.

These comments appear to reflect a tension in information technology professionals' feelings about their user communities. While on the one hand their personal experience suggests that negative consequences—in other words, punishments—do have a powerful effect on behavior, these security professionals were also reluctant to think the worst of people who, after all, are their colleagues and associates and perhaps may even be their friends or relatives. Depending upon who prevails in the interior quarrel about human nature—the little demon on one shoulder or the little angel on the other—some information technology professionals appear to believe people are basically bad and have to be controlled with threats (e.g., of job loss), while others believe that people are basically good and have to be given the leeway and the opportunity to behave as they should. This split casts the problem of influencing behavior in purely black-and-white terms and thereby cuts off debate and creative problem solving about how to influence user behavior. When choosing between people as basically good or basically bad, in the end it is usually the cynics who prevail, because bad things do eventually happen within any community, if that community exists long enough and contains a sufficient number of people. When the cynics do finally win, the tendency is for the organization to veer toward a somewhat draconian approach, as suggested by this comment:

> **I: What works to get employees to do the right thing for information security?**
>
> **R:** Management can access and look at all computer information, e-mail, and office space at ANY time [emphasis original] to ensure that no security has been breached. ... We have reviewed e-mails and warned certain employees, which makes the employees believe this is being constantly watched.

Casting users as basically bad in nature or basically good in nature also misses a critical point that is repeatedly demonstrated in social science research, namely the power of situational influences on behavior. Assuming they have some knowledge of what behaviors are appropriate for a situation, people enact a set of behaviors under circumstances that promote those behaviors. Likewise, assuming they are aware of what behaviors are prohibited in the situation, people may avoid enacting certain behaviors in situations that inhibit those behaviors. Setting aside just for the moment the "inhibiting" and "facilitating" situational influences, one critical prerequisite—for both promoting positive behavior and inhibiting negative behavior—lies in providing the knowledge of what behaviors are helpful and harmful to the organization's objectives. Unfortunately, because information technology skills and the subtleties of authentication and access control are not lessons learned at mother's knee, the rules for appropriate and inappropriate computer user behavior must be spelled out explicitly for many or most users in the workplace. Although small organizations still rely on verbal communication of such rules, in most organizations those in charge make an effort to set out the rules in written form. In short, in most organizations it is the judicious application of organizational policies that provides the essential grounding for influencing behavior. Policy documents and the rules and guidelines they contain provide the "reference standard" that defines the organization's consensual notions of acceptable and unacceptable as applied to interactions with information technology.

Security Policies

In the following discussion, we use the term policy in its broadest sense to refer to formalized efforts to document acceptable and unacceptable organizational behavior. Note that other authors have used the terms policy, procedure, guideline, and standard to refer to various and differing aspects of this documentation process. While acknowledging the importance of distinctions among these terms in some contexts, for our discussion we used the word policy as an umbrella term to cover all of the different aspects of written documentation of acceptable and unacceptable organizational behavior. With this definition, we also distinguish between the several technical meanings of policy—which can refer to various configurations or programming of system parameters or algorithms—and the organizational meaning of policy, which is documentation written by and for people rather than machines. As the following comments suggest, some of our respondents agreed that policy provides the starting point for all subsequent attempts to influence behavior:

I: What's happening here with information security policy?

R1: Information security policy is taken very seriously; over the past few years the company has spent a considerable amount of money on [policy development]. ... As a whole, information security policy is becoming more and more widely implemented across departments and is affecting all users in our organizational structure.

R2: Written and documented information technology policy is absolutely critical. You would not leave your house on a road trip without your roadmap! Policy is the roadmap to security. Without it, how can anyone be held accountable to a standard? With proper written and documented policies, an employee knows what is expected and accepted in dealing with computers and the proper use of the organization's network. They are immediately put on notice of accepted network behavior when provided with a proper roadmap; thereby allowing for sound and enforceable punishment/termination when those expectations are not met.

The only time we noted disagreement on these sentiments was when working with very small companies (fewer than 50 employees), where managers and information technology people alike sometimes expressed the opinion that their firm was too small to have written policies:

I: You were talking about password policies. Can you give me a more general sense of the kind of policies that you do have?

R: Don't have any! Don't have many. There were two or three groups years ago that were working on putting together an acceptable user policy, just two in there, one group, two or three people. As a shell, I don't know where it is. If we don't have it here, I guarantee that we probably don't have it ...

Whether or not it is a wise position for smaller companies not to have policies is open to further questioning, but as we spoke to more people, we learned that they felt it was quite a pragmatic stance. Respondents made clear to us their belief that creating information security policies that are tailored to the business goals, information technology configurations, and operating environments of a firm can be an expensive proposition both in dollars and human effort. The people in most small companies are often stretched too thin to spend substantial amounts of time on information technology policy development, particularly in firms that have only one information technology person (or that outsource all of their information technology needs and have no internal information technology person). As a complicating factor, policy work is never really completed: It is necessary to revisit information technology policies on a regular basis in order to adapt to changing business needs and innovations in technology. The following quote was representative of information security professionals' concerns:

I: What issues do you face with information security policy?

R: We are finding that we consistently have to redefine what is and is not acceptable use of the information and technology at [this company]. What information is confidential and how employees use the information technology at the company becomes very important. … The definition of personal use has also become very gray. For example, e-mail is defined as "not for personal use," however, when an employee receives a personal e-mail but does not respond to it—is it still violating the policy? How can the employee stop people from sending them personal e-mails, when their e-mail address is published on our Web site? The Internet is also defined as "not for personal use," however, when employees download a screen saver for their work PCs, is it still violating the policy? As technology advances, I believe a more specific and defined information security policy needs to be created.

In addition to the burden of creating and maintaining policy, companies need to undertake at least three other tasks in order to encourage and facilitate appropriate user behavior. First, mechanisms must exist by which the policy information can be communicated to users. Such communication generates awareness of the existence of formalized behavioral rules but may fall short in giving users the capability of actually enacting those behaviors. Thus, in addition to communicating policy information to users, information technology professionals must also offer training so that users have the opportunity to learn and practice the behaviors that are expected of them. Although training can give users the opportunity to learn and practice positive security behaviors, this opportunity does not always translate into actual behavior when back on the job. Thus, the final policy ingredient comprises processes and strategies for encouraging ongoing compliance with policies. The enforcement of policy— including the use of punitive sanctions—is often a matter that is left to managers and human resource professionals. Information technology professionals, however, sometimes play an important role in the data-collection activities related to policy compliance. More specifically, information technology people usually deploy and control the electronic methods of monitoring information technology usage in organizations. The monitoring processes often provide the first indication of problematic behavior on the part of an employee. In the following quotes, we hear from information technology personnel on these three interrelated topics: communication, training, and monitoring.

Communication

Turning to communication, we found an interesting distinction in security professionals' preferences for communicating with users. Some security people preferred to cast as many of the company's policies and rules as possible into technical restrictions and limits on what could be done with users' computers. Rather than talking to users directly about the appropriate and inappropriate ways of doing something, they preferred to program the permissions and restrictions into the technology. In essence, members of this group preferred to let the machines do the talking on policy. The following quote was representative of this position:

> **I: How do users know or find out about acceptable uses of information systems?**
>
> **R:** Users usually find out about what are acceptable uses of information systems and what are not acceptable uses when they violate or overextend the boundaries of security that have been put into place on a particular information system. Users know that they must have a user name and password to log on to our corporate network in order to get access to their data stored on a server. If they exceed the number of correct log-ons, their account on the server will be locked out and it will have to be reset.

This strategy may be applicable within larger firms that have high investments in information technology and, as a result, also have the devices, programs, and human expertise to automate these fine-grained prohibitions into their systems. Even with such rich resources, however, it is not always possible to use automated controls to restrict users' capabilities, as the following quote attests:

I: How does this new application affect things?

R: With the installation of this new [production] software program, the doors have been opened to business information like never before. The good news is that a customer service representative can now be the one source for a customer to ask questions about past job history and invoices. However, now that information is public to more employees than before, we now have to trust their judgment in the use of it.

This comment makes clear a fundamental problem with access controls and other preprogrammed limits on users' information technology privileges: Even with fine-grained controls, it is difficult to anticipate everything a user might wish to do. In most organizational environments it is thus a necessity to provide users with a substantial range of permissible behaviors and to allow common sense and organizational policy to guide their enactment of these behaviors. Other security professionals we spoke to recognized that clear and direct communication with users was the best way to ensure that users followed the organization's prescribed information technology policies. The following comment reflects that position:

I: How do you find communicating with non-technical folks about information security issues?

R: I think that being open and honest (as well as drawing some pictures) is always the best way to discuss these issues. All of our policies have been developed by committee to be user-friendly, but, at the same time, have the good of the community at heart. Certainly, more time with individuals would help, but we feel that our publications (in the various handbooks and the technology user guide) are pretty clear on these subjects. I think "doing the right thing" comes really from a moral perspective. If someone truly wants to do something bad, our policies and safe-guards may slow them down, but it won't stop them. So, in some ways, we do have to trust our users. As soon as you connect people together, somebody's going to use the stuff for things you hadn't intended. We just do our best to min-imize the temptation and to respond appropriately when we have a problem.

Note the importance that this respondent places on trust: He sug-gests that there will always be unpredictable and unanticipated uses (or misuses) of information technology such that one has little choice but to place some trust in employees that they will use the complex technologies properly. We also noted that the phrase "minimize temptation and respond appropriately" could almost serve as a mantra for the way that many security people approach their work. Regardless of their positions on trust and temptation, however, most information technology professionals with whom we spoke agreed that communication with end-users was not as good as it should or could be. With only a few exceptions, information technology profes-sionals described problems and frustrations associated with trying to communicate technical information to end-users:

I: How do you find communicating with non-technical folks about information security issues?

R1: It can be difficult sometimes communicating to non-technical people about information security policy because they are just not aware of all the issues that sur-round a corporate entity doing business everyday. They do not really understand the concerns of information tech-nology personnel trying to maintain order and security within the information systems they use every day to do their work.

R2: As with any type of communication, you need to speak a language understood by the target audience. When explaining information security to non-technical persons, the use of analogies and metaphors is necessary.

R3: My experience here has been [that] the computer literacy is not where it should be [among employees]. I don't think that's because people are not smart, but [there is an] unwillingness sometimes to learn. I am not really sure why. ... There has to be a willingness. There has been a dependency on information technology that people take it for granted. ... We want users to be more independent because that will free us up to do something else for the [organization].

R4: People understand the need for security, but are usually unwilling to make the extra effort to practice secure computing.

It is interesting to note that the final two comments in the preceding block focused on end-users' *willingness* to learn what they needed to know in order to achieve better security. These information technology professionals have intuitively grasped the importance of motivation in the learning process, as well as the idea that motivation is as important in learning about security as in learning about any other topic. We heard a variety of opinions expressed on this issue of user motivation to learn, with information technology professionals attributing the problems they encountered to everything from generalized information overload to a specific phobia about technical nomenclature and concepts. The following respondent subscribed to the former view and hoped that better information presentation could improve the dissemination of security knowledge to the end-user community:

I: Can you think of any ways that communication could be improved?

R: We are doing several things. We are redesigning our Web site. We are adding an entire section on security to our Web site, and we will be highlighting in blue to draw attention so that [users] can know how to check up on what they should be doing to protect themselves. People don't want to and won't go four or five layers into a Web site. They need [the information] right in front of them. We also are designing a new ad campaign with a cartoon character of some sort. ... Hopefully if the character is creative enough he might catch the attention of people to pay attention enough to maybe have an impact on helping deal with these security issues.

Whether or not the previous respondents' hopes for the security cartoon character were fulfilled remains unknown, but a reliance on improved information presentation alone seems unlikely to generate the motivation to learn that information technology professionals have found lacking. In addition, it is likely that members of the user community must come to see a convincing benefit to becoming more involved in the enactment of security. Many information technology professionals have related anecdotes to us about how zealous users became about doing backups after losing work to a crashed hard disk drive. The following respondent expresses a similar sentiment with respect to security:

> **I: Can you think of any ways that communication could be improved?**
>
> **R1:** The hardest part about communication is proving the need for information security. Sometimes you have to give real life, recent examples to get the attention of the audience. If it's something that could affect them, you'll have their attention.
>
> **R2:** The ideal solution would be to take one person in the organization on a rotating basis to work with you and spend a whole day watching what you do and asking as many questions as you could tolerate. Unfortunately, we live in the real world; the next best solution would be to provide some method of training about the importance of information security and policy making on a novice user level.

The latter respondent focuses on the value of one-on-one communication and concludes with a more pragmatic approach to communicating security information to end-users: training. This comment crystallizes several of the preceding responses: People will seek out information and learn it on their own—either by asking someone or looking it up—if they perceive a strong need to obtain that information. Otherwise, these information technology professionals suggest that the importance of a topic or knowledge area must be demonstrated to learners through examples with personal significance. Unfortunately, with respect to security, so many aspects of success depend upon preventive and prophylactic measures that most people cannot become motivated as a result of direct personal experience. One would not want to infect an end-user's computer with a virus in order to demonstrate the importance of maintaining up-to-date anti-virus protection. As a result, the organization must mandate users' participation in training. Mandated participation in training can help to ensure a basic level of security literacy among all employees who use computers in their work lives.

Training

Training can occur at many points in the employment life cycle, starting even before an employee is hired and continuing through the duration of the employee's tenure with the firm. The following comments reflect the common practice of beginning the security training process as soon as users come on board with the organization:

I: What's your feeling about security training?

R: Employees must have proper training in a pre-employment interview that outlines, in detail, the importance of and requirements in network security. This interview entails an in-depth overview of the organization's policies and procedures involving all aspects of information technology. The employee [is] required to sign an acknowledgment and understanding of those policies.

I: Has your organization developed or implemented any training in information security?

R1: As part of our new hire training, everyone with or without a security clearance is given a security briefing by the security office as well as a briefing by the [information technology] department.

R2: Just generic new [user] training. This does include some tips and suggestions (passwords, privacy, etc.).

R3: YES! [emphasis original]

I: Who takes this training?

R3: The training is given by company [information technology] professionals; every employee is required to take this training the first two weeks of employment. I feel the training is very effective if the policies are adhered to.

The closing phrase "if the policies are adhered to" makes an important point about the effectiveness of training: Training is useful only if it is actually put into practice when the user is back at work. Human resource professionals call this "transfer of training," and it is the final and most challenging aspect of achieving success in a training program. As the following comment implies, training programs can deliver plenty of useful knowledge and skills within the instructional environment, but if the trainees are not open to learning that knowledge or those skills, they are not likely to benefit from them:

I: What's your feeling about the effectiveness of this training?

R: Our [information technology] department gives training to all new members of our community. It usually lasts about two to four hours. I think the training is OK, but to be honest, the [users] don't really listen when it comes to the security and privacy issues.

As with good communication, one definite key to effective training lies in ensuring that learners are receptive to the message that is being delivered. Another important issue raised by respondents related to the importance of constant repetition and updating of the message. Unlike other areas, information technology security remains in a constant state of flux, with new techniques arising to cope with the newest innovations in the capabilities and functions of the technology itself. In addition, because the sophistication and capabilities of outside malicious agents are always evolving and improving, the kinds of threats impinging on corporate networks are also in a continual state of change. The following comments reflected an awareness of the importance of continual updating in the security training process:

I: What's your feeling about the effectiveness of this training?

R1: All employees are trained on security and usage guidelines. The challenge is refreshing this training over time.

Keeping the awareness of information security policies and new threat information is a constant task.

R2: There is always room for improvement in any type of training. For example, in the 1960s less than 20 percent of people wore seatbelts. Nowadays more than 80 percent do. Of course this did not happen overnight, but persistence, education, and reputation are all causes of the increase of awareness. I operate in the way of reputation. It's kind of funny because usually when anyone from [IS] or myself are around people always say "I didn't do it!" This lets me know that they are becoming more security conscious.

The previous respondent's curious comment about "reputation" bears further scrutiny. While making the rounds through the organization, this respondent found that people were jokingly denying their guilt for whatever bad thing may have happened with respect to information security. Further, this respondent also referred to reputation in the example about seatbelt use. We interpreted this comment to imply the importance of social reminders about the connections between behavior and consequences. When people have some consciousness that their behavior is visible to others—that their reputation is on the line—they are more likely to feel the strong connections between their behavior and the possible adverse consequences. In a car, knowing that you may receive a ticket from a police officer or a rebuke from your spouse for not wearing your seatbelt may influence your decision to buckle up, especially when someone you respect is sitting in the passenger seat and watching what you do. Likewise, consider that people are much more likely to wash their hands after a visit to the restroom if others are present. With respect to information security, knowing that the information technology director, someone in the information technology department, or even a colleague of yours may notice when you visit that gambling Web site may influence your computer-related behavior. These ideas about the importance of visibility of behavior have influenced the designs of networked information technology and the tools the information technology people use to manage it. In particular, information technology professionals have a wide range of tools available for making user behavior visible as manifested in the traffic within and across the corporate network. We refer to these tools under the general umbrella of employee monitoring.

Monitoring

Information technology professionals and security specialists usually become involved in implementing employee monitoring because they have the technical knowledge and security access needed to deploy monitoring tools. In many instances, information technology people set up these tools in such a way as to provide reports and information to managers outside information technology (e.g., in human resources), but even in these cases the information technology people typically have substantial access to the data about what users are doing on, with, and to the company's information systems. Sometimes this monitoring is primarily used for technical reasons—such as avoiding viruses—as the following exchange shows:

I: Is there an information security policy that you know about?

R: Our tech support takes care of that. And they have pretty much set their guidelines and pretty much stick to them.

I: Do they monitor what other employees do?

R: Yes they can monitor. ... They usually monitor right from the server. Mainly it is e-mail and Internet that can be monitored. E-mail they have to because it just comes in and grows, and that is where a lot of your viruses come through and so we have to make sure it doesn't get past that server and they are really good about that.

Monitoring of e-mail and Internet traffic, even purely for technical reasons such as virus mitigation, gives information technology professionals a substantial access to records of employees' activities. This high level of access can generate ethical quandaries by putting the information technology professionals in possession of very sensitive information about employees' behavior. We found that many of our respondents were quite uncomfortable with this degree of access, to the point where they actually ignored or softened policies set by higher management. In this next quote, a respondent expresses a degree of squeamishness about the level of access afforded by the technology in use:

> **I: Do people ever wonder how much access you have to their information, to their e-mails?**
>
> **R:** No, I make sure everybody knows that me and one other person have access to everything. You've got to understand that because we do have access, and I assure them whenever of my personal ethics on confidentiality and all that stuff, I never let them become compromised. So I haven't had any issues with people caring about how much access I have. But, I'll share an incident with you that was a little troubling to me. I worked for a company where there was a disgruntled employee and there was a lawsuit involved. I got a call from a person above me that they wanted me to capture all of this person's e-mail and make it available to them. I know legally that all mail in an electronic system owned by a corporation, business, is a property of that business. But I felt badly about walking a fine ethical line. I felt I would compromise that employee. It was troublesome to me.

The following respondent describes a contrast between the harshness of the stated policies about monitoring and the actual practice:

> **I: Will there be any other information in the system about employees' computer use or activities?**
>
> **R:** We are just writing the policy and we just wrote up this policy statement, which basically says that we are policing everything they say and do all day long. It's not really true. Yes, we do have the tools to monitor, but no, we don't really want to do that. They are pretty conservative here about the policies, but we would rather give people the benefit of the doubt, that they are using the tools given to them in the best interest of the organization. And if they are using them in their own self-interest, so what else is new? Things have always been that way, and probably always will. You can't get out of hand about it.

Perhaps as a result of feelings such as those expressed here, we found that harsh policies and gentle practices were a very common combination in the firms we examined. The tendency for harsh policies probably reflects a desire among managers to protect themselves and the organization against the rare instance when an employee does commit some type of offense with the company's information technology. The preceding respondent continued as follows:

> **R:** There are always a few cases of stupidity, like where I was in my old job and there was a death threat on the voice mail system, and I had to help copy it to be used in a court case against the guy. ... That's about as extreme as it gets, in terms of the understanding of the technology having a real effect on people. Another case, where the local Avon Skin-So-Soft rep would be selling with the use of the company e-mail system. That kind of thing could be discovered, and probably would be discovered eventually, on a case-by-case basis. It wouldn't require a mass monitoring for that. And it wouldn't be a major threat to the organization either. That's my attitude.

The respondent makes a clear distinction between the rare case with significant impact and the more typical problem that may cause some annoyance but is otherwise harmless. The respondent seemed to see value in the monitoring technology at both ends of this spectrum, although the comment about "mass monitoring" also makes clear a preference to leave policy-abiding employees alone. In keeping with this idea, the use of relatively gentle practices—particularly ones that fail to enforce the letter of the policy—seemed to arise from a frequently held belief among information technology professionals that most employees use the technology in ways consistent with the organization's goals. The following comments suggested a certain intentional laxity in enforcing monitoring policies:

I: Do they monitor all [employees'] e-mail?

> **R1:** Well, they don't monitor, they don't monitor. No, no, they don't monitor per individual per se. In other words they won't go into your e-mail and see what is in there. That they don't do, but they monitor as it comes in to see what IP address this is going to and they don't necessarily know who that belongs to but they can see what is coming

in. If there are a lot of viruses coming in then they are getting a lot of hits but actually monitoring and checking people's personal e-mail, no. Not that I am aware of.

R2: I don't want to monitor or even have people think we
are. I would like to make these tools encourage the most
efficient forms of communication: quick, fast, and OK as
long as it goes by certain guidelines. Sort of like the
Internet, with its freewheeling nature. It's like Microsoft,
you can't have people be sending e-mail that can be sub-
poenaed. We don't want litigation. ... But generally, with
reasonable sensitivity, this system can really help. ... I am
hoping that it will make people comfortable that we have
a policy, people know what it is, and if anyone asks anything, we can show them the policy. Hopefully they won't
necessarily look for a minute-by-minute policing of what
the policy says.

As with several other aspects of dealing with the user community,
information technology professionals appear to have mixed feelings
in their attitudes toward monitoring. While managers may hand
down quite powerful policy statements that mandate extensive and
possibly continuous monitoring of employee behavior, some information technology professionals appear to have a strong desire to
maintain their faith in the basic goodness of people and with that
desire an associated preference to avoid prying into people's behavior. As a result, some information technology people appear to intentionally avoid using the monitoring tools available to them or to use
them in a limited way. One respondent who did not wish to be quoted
said that he had occupied his information technology professional
job for many years and that if someone had asked him about monitoring of e-mails, chat, and Web visits in years gone by, he would have
been flabbergasted by the question. He said that he never bargained
for the role of a kind of cybercrime detective. He said that he still
believes that 99.9 percent of the users are honest and are trying to use
the information technology in a responsible way, but that the
remaining 0.1 percent makes it necessary to do all of the logging,
monitoring, and reporting that he does. The following quote from a
different respondent—about the larger issue of policy enforcement

rather than monitoring per se—exemplifies those ambivalent attitudes toward monitoring:

I: How comfortable do you feel with setting the security priorities?

R: I feel comfortable, again, as long as I am involved in what the technology can do for it. I can help them figure out how to spend the money and what solutions might be riskier or likely to work. I like to find out how much I am saving them or what risks I am helping to address. But I also have a social conscience. Privacy needs to be maintained, and our customers deserve that. But I recognize the challenge where they need expedited [service] and the people need information right away, so somehow you have to rectify that discrepancy. If I allow a weakness in security policy, and gain something in [service], from a social conscience perspective, I have made the right decision.

This respondent expressed the idea of how his "social conscience" constrained him from implementing the strictest possible security policy. This idea of social conscience seemed to signify a balancing act among the needs of different groups—privacy of customers, security of the organization, organizational efficiency/productivity, and rights of the employees—that this information technology professional felt responsible for performing. Information technology people work under political and social pressure from multiple constituencies. Further, at least some recognize that privacy, security, or efficiency are not "universal goods" to be achieved at the expense of other desirable outcomes. The correct balance among these forces, however, depends heavily upon the circumstances and mission of the organization. Although some highly placed chief information officers (CIOs) or chief security officers may feel capable of achieving the appropriate balance on their own, most information technology professionals look toward the organization's leadership for guidance on how to resolve the conflicts and dilemmas that characterize the contemporary information security environment. In the quotes that follow, we explore how information technology professionals regard the leaders who set both their priorities and their budgets.

Leader Priorities

In some of the largest organizations, a senior manager in the role of CIO or chief information security officer (CISO) sits at the executive level and interacts directly with the organization's highest-level leaders. In most cases, however, the highest-level information technology and information security managers occupy much lower positions in the organization: mid-level managers or frontline supervisory positions. Except where otherwise noted, the following responses come from mid-level managers with substantial responsibility for information security but without direct access to those inhabiting the executive suite.

> **I: What are the priorities of your organization's leaders in terms of information security? How do you get information about their priorities?**
>
> **R:** Protection of information is the biggest priority. Yet, that is balanced with business needs to share information with customers, partners, etc. All information-security-related policies are reviewed by the organization's leaders.
>
> **I: And do you know what the leadership's situation is in terms of its priorities for security?**
>
> **R:** That is hard to say. I would assume that they are into it but that is not on my end of it so I don't feel qualified to answer that but I am sure it is to make sure things run smoothly and that we don't get hacked …

The preceding comment was a frequent refrain among our respondents: Security managers would say that they had a general idea of what the information security goals of the organization were, but also that they largely had to infer these goals because of a lack of direct communication about security issues from the organization's leaders. On a related note, we heard from a number of information technology professionals about management's apparent desire to avoid deep immersion in the detailed business aspects of running the security operation. The following comments were characteristic:

I: What's up with your bosses?

R: What the new [CEO] is pushing for is—there is no (also my opinion) control at the top—is indicative of how the way things would be and the risk, who would be responsible is all very different for all the people up here: Everybody says "I want to do my own thing, I want to be my own boss, don't tell me what to do," and there is no genuine policy. And nobody at the top seems interested in that, nor do they want to change this [situation], because they don't understand it, the need for this type of thing.

I: What are the priorities of your organization's leaders in terms of information security? How do you get information about their priorities?

R: We meet periodically about information technology issues. I think they share the same concerns as me, although I don't think they truly understand the budget ramifications of some of these issues. Privacy and confidentiality are also critical issues to them and me.

Although this information technology manager was at least meeting with upper management on a regular basis, we noted in multiple instances a kind of language or culture gap between information technology professionals and managers. Although each party saw the importance of the other's role in setting and maintaining the organization's security policies, it was common to find a perception that neither group really understood the other at the level that would be needed to closely engage the organization's overall mission and priorities with the budgets, planning, and technology needed for an effective information technology security operation. The only exceptions to this appeared when an information manager was positioned much more highly within the organization. The following quote came from a CIO with wide-ranging responsibilities for information security:

I: What are the priorities of leaders in regard to infosec?

R: The priorities of leaders (*me* in the case of [my organization]) is to get the right resources and training to my security professionals. Retaining and paying good security staff is an ongoing problem within [my sector]. When employees can be making twice the amount in [another] sector it is hard to retain bright staff who can execute security policies. Additionally, security education and awareness is a high priority.

This CIO's response focused strongly on the resource issues involved in creating effective security: staffing, budget, and training. This sentiment reflected accurately the challenges of business in her sector—an area of business in which information technology was chronically underfunded. Other leaders focused on priorities that fit with their own business environments. For example, the following quote came from a respondent in a financial services company:

I: What are the priorities of your organization's leaders in terms of information security?

R: Probably the most important priority of our corporate officers is the integrity of the data that we receive internally and our customers receive externally. Our company is a securities firm, we are receiving data from many different sources and data is going out in different directions, so it is very important to protect the flow of data throughout our organization.

These comments underscore the importance of open communication between organizational leaders and information technology managers who implement the organization's priorities. Because those priorities depend so heavily upon the nature of the organization's mission and operating environment, and because information technology professionals may not have had training or exposure to the nuances of that environment, members of the upper management team must make the organization's security priorities explicit to information security managers. Note, however, that upper management plays another, more universal role as well. Individuals all over the organization—including most of the members of the user community—look for clues from leaders with respect to what is valued in the organization. The following quotes capture this dynamic:

I: What are the priorities of your organization's leaders in terms of information security?

> **R1:** Organizational leaders ... play an absolute critical role in network security. I firmly believe that security begins at the highest levels and flows smoothly downward when enthusiastically promoted and aggressively enforced. ... It is of utmost importance that organizational leaders assume that role and let their subordinates know that security is a real and serious concern.

> **R2:** Upper management holds the information technology manager accountable for drafting the security policies, overseeing their review, and implementing them. Without support from upper management, security policies often fall by the wayside and never get written, understood, or implemented.

These comments highlight the importance of leadership to the effectiveness of the whole security enterprise. Organizational leaders not only set the firm's priorities, they also encourage and inspire others within the organization to carry out those priorities. Leaders stand behind the organization's security policies; by having personal involvement in the creation and ratification of policies, by following those policies themselves, and by communicating the importance of those policies to others, they ensure that the policies have meaningful and positive effects on the organization. As a parting note on the topic of leadership, this CIO describes the importance of having an "officer level" individual in charge of security and privacy:

> **I: Can you tell me a little bit about your experiences with issues of privacy and security?**

> **R:** There needs to be a security officer for each organization. My organization has been trying to figure out who that person is going to be. In other organizations that I know of, the CIO, that's my job, has received that assignment. Personally, I could do it here, but there is a lot more to security than just the technical issues, like how people actually do their jobs; security and privacy on paper is important as well. So each organization needs to have an officer in charge of it, to keep the information secure and private, and do it in a way that doesn't necessarily destruct the customer service ...

Survey of Information Technology Professionals

With a sincere note of gratitude to the editors and staff of *Network Computing* magazine, who included several of our research questions in a recent survey of their readership, we report here some statistical analyses of information technology professionals' concerns about one particular specialty area of information security: wireless network security. As we noted in Chapter 2, wireless networks provide employees with substantial benefits for mobile data access—particularly while traveling—but these networks also create substantial security vulnerabilities.

The two major vulnerabilities of concern frequently cited by information security specialists are (1) the creation of unauthorized or so-called rogue access points by well-meaning but misguided employees and (2) the use of unsecured commercial or private wireless networks when employees are on the road. The *Network Computing* survey was sent to approximately 20,000 subscribers. Response rates to magazine surveys are generally quite low, and the 2.3 percent response rate (460 respondents) for this survey provides a substantial sample size for analysis, but is unlikely to be highly representative of computing industry professionals as a whole due to biases introduced by self-selection (i.e., into the pool of subscribers) and non-response (i.e., to the survey itself). Nonetheless, these data gave us a view of the range of opinions of a substantial number of people and allowed us to compile some descriptive statistics and comparisons relevant to this chapter.

Respondents included a variety of individuals who self-identified as corporate officer, management, team leader, or technology staff. Despite these labels, the technical nature of the magazine makes it quite likely that most respondents had a significant technical background regardless of their positions in the corporate hierarchy. Respondents reported that their organizations' annual revenues ranged from less than $1 million to more than $1 billion, with the modal response indicating an annual revenue between $10 million and $100 million. Workforce size in respondents' organizations ranged from fewer than 50 employees to more than 20,000, with the average response suggesting a medium-size firm with 500 to 1,000 employees.

The first question we wanted to explore pertained to policies that the respondents' organizations had implemented to influence employee behavior related to wireless network usage. Among all individuals whose organizations used wireless, about 45 percent of respondents indicated that they had a "clearly defined policy" governing the deployment and use of wireless. On the opposite tack, 32 percent said that they did not have policies, 4 percent did not know whether they had policies, and 19 percent had policies under development but not yet deployed. Looking more closely at those individuals who reported that their organizations did have policies, only 46 percent indicated that their organizations strongly enforced the policies. In contrast, 24 percent had "moderate" enforcement, 22 percent had "reactive" enforcement, 5 percent had "minimal" enforcement, and 2 percent had no policy enforcement at all. Taking these two sets of results together, it seems that less than a third of the organizations that used wireless networking had fully deployed policies that were strongly or moderately enforced.

Next, we examined nine critical issues in wireless security, five of which pertained to external threats to a wireless network and four of which related to employees' misuse or mistakes with wireless. Respondents were asked to what extent they considered each issue to be an important wireless security issue; they were asked to respond on a seven-point, agree–disagree scale (commonly known as a Likert scale). We compressed the seven-point scale to three categories to streamline our data display. In Table 6.1 we display the nine items, along with the percentage of respondents who considered the particular issue as important or unimportant or who were unsure of its importance. Data in this table came from approximately 385 responses: About 75 respondents apparently did not feel qualified to respond to these questions, perhaps because of the status of their wireless deployment or lack of knowledge of their organization's issues.

The results in Table 6.1 are sorted in declining order of percentages of individuals who considered each issue important. A column in this table designates whether an issue relates primarily to "outsiders" or "insiders." Outsiders are defined as individuals who are not part of an organization's authorized user community, while insiders are employees and other people authorized to use an organization's information systems. As an example, "malicious attacks by hackers" presumably refers to individuals who are not employed by the company—i.e., outsiders—whereas "rogue wireless access points set up by employees" clearly refers to individuals working inside the company.

Table 6.1   Information Technology Professionals' Perceptions of Wireless Network Threats

Threat	Source	Unimportant	Not Sure	Important
Malicious attacks by hackers	Outsider	6%	5%	89%
Unauthorized access to secure internal network resources by outsiders	Outsider	6%	6%	88%
Tampering with confidential enterprise data by outsiders	Outsider	9%	7%	84%
Rogue wireless access points set up by employees	Insider	15%	9%	76%
Use of organization's Internet connectivity by outsiders	Outsider	14%	11%	75%
Unsecured home wireless networks used by employees for official work	Insider	16%	10%	74%
Unsecured wireless 'hotspots' used by employees for official work	Insider	19%	12%	69%
Damage to the corporate reputation through publicized war-driving attacks	Outsider	21%	14%	65%
Unauthorized non-business use of wireless by employees	Insider	32%	16%	53%

Note: Responses came from N=385 individuals who completed an online survey for *Network Computing* magazine. Original items appeared on a seven-point, agree-disagree scale and were compressed into three categories to streamline the display: 1-3 = unimportant, 4 = not sure, and 5-7 = important. Percentages in each row may not add to exactly 100% due to rounding error.

While the five outsider issues were considered high priorities by a majority of respondents, with three of them holding top positions, we were not surprised to see the problem of "rogue wireless access points set up by employees" appear high on the list (76 percent considered this an important security issue). A majority of respondents rated all four insider issues as important. Interestingly, even for the tech-oriented readers of *Network Computing* magazine, employee behavioral issues were a significant concern in the area of wireless security.

Another interesting finding is that up to 32 percent of individuals considered at least one of these insider issues relatively unimportant from a security perspective. While security priorities undoubtedly differ among companies, we were surprised to find even a hint of a laissez-faire attitude among these respondents, given the results of the interview data. As we dug a bit deeper into these data, we believe we found a reason behind this issue: The pattern of priorities varied substantially depending upon one's level in the corporate hierarchy.

In particular, for each of the four groups—corporate officer, management, team leader, and technology staff—we analyzed which of the eight issues were considered highest priority as well as which of the eight issues generated the most controversy (i.e., the most disagreement among members of the group). Managers, team leaders, and technology staff members were strongly in accord with one another, on average having 88 percent agreement about the ordering of wireless security priorities (average $r = .94$; correlations were calculated by treating each of the nine items as a case, and correlating the set of item statistics for one group with the set of item statistics for the other group). In contrast, when comparing corporate officers to the other groups, on average there was only 56 percent agreement (average $r = .74$) between these groups.

For example, corporate officers rated "tampering with confidential enterprise data by outsiders" higher than did any other group, but in addition there was little controversy among them that this was the most important wireless security issue. In contrast, not only was this issue not in the top spot for any of the other groups, but members of the other groups had some disagreements among themselves on how important an issue it was. Note that we're not suggesting that one group is more correct than another group, only that the concordance about security priorities among the lower level groups is not bubbling up to the officer level. The corporate officers may have an enhanced view of security priorities—from their strategic perspective on the company's business goals—or the techs, team members, and lower-level managers may have a more accurate view from their positions closer to the trenches, but in any event these data suggest that differences in viewpoints may not be filtering across the boardroom-backroom boundary.

Information Technology Professionals' Perspectives on Security and Privacy

In this chapter we used quotes from about 50 interviews with information technology professionals to illustrate how concerns for information security and privacy are demonstrated among those individuals with primary responsibility for the maintenance of information security. These quotes revealed a class of individuals who work at the center of a set of forces imposed upon them by their managers, their user communities, their customers, and other groups who care about the security of information, personal productivity, the effectiveness of the organization, privacy of sensitive data, or all of the above. Information security professionals communicate with upper management but feel that they do not always receive clear signals back. Information security professionals communicate with the user community but do not always feel that they have been heard or that the user community takes their admonitions seriously. Information technology professionals readily use organizational policies as the means of formalizing the rules for acceptable and unacceptable behavior but must rely upon leaders to emphasize the importance of these policies and trainers to communicate the awareness of these policies to the user community. Some see the members of the user community as basically good and trustworthy, while others see the users as essentially troublesome and undependable. Information security professionals possess the means to monitor the behavior of everyone in the user community but often refrain from exercising their full capabilities except in cases of dire need. Despite this reluctance to pry, however, these information security professionals recognized the general importance of influencing user behavior in order to ensure the effective maintenance of security within the organization.

Data from the survey on wireless network security did not contradict any of the findings from the interview data. Two points, however, were emphasized by our analysis of the survey. First, employee behavioral issues do indeed figure into the list of concerns of the technically sophisticated respondents to that survey, even though they might not generally trump the technical security issues. Second, variations in the patterns of priorities among individuals at different levels of the hierarchy reinforced the findings from the interviews that a free flow of data about security priorities between tactical and strategic decision makers may not exist in many organizations.

We close this chapter with a quote from an information technology professional that seems apropos, given the convergence of the interview and survey data on this final point:

I: How much contact do you have with [the top management team]?

R: On a daily basis or as problems arise. We feel comfortable asking them for anything. We're small so we get help right away. The CEO is extremely open. The CIO is kind of bull-headed. In general, I think they sometimes have their own agendas, and they don't come together all the time. Typical! The [Chief Financial Officer] definitely understands the cash, and that has priority.

CHAPTER 7

Employee Perspectives on Information Security and Privacy

In a break from the pattern in Chapters 5 and 6, we begin this chapter with some intriguing opinion survey results about electronic monitoring in the workplace. In 2001, near the beginning of our research project, we conducted an online survey of 257 non-managerial employees with an eye toward finding out what they thought about a variety of new forms of electronic monitoring, including e-mail monitoring, computer monitoring, and video monitoring. The average age of these employees was 35 years, about 65 percent were women, 55 percent had completed at least some college, and their organizations included a wide range of industries and sectors—from advertising, banking, and casinos to travel, U.S. government, and veterinary services. With a sincere note of thanks to our colleague Christiane Spitzmueller, who helped collect these data as part of her master's thesis, we present in Table 7.1 an overview of employees' responses about their intentions to subvert or resist various workplace monitoring techniques.

In response to questions about their behavioral intentions when thinking about monitoring procedures that their companies might adopt, an astonishingly large percentage of employees reported that they would, in effect, game the system. For example, with reference to e-mail monitoring, 65 percent of respondents said they would switch to Web-based personal e-mail accounts in order to avoid having the company monitor them, 63 percent said they might try to change settings on their computers to keep their e-mail private, and 50 percent said they would encourage co-workers to stop using the company system. Although a smaller percentage of employees reported intentions to subvert or resist computer monitoring (e.g., of Web site visits) and video monitoring, a substantial percentage (39–65 percent, depending on the activity) still expressed an interest in avoiding these types of monitoring if they could.

Table 7.1   Employees' Intentions to Subvert or Resist Monitoring Techniques

Item	Would not do this (%)	Not Sure (%)	Would do this (%)
If my company implemented an e-mail monitoring system, I would stop using the company system, if I could, and use another e-mail service instead (such as Hotmail, Yahoo, etc).	9	26	65
If my company implemented an e-mail monitoring system, I would try to find a way to keep my mail private (for instance, by changing settings on my computer).	10	27	63
If my company implemented a system to track employee computer activities, I would try to use my own computer or a shared company computer so that I could not be monitored.	12	29	60
If my company implemented a video monitoring system, I would try to avoid rooms/spaces monitored by the system.	12	31	58
If my company implemented an e-mail monitoring system, I would encourage my co-workers to stop using the company system if they can and use another e-mail service instead.	14	36	50
If my company implemented a system to keep track of employee computer activities, I would change my computer settings to prevent this monitoring activity.	14	38	48
If my company implemented an e-mail monitoring system, and I knew how to circumvent it, I would show my co-workers how to do that.	18	33	48
If my company implemented a system to keep track of employee computer activities, I would encourage my colleagues to try to use their own computers or shared company computers so that they could not be monitored.	15	38	47
If my company implemented a video monitoring system, I would encourage others to try to avoid the rooms and spaces that are monitored by the system.	16	38	46
If my company implemented a video monitoring system, I would try to alter the systems settings to make sure I cannot be video monitored.	17	38	45
If my company implemented a video monitoring system, I would encourage my co-workers to alter the system so that none of us can be monitored.	25	33	42
If my company implemented a system to keep track of employee computer activities, and I knew how to change the settings to prevent this monitoring, I would show my co-workers how to do that.	24	37	39

Note: N=257 non-managerial employees. Original items on a five point Likert scale collapsed to three categories: "Strongly disagree" and "disagree" to "would not do this;" "neutral" to "not sure;" "agree" and "strongly agree" to "would do this." Percentages in rows may not add to 100% because of rounding.

These data were an eye-opener for us, and the results led us to wonder why employees' intentions to subvert or resist monitoring were so strong. Of course, we realize that an important gap exists between expressed wishes or intentions, such as those queried in this survey, and enacted behavior that would involve actually harming an organizational information system or fomenting unrest among one's coworkers. Even keeping this gap in mind, however, it is evident that a substantial percentage of employees in any given organization might have a notably adverse reaction to the introduction of various forms of monitoring—up to and possibly including trying to figure out how to circumvent the system. We believe that some explanation for these reactions is found in the interview data presented in this chapter, and that in particular the final section of the interview report—which focuses on quotes from employees about electronic monitoring—helps to explain how employees feel about monitoring and surveillance techniques. At the end of the chapter, we also present an important "punchline" in the form of a second set of survey results that show an intriguing relationship between monitoring, policy enforcement, and security success within the organizations we studied.

In the interviews quoted in the following section, we focused on reporting the perspectives of employees who use information systems in their everyday work. This group included a wide variety of men and women whose work supported the diverse missions of their organizations. From these interviews, we have chosen to highlight the insights gained from 60 employees at 15 organizations comprising small-to-medium-size businesses from a variety of sectors, including financial, hospitality, healthcare, manufacturing, education, and engineering. Most of the employees we interviewed occupied white collar and professional positions: Typical job titles of our respondents included paralegal, lawyer, software engineer, administrative assistant, nurse, medical coder, and secretary. The persons at the higher echelons of the organizations (presidents, owners, CEOs) were excluded from analysis here because although they, too, are employees and information system users, we discussed their perspectives separately in Chapter 5. Information technology professionals are likewise excluded from this section because of the unique vantage point from which those particular types of employees see the security needs of their organizations. Chapter 6 reports their perspectives.

The types of information systems used by the employees described here ranged from off-the-shelf office productivity tools all the way to large enterprise resource systems connecting many or all of the major departments in the organization, as well as a variety of eccentric combinations of legacy systems in between. Regardless of the type of system in use, we found a remarkable degree of consistency in employees' attitudes and behavior about information security and privacy. As in previous chapters, we found some differences in perspectives depending upon whether the organization had relatively few employees (i.e., from fewer than 50 or almost 100) or relatively many (i.e., in the hundreds or thousands).

In this chapter we focus on employees primarily in their roles as information systems users, even though their jobs may have included other responsibilities that had the potential to influence information protection in other ways (e.g., records management, purchasing). Although these employees' job titles were non-technical in terms of information technology, most of these respondents had substantial skills and knowledge concerning the specific information systems required for their work. We were particularly interested here in the employees' beliefs, attitudes, and actions with respect to information protection as well as their knowledge of their workplace cultures in relation to that information. We examined how employees combined effective job performance with protection of various kinds of information, especially when security problems had no simple or clear-cut solution.

As we explained in Chapters 5 and 6, the on-site interviews used to make our observations were led by the authors and a small group of trained faculty members and students from Syracuse University. Employees were asked by their supervisors to volunteer for the interviews and their responses generally seemed to reflect at least a moderate degree of trust that our research team would keep the responses confidential. Employees were frank with us about both their personal and organizational insecurities and offered up anecdotes about a wide range of topics ranging from their fallible methods of password choice to their failures to follow policies. Employees' frankness with us furnished insights about their motivations, behavior, and in many cases naïveté about information security. In order to protect their identities and those of their organizations, we have edited their quotes as necessary to ensure they are not recognizable. In addition, we have not used the names of organizations, positions, and other information that might make the respondents or their firms identifiable. As noted in Chapters 5 and 6, we have endeavored to preserve the tone and meaning of their comments as closely as possible.

Thus, this chapter tells the story of information protection from the employee perspective. The story is not only about passwords, firewalls, shredders, locks and keys, and fax machines but also about whom employees go to for help and the things and people they rely on for assurance. The story begins with some background: a brief description of users' perspectives about the complex world of information technology in general. We also report on their awareness of security issues as reflected in how they describe basic security procedures such as anti-virus software and firewalls. As a footnote to this section, we present some comments on how regulations such as the federal Health Insurance Portability and Accountability Act (HIPAA) influence employees' points of view on information protection. With this background in mind, we next report how users view problems of information security and their views of their risks and responsibilities in securing organizational information. In this area, we report topics that information security professionals might call vulnerabilities but which organizational scientists would call barriers to positive security behavior. Finally, to close our reporting of the interview data, we examine three issues that have been identified earlier in the book as possible strategies for facilitating positive security behavior: training, policy, and monitoring. Users' perspectives on these issues are presented to further explain their mindsets about their roles in information protection.

Background: Employee Beliefs About Information Technology and Security

In this section we set the stage for understanding how employees view information security and privacy by presenting some representative comments on their general feelings about information technology. Later in the section, we describe more specific perspectives on information security by presenting some responses that suggest a widespread lack of awareness of both basic and strategic information security issues. Finally, we share employees' comments about the information technology professionals on whom they rely for help and their availability and communication skills.

General Attitudes About Information Technology

The employees we interviewed found information technology useful and vital to their jobs. In fact, like some of the managers we discussed in Chapter 5, they described being completely lost when the system was "down" and helplessly frustrated when their tools were not acting as expected. Considering the wide range of job titles, work experience, and skill levels with information systems, it was surprising how many of the employees described themselves in self-deprecating terms with respect to their information technology skills and knowledge. They explained to us that they were not computer savvy, had to rely on others a great deal, and were "dinosaurs" when it came to new information technology. Even people who knew a great deal about the information system in their areas reported that their knowledge of information technology–related tools and jobs beyond those encountered in their day-to-day interactions was minimal.

Some of our conversations with employees suggested that there is an important emotional component to employees' reactions to information technology. We found that employees' general reactions to *new* information technology could be characterized in one of two ways. One group tended to view new information systems as tools that could help them realize their work potential and personal ideals while the other viewed them as sources of confusion and frustration. The latter group described feeling lost in the technical jargon and feared that they would never be able to catch up or keep up with the rapid rate of information technology change, the frequent necessary adjustments to new hardware and software, and the flood of information from the media about the possibilities and drawbacks of new technologies. During our interviews with users, one of the most common gestures made by these users when talking about information technology was hand-waving over the head, indicating that things went "over their heads" and that they did not understand what was said to them about the technical aspects of information technology. The employees' perplexity was compounded by their absolute dependence on people whose focus was not on explaining their professional terminology. Employees such as the one quoted next felt easily disoriented and perturbed by the speed with which they were expected to understand new computer terms and concepts:

I: What is important to you in a new computer system?

R: What I want is a system that is truly user friendly. That I don't need to call someone on the phone to ask a question and then I have to watch them come in and go zoom, zoom, zoom, zip, zip, zip with a mouse and they've totally lost me so I've never learned anything.

Among employees who reported their ages as between 40 and 60, we found that age appeared to play a role in how technology and technological skills were viewed. In addition to finding the terminology intimidating, people in this group lamented that whenever they had finally learned how to navigate their software or computer, something new came along and presented another challenge. Many employees found themselves in situations in which the younger people in the office, often with relatively little work experience, entered with technical skills that were far superior to their own. For example, when we asked one employee about Internet filtering, he explained that many of the high school children he knows are computer wizards. This employee described his 18-year-old co-worker as a "kid who can actually build a computer from the bottom up." In his view, this situation made the idea of trying to block Internet access from that younger employee and others like him futile at best. "Of course he's going to know how to tap back in, you know, and get it going again." Older employees also explained to us that at home, they relied on children to help them with all kinds of computer-related activities. At work, this reliance on others translated to a feeling of hope that information technology employees would show them things in a simple enough manner that they could understand it despite their lack of background in information technology. Often a co-worker or information technology professional sat down and taught them one on one.

Beliefs About Information Protection

Employees we interviewed seemed to view information protection similarly in some ways to how they view information technology generally: They knew that it was useful and necessary but at the same time could be frustrating, mysterious, and overwhelming. Like many employees, this educator found herself not only uninformed about security issues but also hesitant to ask questions:

I: Can you think of any security-related advice for the information technology staff?

R: I don't know. I can't think of anything, because again I don't really know how the security part of it works. I personally sometimes am reluctant to ask for details of how this technology stuff works because I feel like it's stuff that everyone else knows and I should know. I feel kind of dumb. And I also think there is that assumption that [educators] don't care about how things work, they just want it done. I think that's very unfortunate, because I would love to know how it works.

Among employees who reported care and concern for information, the most common motivations for caring were based in concerns about the human impact of confidentiality or privacy violations that might result from an information security breach. These concerns for human impact worked in two directions: *out* toward a consumer for customers, clients, or patients and *up* for the principals or owners of the organization. First, employees expressed empathy for their customers, clients, and patients; on this basis they wanted to protect their clients' personal information and prevent harm from coming to them. At one social service agency, for example, two employees said that they felt that it was important that caregivers were sensitive by keeping their voices low and not calling attention to embarrassing information:

I: What could be done to improve the [confidentiality] situation?

R: I would like to see more people out there reminding the others not to say [private or personal] things out in the hallway.

I: Is that a main concern of yours now?

R1: I'm looking at more dignity and respect, I guess. They're not out there yelling so-and-so's got a [urinary tract infection] or anything like that, but just a little more dignity and respect, just a reminder.

> **R2:** The client's privacy has been taken away. You are dealing with clients who have special needs and things they don't want anyone to know about.

As the quotes here suggest, in healthcare organizations and social service agencies, employees often perceived their most important information protection duty as relating to the protection of patients and clients. Here we also see that information protection on the ground often includes issues other than the security of digital data. Employees in other types of organizations besides healthcare also held the protection of client information in high regard. One example of this was a financial employee who explained his core mission:

> **I: What are the main security concerns for you in this organization?**
>
> **R:** Probably the client information. ... That's our No. 1 objective, to serve the client and protect their personal information.

Along the same lines, employees reported being aware of the critical nature of their task and being very concerned about making mistakes and passing information to unintended recipients, with possible adverse effects on the clients. In one case, an employee who worked for a youth program was very protective of information related to her young and vulnerable clients. The respondent explained to us that the clients would not participate in the program if they thought there was a chance that their identity would be exposed:

> **I: How do you feel about protecting the information you deal with every day?**
>
> **R:** Unless somebody is giving me money, they aren't getting any information from me. (laughs) [Other organizations are not as careful] so we give them bogus identification numbers for the clients. Even though it is not done to hurt the client, somebody is not being secure about their information. Somebody is sharing information without that client's knowledge. I am very concerned about that.

Next, employees also reported an ability to put themselves in the shoes of their organizational leaders: They did not want to be responsible for compromising the network or other organizational resources for fear of legal problems that might affect the owners or principals. Employees in healthcare and in for-profit firms also expressed concern for the complex web of outside regulations that affect the survival of their organizations. Finally, users indicated that they cared about information security because they felt that taking care of organizational information was an important facet of their jobs and—done right— would reflect well on their status in the organization. Employees reported pride in their performance at work and the desire to be more successful—both individually and collectively. Many employees told us in a variety of ways that they prided themselves in "going the extra mile" for their clients, co-workers, and their organizations. Employees from a wide variety of organizations said that their No. 1 responsibility was to their customers. Employees also watched out for each other and were concerned about each other's well being, as suggested by a payroll clerk who told us that it was "the worst thing in the world" to make a mistake in another employee's paycheck.

In terms of service to the organization, employees repeatedly depicted their busy and demanding workweeks and their willingness to go to the office on evenings or weekends to complete critical assignments. Given the common practice of tying policy enforcement to draconian job actions (e.g., suspending or firing an employee), we found it interesting to note that users tended *not* to present simple self-interest as a motivation for maintaining security. This idea suggests that using threats of suspension or firing as a method of inspiring adherence to information security policies may not provide the most effective method of motivating employees to maintain positive security practices. Language conveying such threats may be necessary for legal reasons, but we think these results suggest that threats may have minimal effect on the typical worker in energizing improvements to security practice. In contrast, suggestions concerning how security improvements may help to protect the well-being of customers, co-workers, and the organization as a whole might have a more substantial motivating effect for employees.

The Value of Information

Among employees we found what we believed to be a widespread naïveté concerning the value of the organization's internal information resources. Similarly to managers, employees universally recognized that some types of information, such as a patient's test results at a hospital or doctors' office, were sensitive. The value of business information, however, did not seem well recognized, either in terms of the amount of time needed to re-create it if it were destroyed or in its potential value to a competitor. In the following examples, note how the employee does not believe that customers' account numbers or addresses are sensitive information:

> **I: What kind of information do you have on your computer? Is there anything that you would say is sensitive or has to be kept confidential?**
>
> **R:** Not on my part, no. I have access to the product codes— our products, customers' account numbers, their addresses, the routes, you know, the drivers that take those orders—but otherwise no.
>
> **I: It's not something that you would consider sensitive?**
>
> **R:** Right, right.

Likewise, a sales associate from the same operation was not particularly concerned about the safety of her information:

> **I: What would be your major concern regarding the security of whatever information you have on your computer?**
>
> **R:** On my part, our department here, I don't think we really have to worry about too much. The only thing that would worry me would be somebody changing an order that I took— changing it and making [the order for] even more of a product or less than I had originally ordered without me knowing. But otherwise, [I have no concerns] for our department really.

At an educational institution, employees were similarly uninformed about the value of organizational information. A library worker whose comments follow did not think the information she dealt with on a daily basis was particularly sensitive, as opposed to the kinds of information she used personally from her home office:

> **I: What can you tell me about how you manage passwords and that kind of thing?**

R: My password, everyone probably knows because I change it very seldom. And I use it for everything, but most of what I deal with is not particularly, well, I don't have anything here that I wouldn't want somebody to see. It is easy for me to remember so I just keep it.

I: Is there an electronic prompt that comes on and reminds you to change it?

R: Yes, about every six months or so.

I: Can that [password] be changed back to the old one?

R: Yes, I go back and forth [selecting a choice of one or two passwords]. So I am an open book. And as far as here goes, I'm not in a position to have confidential information so I have nothing here that I wouldn't want anybody to look at. I have no problem with that. If it were at home I would feel differently about it, because there are too many things that can happen. If somebody gets your credit card number or whatever, or gets into where you keep that information, but I don't have anything like that here.

I: What situations might happen at home then that worry you?

R: You know, strangers or someone coming in. It is a whole different situation, and I don't do things like that here so there is no need for me to have a password secret.

Some times employees did appear very knowledgeable about the importance of protecting potentially damaging material. For example, in the following quote a laboratory researcher shared his concern about potential leaks of destructive information. In this case, the laboratory contained hazardous materials and the revelation of this to a wider community outside of the institution would have been awkward:

I: What types of confidential information would be troublesome if leaked?

R: There are things that have happened in the lab. I can talk about it now but at the time it was very sensitive. We have [specimens] in a freezer in the lab that it turned out were a health risk. The thing had not been continuously plugged in, unfortunately, and most of us were in the dark about it being a health risk, but we knew it smelled really bad. We did not know about it and discovered we had very complicated procedures [for handling these materials]. It's not something I wanted broadcasted around.

Fear of publicity related to rotting refrigerator contents is probably a relatively unusual instance of an information-protection concern. A more representative example of an employee's understanding the significance of organizational data was evident in this quote from a school employee:

I: What are the principal security concerns with your organization?

R: We deal with very sensitive data and any discussion of that is not related to our work, our job. You simply do not share that, or even show that you know it. It is not our data to do anything with, we are just custodians of it.

Knowledge of Security Tools

As reported in Chapter 6, many information technology professionals are aware of users' important roles in the maintenance of basic, frontline security techniques—such as anti-virus protection—that help to keep the organization secure. Looking across our whole body of interview data, we found among employees a significant lack of knowledge and skill at using basic security tools. This deficiency may spring in part from users' lack of a strategic sense of the overall goals of information protection in their organizations. A further problem, indicated in our transcripts, is that employees seldom understood the limitations of their knowledge of the overall security situation. Users felt that as long as they took steps toward security in their own area, they were not being negligent in their duties. Using anti-virus protection as an example, we found employees to be in many instances uninformed and apparently unconcerned about information security and the implications of their actions for the larger system. It was unnerving to learn how many employees—particularly from smaller firms—reported having either no regular updates or no anti-virus protection whatsoever. This quote from an accountant at a small financial services company was typical:

I: Do you know if there is any anti-virus [protection] on your computer?

R: Hmm. (long pause) Yes. There is a system that pops up one day a week that scans the computer system. Right now, my computer does not have that.

I: It doesn't have anti-virus?

R: It does have something on there, but I have it locked off because it is too slow. I can't get to any of the screens.

I: So you turned off the anti-virus?

R: Yes. I turned off the ...

I: ... [Brand name] anti-virus ...

R: Anti-virus, yes. I had problems with my computer and when they reloaded the whole system, if that's on, I cannot move within my screens. It gets stuck. (laughs)

I: And did you speak to the information technology person about that problem?

R: I spoke to a gentleman that, yes, handles the computer systems and he sort of ignored it. He just said OK.

I: No steps toward ...

R: I don't believe so.

I: He knows you turned off the program?

R: Yes, he does.

I: You don't know what will happen toward finding a solution?

R: Correct. (laughs)

I: That's fine. I just want to make sure I understand everything.

This exchange highlights the oft-discussed concern of the balance between productivity and security. This worker from a small firm shut off virus protection on her computer because it interfered with her ability to get her job done. She further indicated that the information technology person at this organization was aware of the problem and yet did not seem concerned enough to develop an immediate solution or response. This situation harks back to a comment we made at the end of Chapter 2 about the role of information technology amateurs in small businesses. The firm that employed the worker just quoted was small enough that it leased most of its computers and outsourced the installation and maintenance of its network. As a result, the firm had no in-house information technology professional but rather depended upon an "information technology amateur" (an employee in another job role who served as a local information technology expert), together with occasional visits from one of the outside vendors. We found that small firms of fewer than 50 employees were quite likely to be lax about basic security measures such as anti-virus protection. In this example, an employee at a small company explained that she did not even understand the interviewer's question:

I: Do you know if there is an anti-virus on your machine?

R: I keep getting one [a message] that says we are quarantined anti-virus. I don't know if that's what you are asking. They do have a program that is supposed to catch a virus. And I am not very good with the computers. I just do what I am told to do. I don't have a lot of education.

In many places, users do not perceive security as an organizational or personal priority. Employees who were invited to talk with us about security often wondered why they were the lucky chosen ones and told us they were surprised to be included. The second of the following comments, made by a customer service representative, echoes the voices of many employees who had not given the topic much thought or attention:

> **I: What do you hear about security from the information technology department?**
>
> **R1:** Not much. System passwords, and that's pretty much it. Informing us of what's coming up.
>
> **R2:** It [security] is not a big topic of conversation.

Even small companies that were quite technically sophisticated were not immune to the problem of deficiencies in the basic steps of information protection. The following quote came from an employee at a small engineering firm. This individual seemed knowledgeable about many basic security procedures but was missing virus protection:

> **I: So you probably keep that pretty secure, right? How do you know what to do in order to keep problems from occurring like that?**
>
> **R:** I try to stay up with their updates or with their software installer or whatever it's called. I let that run once a week or whenever they are recommended. I try to make sure to stay up on the updates. I have it set up so that you need a username and password to get into it. One thing I know I failed to do so far was that I haven't invested in any anti-virus program—something which I probably should do.

The final sentence in this quote suggests that it is not only awareness that is lacking. Other barriers seem to impede employees' ability to protect their information, including a lack of resources or low organizational priority given to security. In the following quote, a newly hired paralegal shows that she is acutely aware of the security risks in the organization but is not yet in a position to make much of a difference. Note that although her language is not technically sophisticated, her description shows higher security awareness than her boss:

> **I: What are your main security concerns for this organization?**

R: I think probably the one that [the boss] really should address soonest is that the receptionist's desk is out in the hall and it is not locked up. None of the machines are turned off at night. It is currently sort of security through obscurity. Once in a while they forget to lock the front door, so the building isn't even locked. Or during the day, you know, if my boss goes on lunch and we're all locked up in our offices, it [the receptionist's computer] is just sitting out there waiting to be seen. There is [a tenant] across the hall who is a criminal lawyer, so he has criminals in and out all the time, just passing through the hallway next to that computer all day long. So that is a big issue; that the physical security of the machine out in the hall because it's hard-wired, you know, linked by Ethernet to everything else. So, that's not a good thing; that should probably be addressed. General security of the building is not particularly strong. I don't know how security analysts work with that sort of thing, like measure against the amount of crime in the area, how much you need. Obviously, in this kind of place, I don't think this place has ever been broken into, but it's just because, I suppose, nobody's tried. It wouldn't be hard, as [the boss] said himself in our last meeting. And then we probably could [invest in more secure firewalls]. Some measures have been taken in terms of security on the machines, but mostly it has just been [brand name] personal firewall on each machine, which is not real super powerful sort of security and if anybody who was a practiced hacker wanted to get in, I'm sure that they could.

I: It would be very easy?

R: That's right. I mean, it's sort of been as it is, out of the box. And then we get frustrated because it's screwing up and not working right, so we just shut the damn thing off and then you forget that it's off, you know. Or it's interfering with, you know, other processes, and you just, you know. I don't know exactly what all he's even got on his network, but it doesn't feel like it's probably going to be enough for the long run, for the kind of highly sensitive information that he's storing. I mean, so far so good; there haven't been any problems, but all he'd need would be one break in by the wrong person and a lot of people could be victims real fast and he could find himself in a big lawsuit. You know, he's not going to listen to just me, we'll run this by [the owner] and see what he thinks once some experts come in and say, you are taking some steps and that's good, but you really should think about taking some more.

This quote and some of the previous material make evident a pervasive conflict between awareness and power in the organization. Frontline employees may have detailed knowledge of security problems and barriers in their specific and narrow areas of familiarity, but their lack of positional power in the organization may make it difficult to translate that awareness into some action that managers will condone and support. It is also likely in many cases that these "micro" level security concerns would need to be balanced against larger strategic security goals: Managers may consider the resultant compromises as their purview and may not want employees to be vocal about their specific concerns. Employees who have few concerns about security or who choose to ignore them have a kind of peace-of-mind advantage in that they are not caught in the vise of knowing what to do but not being allowed to do it.

In addition to essential security measures meant to keep workplace computers safe, employees also have important roles in maintaining business continuity through information management and storage. One area of business continuity of significant importance to companies of all sizes pertains to data backups. In some organizations where we conducted research, we found problems with backups not being done, tapes not taken off-site, and general lack of attention to the importance of this essential business continuity measure. The following example was extreme—most organizations we visited had a more reliable strategy than this—but was not unique in showing major problems in the maintenance and handling of backups. An employee at a government agency explained how the organization's information system is not being backed up:

I: What can you tell me about your security concerns?

R: If something occurs, you know, this business is gone because we don't have a backup.

I: Is the backup procedure now resolved?

R: We did have an issue. Right now, it's not completely resolved. Once we found out that there were not backups, we started using a tape backup that has been implemented within the last, probably, 30 days. The problem now is that the tape is supposed to be on automatic run and it's not happening that way. We went through one week fine but then the tapes weren't overwriting and I don't know why. Our information technology person could probably tell you why. So now he's doing a manual backup before he leaves. If he's not here and someone else doesn't know how to do it, we're not getting a good backup tape ...

Even employees who may be highly knowledgeable technically find that security issues can fall through the cracks. Although it did not happen too commonly, sometimes employees expressed the desirability of learning more about the "big picture" of security. This quote from an engineer exemplifies this desire:

I: Do you have any other concerns about security that we haven't discussed?

R: As a bunch of engineers, we think of security in terms of firewalls and encryption. We have a hard time thinking of security in terms of procedures, and what happens to those few pieces of hard copy at the end of the day. The minute it's no longer a bit on a magnetic medium we tend to lose sight of it. So any kind of guidance on how to handle the larger picture of security rather than the micro picture of bits on disk would be helpful.

Attitudes Toward Information Technology Professionals

To close this discussion of beliefs about information protection, we also report on employees' perspectives on the people who support their efforts to keep the organization's information safe and available. In general, we found that employees in the organizations we visited had positive feelings for their information technology departments. Additionally, they appreciated both the enormous scale of information technology professionals' tasks and their resource limitations. Information technology professionals, their daily schedules, and their work activities were considered both mysterious and worthy of a basic faith that all of the right things were getting done. The comments that follow depict this range of feelings and experiences. Positive feelings about information technology professionals were reported so frequently that this type of comment could fill a chapter in itself:

I: How are your interactions with the information technology staff?

R1: Our information technology person really does her job. She is great. She is like a system in herself because she knows everything. If there is something funky, she catches it. The way she operates, it really helps me.

R2: She helps me whenever I need it. She sits down with me one on one, and that's what I need.

R3: They are very good and they are especially [good] at working with the new systems and making sure that the security of [our medical] records [is] maintained.

R4: He is great. He doesn't talk over everyone's head, you know?

I: Do you have any suggestions for the information technology department or comments about its priorities, particularly in terms of security?

R: I think they do very good with security. You know, short of interfering with your daily routine, I don't know what they could do differently short of taking responsibility of turning everybody on and off everyday, which, who has the time for that? I frankly don't know what more they could do at this point. I think they've got the bases covered. Anything else I think they're looking at an entire agency revamp and without many, many dollars that just is not going to happen.

For the typical user, information technology people and skills are shrouded in mystery, a fact that was noted by the employee in the following quote:

> **I: What advice would you have for information technology staff members about security or other topics?**
>
> **R:** I don't know how to give advice about it because I don't understand their jobs. The work that information technology people do is almost as mysterious to me as the information technology stuff itself.

Even though information technology staff's methods were sometimes baffling, many employees felt that information technology workers were often able to handle problems without much trouble. They respected information technology workers for their skills and patience. Even though employees felt that they did not know anything about what the information technology staff actually did, they knew that the outcomes were successful:

> **I: Do you have spam filters here?**
>
> **R:** Yes, actually they do. If I leave on a Friday and come back on a Monday, I'll have over 300 e-mails. So I went to [our information technology staff] and told him that I am so tired of getting e-mail about wanting my boobs bigger. I don't need them, thank you. So he would go in and do whatever he did and he would say okay, now check your e-mail and see if the stuff you are getting is any better, and it really has been. It's been great.

Employees also recognized both the unconventional role, the importance of the job, and the value of information technology personnel. The following excerpts from social service staff members were characteristic of this group:

> **I: What can you tell me about your interaction with the information technology staff?**
>
> **R1:** I count on her [the information technology staff] in a lot of ways, not just the computer. It's almost all on her shoulders, so to speak. To try to get things organized so the program runs smoothly, and she has everything she needs

without us having to duplicate, triplicate the forms—that's hard. It must be difficult for her, having us on her case all the time.

R2: I have a lot of faith that these guys have done their homework. I don't know their jobs but I know that they have done their homework and that there won't be any problems with [unauthorized people] getting in through our network.

Employees such as the professionals quoted next were thankful for the fact that their information technology personnel were responsible for difficult tasks that were beyond their expertise:

I: When do you have contact with the information technology people in your organization?

R1: When [the information technology manager] says to do something or if [he] says that he has done something, I have enough faith that [he] is a good person and that it's the best thing for all of us.

I: Are you aware that he is doing these things?

R1: Yes. I am aware that he is doing these things and I'm happy that he's doing them because then I don't have to think about it myself.

I: Do you have any concerns about the security of your information?

R2: I am hoping that they have a really good virus protection package. (laughs) I am trusting that they have a really good virus protection package. (laughs) I hope that it is not a misplaced trust. Here, actually, they are very aware of the problem. … I truly trust the computer folks [here]. They would not let our system become vulnerable.

A few contrary voices were heard among the general adulation. A few problems seemed to spring more from the information technology staff's communication skills than from its technical competence.

This excerpt from an interview with a healthcare employee described a common frustration about information technology professionals:

> **I: What are some of the troublesome tasks in your daily work?**
>
> **R:** I know if I hit Shut Down and take it back to the main menu and I hit Reboot, it goes away. But if it is a major thing, bigger than I can handle, then I call [the information systems department].
>
> **I: How do you find dealing with them?**
>
> **R:** Oh, if you can find them, you are lucky, because they are never in their office. I don't know where they are, but they are never around. You can page them three, four times, and they will call you back. Or it's in the middle of the night and they can't come in. They are not exactly very user friendly.
>
> **I: Once you can get it touch with them, do they help you?**
>
> **R:** Yes, they usually come in and take care of it. Then, they don't say that they are leaving and that it's been taken care of. They walk out of the building and you are still sitting here going, "Did they fix it?" Then you look and see that it's been fixed. The ones I have dealt with are not very personable.
>
> **I: What is your impression of computer people?**
>
> **R:** They are very to themselves. They are not, people-people, you know what I mean? That's why they hide behind their little computers.

In a minority of cases, employees related some of the common stereotypes of computer personnel in their descriptions, including the notions that they are poor communicators and inaccessible. Interviewees sometimes suggested that employees generally expect information technology staff to talk in technical terms that they would not understand and would find frustrating. More typically, however, we heard from employees that they considered that their information technology departments worked very hard to ensure "uptime"—that the employees' computers and other systems were available for productive work. This sentiment reinforced our sense that employees often saw benefits from information security to the extent that it kept their systems from becoming inoperable as a result of hackers, worms, or viruses.

Perhaps as a result of their lack of understanding of how hackers, worms, or viruses do their evil deeds, employees frequently suggested a sense of helplessness and attendant anxiety in face of "bad things" that could happen. In this example, a human resources employee from a large financial services company told us that he does not know much about the possible negative consequences of inappropriate behavior. He suggested that the technical vocabulary used by information technology professionals to explain their vulnerabilities was beyond his grasp. This general unease may be indicated by his somewhat unfocused rambling about possible disasters or embarrassments:

> **I: What are your main computer security concerns these days?**
>
> **R:** I'm a novice in trying to do anything computer-wise. All of a sudden I watch these TV shows and everybody can hack into everything. I don't know if any of that is true or if that's just television. I would have to say that the vulnerability of [our] access system, that people get into. Our information technology person tells me it's on a drive with this and that, whew [waves hand over head]. But I would imagine at times that that system is vulnerable to somebody who knows what they're doing. The same is true with the [brand name] system, even though I have a password. Knock on wood. To date it hasn't been broken into or ever been compromised. But I don't know. I don't know that much about it, that's my only concern. I don't know how you do that type of stuff. I turn it on, type in my password and I'm good to go. But a lot of inappropriate people have access to it. I don't know how the company is run, but maybe the automation person shouldn't have access to payroll information. I don't know, maybe they do. If they do, that's fine. But several assistants also have access to it.

Those are questions I don't know. Every once in a while when you're driving home you start thinking about that stuff, somebody runs a stop sign so you're off to another thing. But in turn, those things concern me. I trust everybody in automation. I have no concerns about those people at all. But yet, when you look at somebody's salary then all of the sudden that can sort of temper your judgment as to he or she makes more or less than me type of thing. But that would be my only concern. Plus the social security number I would have to say that the more of a nosiness to look in there I don't think they're going to get in there and take my social security number. I'm not worried about that.

I: "They" meaning [whom]?

R: Well, whoever, employees, whoever. I don't know if you can get in from the outside, I really don't know that. But that would be my concern, just knowing what somebody makes and then them saying, well I know that you make this why don't I make that? That would be my concern.

There are several things worthy of note in the preceding discussion. First, users like this one often rely on trust and faith and "knock on wood" because nothing "bad" has happened yet. At first expressing trust for his co-workers, he follows with some questioning thoughts. Not privy to much insider knowledge about security, he still has enough to feel a bit insecure and nervous. Not knowing all of the technical details, he relies on guesses and imagination to fill in the holes. In effect, he has no way to accurately judge the risks involved in protecting organizational information that is important to him. As with some managers whom we described in Chapter 5, employees sometimes had a mistaken belief that the complexity and obscurity of their information systems would thwart any attempts to damage or destroy information; as a result they made low assessments of risk. The following financial professional viewed security risks in terms of what he personally would find difficult to do. By assessing others as having low skills, he thought his information would therefore be safe:

I: Can you recall anything like that [a security breach] happening?

R: No, because I think most people probably wouldn't know where to go in the software to get that but if they did want to, it's probably pretty easy.

I: It's not restricted at all?

R: No.

I: No, and have you spoken about that to anyone, I mean, have you made it known to people that it could happen?

R: I think we probably discussed it, but I mean, he has such a hard time trying to find it himself that he probably just figures that nobody else would be able to find it either.

I: So what kind of information do you have in those?

R: It's all the financial statements and the financial information, but not payroll.

External Regulations and Information Security Awareness

External regulations were welcomed by some employees as an opportunity for helping to reinforce good practice but regarded by others with frustration, incomprehension, and fear. Employees wanted to make sure that they were doing what they were supposed to do, but in some cases security and privacy regulations seemed overly complicated to them and made their work flows increasingly cumbersome. In a few organizations, however, employees knew little about privacy and security regulations and as a result seemed unconcerned about them. This employee at a large financial services company was typical in claiming not to know anything about regulations that governed his use of information:

I: How do you think laws affect this organization's handling of information?

R: I really don't have a clue, to tell you the truth.

Note that this response is particularly dismaying, given the importance of the recent Sarbanes-Oxley and Gramm-Leach-Bliley legislation on the integrity of financial information. In contrast, most of the users we asked had at least some direct contact with procedures that were regulated by the federal government or the state. Employees felt that they had no choice but to comply with a variety of strict, complex, and overlapping outside regulations. This was particularly evident in the healthcare sector, where a worker in medical records explained the dilemmas of working in her department:

> **I: It sounds to me like there are a lot of different rules in terms of who is allowed to see what.**
>
> **R:** Yes. There are lots of different rules. Not only are there the few things I mentioned, but then there are state rules about what they can have access to. When the Department of Health comes in, we need to review records and then we have to release that. There are also many other types of rules according to subpoenas that we receive; for example, if it's family court then we need to have the subpoena signed by a judge. There are a lot of different rules like that we have to manage in our department. I really hesitate especially now with HIPAA to release just anything, and before we pretty much felt like, well, the patient is over there and we should release it, but very often I don't know if the phone call is actually an emergency room. It could be the person's aunt. So we have to do a lot of verifications either with phone calls and faxes to make sure that we are sending it to the right person.

Essentially parallel concerns surfaced in the financial services sector, as this insurance company worker attested:

> **I: How does information security fit in with your work life?**
>
> **R:** With the advent of privacy acts and whatnot over the last several years, we used to be able to draw on this information. We're interfaced directly with all of the states we do business in, either directly with that state motor vehicle department or third-party vendor that accesses this for us. We used to be able to take that information and give it to the business owner and say, yeah, this guy is OK to drive your vehicles, no this guy isn't. Well you can't do

that anymore. So now we have to be very, very careful. We can only say that once we've got that information, this person is eligible to drive your vehicles or not.

This comment highlights the influence that awareness of outside regulations has on employees' decisions to release information outside of the organization. While some employees reported their beliefs that such regulations decreased service quality, others explained that changes in outside regulations have helped a great deal in some organizations—sometimes as a motivator for being more diligent— and could be used to continue improving the quality of the information protection. We got more than one hint of the idea that employees saw a salutary effect of external regulations on their bosses, who as a result finally began to take security and privacy issues more seriously. Here, a healthcare worker describes the situation on her floor:

> **R:** I think under pressure sometimes we might have some staff members who would just give it [information] off. You know we don't want to interfere with the continuity of care of the patient, but yet at the end we are trying to protect that patient's privacy at the same time. So, it's been very touchy I think since HIPAA. We have been made much more aware of what we are actually doing.

Vulnerabilities: Users' Perceptions of Barriers to Positive Security Practices

This section examines users' explanations of factors that they felt inhibited their ability to work in a more secure fashion. Employees reported the following barriers to effective security: a low level of security awareness among their bosses, coupled with low prioritization, problems with the physical layout or condition of the office or building in which they do business, the challenges of legitimate sharing of information with outside parties, and the difficulty of securing sensitive data on portable devices. These concerns were repeatedly raised by various employees in different settings. While these barriers are mentioned frequently, and therefore warrant review, we found that they reflected only a tiny fraction of the employee-related vulnerabilities mentioned by information technology professionals. In the following discussions, we found that some employees evidently did not recognize the limitations of their vantage points while others were aware and slightly disturbed by their lack of big-picture perspective.

Behavior and Attitudes of Bosses

In some organizations we visited, employees realized that organizational information was insecure. The difficulty they encountered arose from the fact that they reported to a person higher in the organizational hierarchy who had fewer concerns for security or less of the relevant knowledge that would help to make those concerns manifest themselves. Employees reported that they felt it would be difficult for an employee to "train" his or her boss on how to keep organizational information safe, particularly when the boss was perceived as lacking fundamental knowledge of information technology:

> **I: What are the priorities of your supervisors regarding information security?**
>
> **R:** My boss, the chief financial officer, is very computer illiterate, so he doesn't even do a lot of his stuff on the computer. He still does a lot of handwritten notes and spreadsheets and what not. He's got a lock on his desk, but we all know where the key is so ... (laughs)

This comment resonates strongly with our report in Chapter 5 of the many high-level managers who lacked the most basic information technology skills. The comment and others like it reflected a feeling of despondency on the part of employees who had "computer challenged" bosses in that they saw as hopeless their efforts to educate people higher up in the organizational chain about security priorities. Some employees seemed to believe that information security could not really be a high priority within the organization if the organization's leaders had not taken the time to learn basic information technology skills and concepts.

Physical/Office Layout

Because employees often worked quite literally on the front lines of their organizations—working with customers, clients, patients, and other individuals who also had physical access to the organization's facilities—they were most likely to encounter information security and privacy issues related to physical space. Whereas information technology people worry about the ethereal world of data on networks, and managers sometimes enjoy seclusion from most physical security concerns as a benefit of having lockable offices, employees in the front room often wrestle with security and privacy issues related to faxes, paper forms, exposed computer screens, and verbal disclosures. From healthcare workers we heard a number of stories about "life before HIPAA"—when patients' sensitive information was not always well protected (e.g., "John Smith, please come to the lab for the results of your erectile dysfunction test"). The following response from a nurse supervisor contrasts the positive intentions of the nursing staff with the limitations of the physical space in which they work:

> **I: Did you observe [other employees] being guarded about confidentiality prior to HIPAA?**
>
> **R:** If you saw the physical layout in my unit in particular, you would see that it is just a row of 38 beds all in a row basically. It's very, very difficult to maintain confidentiality. There are many incidental exposures to medical record and patient information. We are always trying to come up with ways to best protect the patients, even though we are very limited in what we can protect because of our physical layout. When we are inputting data into the computer, we angle it the right way so that people can't see what's been said. Because we don't have a desk to put the medical records, we flip them over or close them and make sure they are not open for everyone to read. We make sure that phone calls are done in the most private setting that we can, if we know it is going to involve patient information.

Security of Data on Portable Devices

In several of the organizations we studied, the employees believed that their internal policies and equipment were more than sufficient to protect their information while it was in the building or on the organization's servers. What worried them more was that they were increasingly carrying data with them, usually on a laptop computer or a removable disk drive, either to work at home or for business trips.

They were aware that using data on a home system did not carry the same level of protection as the system at work but were hard pressed to find an alternative. They also noticed that their co-workers were carrying highly sensitive data on portable media and they did not feel comfortable with that. Even at an engineering firm, where we expected a high level of security awareness, we found that security-related behavior did not meet that standard. The following quote from an engineer at that company reveals several barriers to security. This employee's frustration was apparent because he recognized that there was a problem and attempted to solve it but was unable to find a reliable solution:

I: Do you have any other concerns about information security that you would like to discuss?

R: We have a firewall at the office and we have these [security] zones and we have a requirement for anti-virus software and so on. But then people go and work at home. For instance, I have a notebook, which never leaves my side. I am out there at that demonstration, as well as preparing for it in our low-security zone, and then I go home and I hook up behind a cable modem. So there's all this migration of information from one computer and one [security] level to another. Another guy at the office doesn't have a notebook but he does probably 40 percent of his work at home on his [personal computer] there. So he's constantly transferring data back and forth on one of these little USB drives or via e-mail or via file transfer or whatever. So information moves from host to host, hosts move from network to network. The worst situation of all is when I'm at home I have a firewall. Firewalls have been offered to all of our employees. You know those little $49 boxes from [a company]. We bought a bunch of them a while back and said, "Anybody who wants to operate at home, take one of these." Now I don't know for a fact that every employee is using that offered asset, nor using it correctly, but at least it's been offered. But then I go to some hotel and I plug into the hotel's Ethernet in the room, or I go on the hotel's Wi-Fi. Now I have a problem. Sure, I downloaded personal firewall; well, I ultimately ended up buying [brand name], but it doesn't work worth a damn. Real firewalls are orders of magnitude superior to pseudo firewalls that run on the end system. Because any time I try to do anything, the firewall pops up and says "such and such.exe is attempting to access port such and such." Well how the hell do I know whether that is a legitimate operating system component attempting to do something that it needs to do in order to provide the services that my applications require, or if it is evidence of some attempted or successful intrusion? I have no clue. And so initially I say no, and after I've said no two or three times and I discover that I can't do what I was trying to do, then I start saying yes. And it's atrocious.

After confronting these types of "atrocious" situations, users sometimes took the situation into their own hands and showed great perseverance in looking for ways to keep their information safe. In the case just described, the engineer decided to "lug yet another piece of technology around" when he traveled. He continued by saying that carrying a hardware firewall with him seemed "ridiculous" but it was the only thing that he could think of to do to provide "a combination of functionality and protection while on the road." One other interesting aspect of this quote is the combination of the technical sophistication of this respondent and his recognition that most employees would have no clue what to do when faced with the choices presented by personal firewall software. We heard similar sentiments from information technology professionals who were concerned that the complex and obscure nature of many security tools made them difficult for regular employees to use. An analogy springs to mind: Modern word processors represent several generational steps of improvement over early text editors, and those steps have made word processing highly accessible even to novice computer users. Perhaps similar advances in personal information security tools are also needed, because usable security tools for non-experts are essentially non-existent at present.

Need to Share Information

Another barrier perceived by users was that they had no choice but to share information with other people or organizations. The ubiquitous nature of outsourcing and the increasing trend for businesses to be electronically connected with their suppliers and customers has created numerous situations in which employees are expected to facilitate transactions and movements of information, but in a guarded way that protects the best interests of the firm. The mandatory nature of such sharing and employees' beliefs that they lack expertise in the necessary processes can contribute to feelings of apprehension, as shown in this quote from a financial services agent about the company where he worked and the friendly wager he made about their vulnerability:

> **I: Is there any event that has happened in the past that has changed the way you work or has made you more concerned about security?**
>
> **R:** My biggest concern right now is that we have made an arrangement with another organization so they can now come in and use the same data that we are using. And I am concerned that it is not protected correctly. I am concerned. ... They are a competitor of ours, and not a friendly competitor. I think with their expertise and with what limited expertise we have here, if they wanted to get that information, I am a firm believer that they can. Actually I have a $100 bet that they probably can. That's what I am a believer of. I don't know. ... My personal opinion is that we should not have had an arrangement with them, period. To be married to one person is enough.

Sharing of information with competitors was a difficult issue for this employee of an engineering firm as well:

> **I: How extensive do you see the threat of your competitors being interested in trying to steal your project and project plans?**
>
> **R:** On the one hand, in my career, I have only had two instances of clear-cut "somebody stole my intellectual property" and it hurt me. And in a career of 20 years plus and climbing at this point, that's not bad. We're pretty low profile and low visibility. It's not like a lot of our competitors know we exist yet. Then there is the flip side. For instance, I've been in direct face-to-face negotiations with my direct competitors recently. We've had customers say

hey, we've got a duplicative program here. Company A is working Program One and Company B is working Program Two and these two programs are 98 percent overlapping and we're not going to fund either one of them any further until the two of them get their act together. So I had lunch with a guy and I said, "as I understand it, you're my direct competitor and we wouldn't even be talking except that the [customer] says neither one of us is going forward until we do." He said, "Yeah, that sums it up about right." So all of a sudden now, I am in the mode right now of sharing information with the last people on earth that I would want to be sharing information with, except that we've been put in the situation where we have no choice.

I: So as a future issue, it's quite possible that a competitor could be quite interested in finding things out, whether it was by dumpster-diving or network hacking.

R: Yeah, and given the nature of our company, the network hacking, if successful, will be a far more effective way of mining our data.

These issues represent just a sample of the problems that employees encounter in protecting information. We found it interesting that all of these problems had a practical, everyday flavor to them: They were not grand challenges or big-picture concerns but rather troubles that employees encountered in the process of simply getting their jobs done. In several instances, the problems also had important aspects that were not in the purely digital world of firewalls and routers but rather in the physical world of printouts and faxes. In addition, many employees' responses indicated that they lacked an understanding of the overall security picture. The following example shows that this employee understood quite well that he had only partial knowledge of the activities of his co-workers:

I: How well do you think your co-workers and other staff follow proper information security procedures?

R: I don't know. I can't answer for other people.

I: I guess you have a login and a specific protocol?

R: Yeah, I'm in my own little world. I know we do what we are supposed to do, or what we perceive we are supposed to do. I don't know what anybody else does.

During another point in the same conversation, this employee said the following:

I: What are your leading security concerns for your organization?

R: I am very fortunate, I guess, in that I don't really have too many concerns about information leaks. I don't send any [sensitive] information via e-mail. ... The administration has to worry about the security aspects. They tell me what to do and I implement their policies, and fortunately the technology department has their set of criteria they have to follow. I am fortunate that they have already done their homework.

Another employee at the same institution said that he felt the same way about his knowledge of the security priorities of the organization:

I: What is the leadership's situation in terms of their priorities for security?

R: That is hard to say. I would assume that they are into it but that is not on my end of it so I don't feel qualified to answer that. I am sure it is to make sure things run smoothly and that we don't get hacked or whatever you want to call it. That is out of my ... that's just common sense.

In the quote that follows, the user believes that the security situation may have been compromised by lack of consistency in skills and awareness across the entire organization. One complaint was that, for a variety of reasons, security meetings were convened without a representative from each department, leaving a situation in which the security status of everyone was highly dependent on the awareness level of each individual team leader. At the same time, he thought that the variability found in different areas within the organization caused inconsistent and even contradictory results in behavior:

I: How does the administration handle security awareness?

R: If there is a pushy team leader who is doing it right, we will all be doing it right. If the pushiest team leader is doing it wrong, then guess what, we are all going to be doing it wrong. I think that the management of the human use of technology and an organizational approach to that would probably be one of the most powerful pluses we could do relative to security. I say that almost in ignorance of the level of technology security solutions that are being put in place. I don't know what they are but I probably know better than my peers. We would benefit greatly from our staff being better educated to these issues. It's all a sliding scale, I just think the problems slide along the scale, up.

Echoing this desire for better information about security awareness issues, a clerical support employee expressed a strong desire to become more knowledgeable and involved:

I: If you could say something anonymously to the administration about the changes you would like to see happen, what would you say?

R: Security wise? I think they need to communicate constantly and I think their most important source of information is their employees and also their greatest strength. But other than that it has been a great place to work. I have always been involved.

I: What would you like to see happen in terms of communication?

R: Not necessarily meetings, but information in general, on what the plans, what is coming down the road, because obviously our top administrators have a plan. ... It is not just one of those general [plans where] "we want this to be the best place it could possibly be that is nice and you want that," but I want to know personally, I want to know how they plan to get there and what can I do to help. And I just think that, some of that is being done, but evidently not enough to please me or I wouldn't have mentioned it (laughs). ... [I want to say to them, "You should be] more open, trust your employees that they are going to do the right things and use them."

I: That sounds like a great attitude.

R: Yes, the people [other employees] here are very good and when they have been asked to do things they have been willing to step up to the plate. I have been here through many changes, there are more to come, and I like to be a part of it.

User Perspectives on Training, Policy, and Monitoring

In the previous section we focused on several specific issues that seemed to interfere with the enactment of positive security behavior—attitudes of bosses, physical office layout, information carried on portable devices, the challenges of careful sharing of information outside of the organization, and the often obstructed viewpoints from which the ordinary employee sees the organization's security status. Here we turn our attention to three of the common solutions used by organizations to mitigate problems of information protection: training, policy deployment and enforcement, and monitoring. We addressed specific questions to employees about these issues and got responses suggesting that, from many employees' perspectives, most organizations are not doing the right things in any of these arenas.

User Training for Information Protection

Our study showed us that users need more training in information technology and security. First, users tell us they are very excited about training. It is common for them to say that they would "love" to get more training. This attitude contrasted starkly with the beliefs of information technology professionals (reported in Chapter 6) that employees were not interested in security training. Second, it was clear from employees' analyses of their vulnerabilities and possible security solutions that they were in need of some up-to-date training in many areas. In fact, many employees told us they had not received any training since they started in the position at their organization.

Also, we found that the training that was given was not frequent enough and did not always include all of the people who would have liked to be invited. When a security issue arose and individuals were invited to learn more about it, the select few who knew the most about information technology were typically the ones invited, rather than having the session open to other employees who might have been interested. Finally, users sometimes felt confident handling normal situations but did not know what to do with situations that fell into "gray areas," in which answers were less clear cut. Unfortunately, with security, it is precisely those ambiguous, infrequent, or exceptional situations that can cause the most difficulty. This sales associate described a common situation in which information technology/security training was not very frequent:

> **I: Do you receive any training about security?**
>
> **R:** When we first started.
>
> **I: And not after that?**
>
> **R:** I've only been to one computer class and that might have been two or three years ago and that was it.
>
> **I: Was that when the program changed?**
>
> **R:** Yes, I think we started [brand name], I believe, or something. It was two, three years ago.

This idea of inadequate training was echoed by users such as this accountant from a small insurance company who said that he and his co-workers would like to take advantage of more training opportunities:

> **I: What can be done to make your computer system more secure?**
>
> **R:** They update the versions but the only thing that we would love is proper training. Certainly, we look into every training possibility but it's too costly so … my main complaint about this system is the training.

Training was sometimes reserved for handpicked employees who may have already been more tech-savvy and interested in security. This sales associate gave a typical comment in this vein:

I: So basically you would say you have training when required, for example if you need it for a new program?

R: There are other things that I'd like to see, but I'm not one that gets [chosen]—a lot of us don't get picked to go to those training [sessions].

Users told us that there were many situations related to security in which they did not know what to do or whom to ask for help. This healthcare employee feels many times there are policies but that there is a lack of clear-cut procedures about what to do in unusual situations:

I: What were you thinking of?

R: I was just thinking of a physician who was telling me that he had a patient that he has done a biopsy on. And he had been playing a phone contact back and forth, saying "This is Dr. So-and-so, please call me," and it went back and forth. Finally he left the information on an answering machine: "You got your results and your results are this." And [the director of security] hit him with a HIPAA violation. I think there needs to be more education about what you can and cannot do, you know, and there are still a lot of gray areas as far as answering machines, even if the patient gives you permission to leave a message on a machine, because we do that all the time. We call the patient the night before to let them know what time they come in for surgery and if we don't get hold of them, we usually leave a message. But if your family doesn't know that you are scheduled for a procedure, we give the patient a letter saying that we are going to call them at this time, you know, we give them a way to keep it secret ... so there are the gray areas though, you know?

From this quote, we see that even the most basic data management procedures can be problematic for those who do not feel properly trained. The technical nature of many aspects of information security and the difficulties in communication across different areas of expertise may cause a lack of confidence for some of these employees. Several problems arose from users' difficulties in understanding technical jargon and their lack of confidence in their information technology skills. Other problems sprang from the low priority that security has in the eyes of some co-workers and the fact that responsibility for information security is mostly delegated to information technology professionals. These situations allowed users to invoke a variety of excuses for not finding or following good solutions for information technology security problems. The motivations behind these excuses may have been innocent but their actions, even when altruistic in their eyes, may not contribute to the well being of the organization in the long run. In some organizations, employees use informal "buddy systems" so that they can access their co-workers' information in the event of an absence—an example of a non-malicious bypassing of good security practice. Although a few employees, such as the clerical support staff member quoted next, viewed the practice as a vulnerability, it was more common for employees to consider password sharing mainly as a harmless way to gain some convenience in helping out their co-workers:

> **I: What new steps do you think can be taken to improve security within your department?**
>
> **R:** See, I still think the password system [at our financial services company] is a joke. When we have people out in our department we have to check their e-mails. So therefore we have a buddy system.

The following quote from a hotel employee also describes this common practice and suggests that he does not consider it particularly troublesome:

> **I: How are information security priorities communicated to you?**
>
> **R:** They [information technology staff] just come down and say "OK, we're changing the passwords" and you change your passwords and away you go. I mean it's really just not that big of a deal. [In this department], I mean there are only four or five people. Ten people actually. But

somebody comes in and tells the other one we have got to change this, and everybody changes it.

I: Do they [information technology professionals] change your password for you or do you change it yourself?

R: Usually, most of the time you just change your own. They say OK, change it and this is what you're going to use. We try to keep them common only because a lot of times you're using somebody else's desk. So if you want your own security for a certain time you can put that in. If you're using general information then we all use the same [account].

As at many of our study sites, the same practices were noted at an organization where it was ordinary protocol to share passwords:

I: What else can you tell me about passwords?

R: Recently we had something happen where one of the secretaries had to leave because her parents were ill. It was on short notice and away she went, so I had to be the secretary. Generating things on the computer, I needed to get into her computer as her. Getting in as me didn't help at all. The fact that I knew her password was very helpful.

The preceding quotes, typical of what we encountered, suggest that employees are not so much malicious in their password sharing as they are naïve about the harm that this practice can cause both them and their institutions. Employees frequently asked for positive behavioral examples to help remind themselves and one another of appropriate procedures. The following quote from a professional employee shows that she would have welcomed changes in the norms regarding best security practices:

I: You were telling me that sometimes employees forget about the need to keep personal information private. What do you think could be done about that?

R: If they just had a constant reminder, everybody, even you, if you're walking down the hall and you notice somebody saying something, maybe you shouldn't say that, you know, take it in the other room. So not just the [professional staff], but it should be everybody working together, just to remind each other.

Policy Deployment and Enforcement

Security policies—and in particular acceptable use policies (sometimes referred to as AUPs)—represent one method by which organizations try to influence the computer-related behavior of their employees. Our interviews with employees generally showed a lack of awareness and understanding of their organization's security policies—in those instances where formally documented policies actually existed. We also encountered a tendency for some employees to brush off information security policies and practices as basically "common sense" and not worthy of in-depth consideration, as the conversation with these two employees suggested:

> **I: Did you ever learn about security policy during training?**
>
> **R1:** Yes, we did at the [organization-wide information system] training. But every situation is different and you kind of have to feel it out and if you are not sure, you call your supervisor.
>
> **R2:** Yes, it's just common sense. That's the biggest thing.

If there was a policy at this small legal services firm, it was not clear to one of the newer employees, a paralegal who already knew quite a bit about the other aspects of the business:

> **I: I understand that you outsource most of your information needs.**
>
> **R:** Right, the networking stuff is outsourced, correct. We need technical support.
>
> **I: How do [the outsource technology people] communicate their security priorities to you?**
>
> **R:** I don't know. I don't know that they have, in terms of like, you know, having a formal policy, you know, "this is

what we do for all our clients, blah, blah, blah," I don't think so. I think my understanding of that relationship is, there's a problem, we call them in; we have a new need, he [the owner] calls them in and they deal with things ad hoc as they go. I could be mistaken or maybe he has a policy, but he has failed to make it clear. I don't know. So, that's the answer to that one.

This new employee was "sure" that there were some policies but she did not know what they were. This organization was not unique in providing only minimal security training to incoming employees. Even veteran employees who know about a given security policy sometimes found it difficult to follow, however, but not necessarily because they were consciously trying to subvert or bypass organizational rules. Instead, they may have decided to ignore policy for a business purpose that they considered important—such as maintaining rapport with clients—as suggested by the following verbatim answer from a customer service representative:

I: Do the policies allow for someone to get personal e-mail?

R: Oh you're not supposed to receive them. But that doesn't stop it from happening. You can receive an e-mail and you can write back and say please don't send me [this], I really shouldn't be receiving personal e-mails. And people still send them to you. I do have some issues regarding that because some customers have been with our organization for over 20 or 30 years. They have developed a relationship with a lot of the service reps so therefore every now and then a personal one kind of breaks that, and it's sent. I'm not going to tell a customer "don't send it to me." The loyalty and comfort level is there, I'm not going to do that. Maybe you don't respond and go back and forth as much as you would, but you still accept it.

Users often viewed compliance with policy positively, in effect equating policy compliance with professionalism and ethical behavior. These employees appreciated when they were involved in policy formation, and the resultant security policies were expressed clearly. The following quote from an employee expressed a widely held belief that personal ethics control security-related behaviors and that these ethics are often compatible with organizational beliefs:

> **I: What are the rules for acceptable use here and how did you learn them?**
>
> **R:** Good question. I just try to be professional. I try to be within what I think is the professional range. I don't send out blanket joke e-mails, that kind of thing. I think it is more etiquette than anything else. I know they take care of blocking Web sites … that I probably wouldn't want to be on anyway. So it isn't anything that I do myself.

Employees appreciated management's giving them a clear explanation of security policy. Following is an excerpt from a joint interview with two employees who shared a commonly held belief that they should comply with security policy as long as they were provided with a rational explication of the reasons behind it:

> **I: When you receive new information about information security policies, how do you feel about it?**
>
> **R1:** I'm like, whatever, I'll do what they say.
>
> **I: Really?**
>
> **R1:** It's part of my job. If there is a reason for it, I will comply.
>
> **R2:** They wouldn't implement something if there were no reason for it. If it affects me in a way that I can't deal with, then I will talk to my supervisor.

This final comment suggests a strong degree of trust in the organization's policymakers. The idea that "they wouldn't implement something if there were no reason for it" suggests a belief that all of the organization's security policies were well thought out and appropriate. A similar belief is expressed in some of the material on employee monitoring that follows.

Employee Perspectives on Workplace Monitoring

When examining how employees felt about electronic monitoring and surveillance, we found two essential perspectives. One group asserted that the concept of trust played a very important role in its beliefs and attitudes. The other group, consistent with the survey data presented at the beginning of the chapter, was skeptical of monitoring for a variety of interesting and sometimes unexpected reasons.

Many of the employees with whom we spoke apparently had very trusting attitudes toward a wide range of other people: They expressed trust in outsiders, co-workers, and themselves. Many employees also expressed substantial trust in their management's ability to responsibly collect and protect sensitive data. They seemed largely unaware of (or at least reticent to express) the possibility that management might not trust *them* and might monitor their computer use for a variety of purposes. Many seemed to have little awareness of the monitoring technologies in use, the frequency with which they were monitored, who had access to the data, and so forth. Even in firms that had written policies that employees were obliged to sign at the time of hire, we found that very few employees could accurately describe what was being monitored or how it was being monitored. We found that many employees believed that as long as they did not misuse organizational property or information, they did not have to worry about security or monitoring. One clerical support employee at a large financial services company explained why she does not give the topic much thought:

> **I: What do you know about the acceptable use policies here?**
>
> **R:** It's been indicated to us that it [the organization's computer system] shouldn't be for personal use.
>
> **I: So there's a handbook or guidelines?**
>
> **R:** You sign up. When you're hired you sign something and then, occasionally, it's sent in an e-mail to remind us that you're not supposed to be doing "forwards" [e-mail forwarding, of jokes, etc.] and that kind of stuff: recreational use of the computer.

I: Do you know if your work is monitored regarding this?

R: I would think it is. I don't pay very much mind because other than an occasional e-mail to an individual in the family every three days or something like that, I don't mis-use it, so I don't worry about it.

We found this to be a very common attitude: "Because I personally am honest, I do not need to worry about how my behavior is being tracked." To put it bluntly, we found that employees in many of the organizations we visited did not know whether or not they were being monitored. These responses from three customer service representatives in the same firm supported these ideas:

I: Do you believe that your daily activities are being monitored by [the information technology department]?

R1: I don't think so.

R2: I don't think so, I think some of it is, such as proper use of e-mail …

R3: Sometimes you'll get a note "you're not supposed to use e-mail for these purposes," so somebody's obviously monitoring at some points, but I don't think they monitor it all the time.

The following quotes from a variety of settings show the trusting nature of employees as they considered whether or not their work activities were being scrutinized electronically:

I: Do you know if your work is being monitored?

R1: From my understanding, no. I don't see any reports and I don't believe [my supervisor] sees any reports either as to who is doing what. I do believe that they can print out how many transactions somebody did but we don't pay any attention to that.

R2: I don't think there are any restrictions. We sign something when we first start working, when we do our paper-work, and I think that says no personal use, but I don't think there's any type of restrictions. I don't know whether there's monitoring or not.

Although it is possible to conclude that these employees were simply clueless or naïve, the implication that we drew from comments like these was that the employees trusted their organizations not to abuse their capabilities in monitoring employees. Related to this, a culture of trust was seen by many as something quite positive for their organizations. This situation is described in the quotes that follow, from a customer service agent who reported that her small organization was like a family. The employee's initial response of laughter about the question itself quite possibly reveals as much about the organization and its informal culture as the rest of her explanation. She appeared to imply that the very idea of monitoring in the firm's intimate and friendly atmosphere was ludicrous:

I: Do you know if your work is monitored?

R: (laughs) I don't really think so, because I don't think that anybody in [our company] as far as I know misuses the Internet, and if it was monitored, it probably would be brought to the attention of the owner. And I wouldn't even know that until he addresses that issue. We don't, per se, babysit. We are a small company. And it is still more like a family business type, not a big corporation where we would have a whole lot of chain of command. Everybody wears a lot of hats, we do a lot of different jobs; there is not one specific job. And we do have a trust basis. If we saw somebody that was always on the Internet and they were out shopping or something like that, we would address it. If it became a problem, we would, but we don't really look over anyone's shoulder.

I: If you saw a problem tomorrow, would you react by telling them [the co-worker] up front? Is that what you mean by a trust basis?

R: Right. Even if someone did start [misusing the Internet], we would just say that we don't use the Internet for our personal use, only when it is necessary. Something like that. We do our licenses via the Internet. We renew our licenses for the industry via the Internet. We ask that if they are going to use it, to do it during their lunch times or before and after work. That is told to them when they come here. After that it is a trust basis.

We found that "trust basis" was a common expression among managers, employees, and information technology professionals alike—particularly in smaller organizations. The phrase seemed to indicate something of the family-like nature of the smaller firms— that the strength of personal connections and relationships among the members of the organization helped to ensure that everyone kept his or her behavior within the expected organizational norms.

Along the same line, many users thought that the administration had a right to monitor them as long as they were told about the procedure and consequences ahead of time. In the following conversation, two hospital employees discussed their response to hospital monitoring (these two respondents participated together in the same interview):

I: How do you protect client information?

R1: They are definitely strong on that and we do try to do the best we can and its kind of hard because we don't have a window and it's all open, so it's tough because you talk about situations and sometimes you have codes for reasons and stuff, and you don't realize that there are people in the waiting room who can hear it.

I: So what about that concerns you?

R1: I'm concerned about people's privacy.

R2: It's truly not private.

I: What about on the phone or e-mail?

R1: We're not allowed to discuss any medical or personal information about patients through e-mail. And they do check that.

I: They check your e-mail?

R1: Yes. Anything that's done on the system, they can check.

I: And do you feel that is reasonable?

R1: Yes.

R2: Yes. They are paying me so you know ...

R1: They have to monitor somehow and if this is the way. ... They need to get rid of people that are discussing patient care unless there is a necessity because they do go from department to department. Sometimes from an inpatient to an outpatient. Then fine, we'll discuss it but if we are just doing it to be nosy, then, you know, you don't belong here.

I: So they have a more proactive way of doing things than a reactive way?

R1: Yes.

R2: Yes. Exactly

I: And that works well?

R1: Yes. I think so.

R2: Fair warning.

Some employees even embraced increased monitoring because they believed it would make them look good. Highly positive appraisals, such as the following from a data processing clerk, were relatively infrequent but poignant because of what they revealed about how these employees felt about themselves and their jobs:

I: What do you think about the arrival of this new information system?

R: I think the [new system] will help with a lot of feelings in some departments that this person works harder than I do or I work harder than this person. It will stop the rumor mill because it will say you've processed eight [orders] and she has processed 20. Uh, there is something wrong with this picture—the workload isn't equal, let's distribute it a little more equally.

In contrast to some of the smaller settings, larger institutions included more employees who were skeptical, apprehensive, or aggravated at the prospect of their employer putting into place or increasing the monitoring of their work activities. Some employees were concerned because they viewed monitoring as an implication by management that they—the employees—were not trusted. Others thought that the information garnered about them through monitoring did not accurately reflect their workplace activities. These two employees contended that their personal ethics, and not monitoring, motivated them to behave properly for the good of the company:

I: How does your department handle monitoring of employee behavior?

R1: We are on the Internet all the time to find software. Every now and then when you go to look for something, you end up someplace else, and we joke around, "Don't tell [the information technology person]," you know? People pretty much follow it, and they don't abuse it.

I: Why do you think they don't abuse it?

R1: I think it's, I don't want to say, (pause) professional. ... It is their ethics and the sense that "I know what I am here for and that [abusing Internet privileges] is not what I am here for."

R2: I have no accountability professionally to the information technology department. I do that [comply with policy] because it's the right thing to do.

In another case, a professional service provider contemplated leaving her job if a new system was implemented in such a way that it would impinge on her current level of autonomy at work. The planned system—referred to as the "scheduling" system by the interviewer—would have given management the opportunity to review and compare the client loads of all of the different professional staff members:

I: What do you think of the proposed new scheduling system?

R: I don't even know whether I want to stay here if someone would do it. ... Okay, if they would just back off and let me do my job. (laughs)

In the following quote, a professional employee explained that she and her colleagues had been participating in conversations about the possibility of unionizing. She felt nervous about the intentions of the administration and the political and potentially dangerous aspects of her involvement in those activities, and she did not want any of their conversations to be made public. Her quote gives her explanation about her union activities and the discomfort she felt about the risks involved:

I: Do you ever have concerns about the security of your information?

R: Well, that's an interesting question. I mean, I was involved last year in this process of trying to get the [workers] unionized, and I was really uncomfortable with, like, thinking, because I know that [my manager] is very much opposed to it, she has made all sorts of comments, and I mean I really began to think that it was something that would influence whether or not they would ask me to come back this year, so, and I had a sense that [the organization] as a whole (laughs), you know, I mean, the statement came out from [high-level manager] that blah, blah, blah, all this stuff. I mean, in some ways, huh, that's interesting. Because, yeah, I mean, sort of the subversive stuff (laughs) that I think it's really important that people are able to [talk] without having sort of a level of surveillance is important to me. Other than that, I can't think of anything that I would care that anybody had access to.

I: How did you handle that?

R: Oh, we just suggested that we carry on a conversation using e-mail accounts that were not connected to [the organization], so that we would use our [free e-mail] accounts or whatever, and then have our listserv through that, and that felt fairly [safe], you know. For some reason, again, I felt that it was, that probably displays how I don't know how that works, (laughs) there's a false sense of security. (laughs)

As opposed to this hesitant yet somewhat trusting employee, anger and fear were emotions felt by some employees at the idea that monitoring capabilities would not be used appropriately or sensitively. The individual whose words follow was a relatively new employee who shared his thoughts about the possibility of a centralized computer system with increased monitoring capabilities. Our interview was almost finished when he expressed his concerns in this way:

I: Do you have any other questions?

R: I have had the problem in the past that people try to quantify things too much. They make a justification for wanting to monitor us, and that's not really a problem in itself, because I know we work hard here. It's just that (pause), well, the numbers don't always reflect the reality. At my old job they started having us write down how much time was spent on each activity. Sometimes you spent a lot of time on something that was beyond your control and it ends up looking funny. You end up spending a lot of energy on making it look okay. My fear is that there would be repercussions for me if it looks worse on paper than it really is. That's why I worry about the computer too. There are some situations where it looks like we are letting people build up a balance but we're really not. They think we haven't taken care of things when we really have. That bothers me. I want the computer thing to be worked out first before they use it for that kind of thing [monitoring].

This employee was one of many with this type of concern. Employees at a government agency expressed anger at the way they felt their administration had abused its monitoring capabilities. Even before the implementation of electronic monitoring, employees felt they had been excessively tracked and recorded. The arrival of a new computer system was met with intense pessimism, as the employees imagined they would be harassed relentlessly. These two employees' irritation is displayed in their comments about the prospects of increased accountability for workers' time:

> **I: Why is management interested in [implementing a new system in which clients have to sign something verifying provision of service]?**
>
> **R1:** They think that we [employees] are wasting time, and that they [management] have no accounting for our time. That they will have closer tabs on us. But you hear in the back of the office sometimes, "I don't want to be treated like a baby. I don't want a babysitter. I am here to do my job and however long it takes, it takes."
>
> **R2:** I don't mind documenting it [my time], but I should be trusted.

Finally, another sentiment uttered by employees was apprehension about giving up flexibility in their jobs. For some people that meant having freedom to use organizational information resources during their lunch hour, while for others it was related to the common practice of leaving the office for brief periods to conduct essential personal business. With the prospect of increased monitoring came trepidation at the prospect that employees would be either compelled or forced to remain in their offices for the entire work day. The professional employee whose quote follows was agitated at the potential effects of a new centralized service-scheduling system:

> **I: What are your concerns about the implementation of the new system?**
>
> **R:** I feel a little bit apprehensive of giving a schedule of all of my free hours because I frequently can reschedule people on my own during the week. I try to fill every hour [as requested by the center] but I like the flexibility if I have to go and pick up my daughter at school because she is sick, I can just fly out of here in a free hour and get it done.

To summarize this section, we found a range of employee perspectives on monitoring, although these generally fell into two camps. In some organizations—particularly smaller ones—there was little concern about monitoring and little awareness of what kinds of monitoring were being conducted, even in organizations that were in fact using a variety of monitoring techniques. In these organizations, employees frequently reported sentiments about their own ethicality and the degree of trust that they felt in the organization's capability to treat them fairly with respect to monitoring practices. In other organizations, employees expressed substantial reservations about monitoring, generally on one of two bases. First, some employees felt that giving managers the opportunity to make employee data more visible also implied a loss of autonomy. In effect, the sentiment was that if managers can see what I'm doing, they will want to control it, to the detriment of my work or non-work freedom. The other basis for employee concerns about monitoring pertained to the inability of monitoring techniques to give a clear picture of what employees were actually doing. Here, employees felt that their honest and productive activities might sometimes be erroneously detected as inappropriate or contrary to organizational policies.

Overall Recap of Interview Data

In summary, the preceding interview excerpts offered employee perspectives on matters related to information security, privacy, and monitoring. Although many employees had very positive feelings about the information technology personnel who supported them, quite frequently they found the information technology itself somewhat mysterious and confusing. These feelings extended to the technical aspects of information security as well. Despite these feelings of confusion, however, employees were eager to protect the personal information of their clients and customers. Likewise, they saw great value in keeping their organizations from getting into trouble as a result of breaches of information security. Users viewed the following as barriers to security: the security awareness and behavior of their managers, the physical layout of the workplace, the need to share information with others, and the need to work and transfer data off-site. Some employees expressed a wish to understand a more comprehensive picture of security priorities and frequently hoped for improved and more frequent security training. Policy awareness and awareness of monitoring techniques in use were generally quite low in the organizations we visited, and some employees expressed a slight disdain for policies along with some suspicion of monitoring techniques.

A Survey of Employee Beliefs and Information Security

To conclude our examination of employee behavior, we conducted an employee security survey to shed some light on employees' beliefs about security-related behaviors and issues. This survey used elements from the same data set reported for the simple comparison of managers and employees that was described in Chapter 5, but we analyzed those data in a more sophisticated and complete fashion for this chapter. Specifically, we assessed employees' beliefs about their business units' information security in five areas: training and awareness, security self-efficacy, security culture, monitoring awareness, and enforcement of acceptable use policies. In addition, we asked employees how successful they thought their organization would be at avoiding future information security problems.

Employee beliefs may play two important roles in answering these questions. First, as hundreds of psychological studies have demonstrated (based on the Theory of Planned Behavior; Ajzen, 1991), beliefs about the importance or desirability of a particular behavior have a profound influence on intentions to perform that behavior. Beliefs shape a person's thoughts as to how desirable a certain behavior is, whether other people will approve the behavior, and whether the behavior will lead to worthwhile outcomes or unpleasant ones. Behavioral intentions, in turn, influence actual behavior given situations that provide individuals with sufficient latitude of action. In a related idea, beliefs about self-efficacy can create or release constraints on behavior (Bandura, 1977). Self-efficacy is a particular structure of beliefs that individuals have with respect to their competency or ability to successfully complete a particular task. Individuals who feel a strong belief in their own competency to perform a specific task are both more likely to undertake that task in the first place *and* more likely to succeed in the performance of the task. Projecting these ideas into the area of information security, it seems reasonable to suggest that employees who believe in the importance and value of information security and who feel a sense of competence about their duties in the maintenance of security are more likely to enact behaviors that they believe will promote security. Whether these behaviors have any measurable effect on actual security outcomes—either positive or negative—remains to be demonstrated.

Secondly, analysis of employees' beliefs can help in the diagnosis of the status and conduct of information security in their departments or business units. Here we draw a parallel to the measurement of morale or cultural characteristics in organizations. To make an estimate of morale in a group of employees, one averages individuals' reports of job satisfaction and related measures to create a summary for the business unit where the employees work (see, e.g., Bruce & Formisano, 2003). Likewise, when researchers are interested in the organizational culture or cultural characteristics of a group of people, they estimate the standing of the group on the cultural measure by aggregating across the responses of a representative sample of individuals from the group. In these ways, aggregate measures can be meaningful and useful as summary representations of a group phenomenon. To be reliable, measures of both morale and cultural characteristics depend upon the cancellation of various types of error that occur when obtaining reports from samples of individuals. As Surowiecki (2004) documented in his book *The Wisdom of Crowds*, estimates of both subjective and objective phenomena obtained from groups of people are often more accurate than those of single individuals. In some cases Surowiecki and others attribute this accuracy to a "Goldilocks-like" cancellation of errors or judgment: Some people guess too high while and others guess too low, but the average of all guesses tends to be just right.

Beliefs are by their nature subjective, however, and may be accurate or inaccurate reflections of reality. So we also collected somewhat more objective data in the form of expert opinions of the effectiveness of the information security programs of these employees' organizations. Using these expert ratings as a target for analysis, we probed employees' perceptions of training and awareness, security self-efficacy, security culture, monitoring awareness, and enforcement of acceptable use policies to examine which among these was actually effective at predicting the security experts' ratings of security effectiveness. The results reported in the following section suggest that employee belief systems and reality did not always match up very well.

Description of the Employee Survey Study

During the final year of our data collection for this research project, we conducted research in 14 different organizations. The organizations ranged in size from six employees to approximately 2,100 employees. Within the larger organizations, we had information on several different business units within the organization. Counting each business unit separately, we had data on 39 distinct business units. In each organization, we conducted a security audit with the help of an information security expert at Syracuse University, Dr. Roman Markowski—an individual who is a founder of a software company, has designed secure networks, and has taught technical security courses in the university's computer science program. Two of his graduate students assisted our group with the information security audits. Note that we gratefully acknowledge Dr. Markowski's contribution to this study, but we also take full responsibility for any mistakes or misinterpretations in our compilation, analysis, and report of these data.

Within each organization, we requested participation by employees in completion of a brief, online security survey. Looking across the 39 distinct business units, we had as few as three responses from some business units and as many as 185 responses from one business unit for a total of 729 responses. These responses included those of regular non-information-technology employees as well as non-technical managerial personnel (generally no higher than director level; note again that these data come from the same data set as reported in the manager-employee comparison of Table 5.2). Although it was not always possible to calculate an exact response rate, many of the smaller organizations had a 100 percent response rate from their employees while others had response rates as low as approximately 33 percent of individuals who were asked to complete the survey.

For each organization, the security audit resulted in a comprehensive printed feedback report to the organization that contained descriptions of the company's information technology setup, positive findings about security, a catalog of important security flaws found at the company, and recommended solutions to those flaws. These reports were always delivered after all of the employees had completed the online survey, so employees were unaware of the experts' conclusions when they completed the survey. On the basis of these feedback reports, as well as spot inspections of the premises, interviews with key personnel, and information about the community of computer users, a team of six judges with experience in organizational research and information security provided an overall security performance score for each of the organizations. In addition, the technical security professional and one of his graduate students also provided scores, for a total of eight security assessment scores for each organization. These scores were averaged and assigned to all of the organization's business units to provide an overall security score for each business unit.

As indicated by the contents of Table 7.2, our online employee survey consisted of 10 items designed to elicit employees' beliefs about security in five areas: training and awareness, security self-efficacy, security culture, monitoring awareness, and enforcement of acceptable use policies. We used a statistical procedure known as principal components analysis to help make decisions about pairs of items that should be combined to make a composite. When two items on a survey ask a similar question, it is often better to combine their responses—usually by averaging them—in order to reduce the total number of separate statistical tests being conducted in later analyses. Table 7.2 shows the text of the items and how they were combined. Note that the people responding to the survey indicated their level of agreement with each item on a five-point scale, the process known as Likert scaling. For these analyses we retained the full precision of these five-point scales.

In summary, for each of 729 employee responses we had five predictors—training and awareness, security self-efficacy, security culture, monitoring awareness, and enforcement of acceptable use policies—and a subjective outcome variable. For each of 39 business units we also had an *objective* overall security assessment score provided from our expert team of security assessors. Using these data we aggregated employees into their business units and conducted analyses at the business unit level. These analyses highlight the relationships between normative beliefs held by a group of employees in an area of an organization and the security outcomes for that area, both subjective and objective.

What Do Employee Beliefs Predict About Security?

Statisticians typically refer to the type of statistical analyses described in the following section as "multiple regression." This technique describes how well a particular set of input variables predicts

Table 7.2   Employee Survey Configuration

Survey Items	How the items were combined
There's a lot I can do to keep the information I work with on my computer secure. I feel confident that I know how to choose secure passwords for my computer accounts.	These two items were averaged to create our measure of security self-efficacy.
My company provides useful training to help employees improve their awareness of computer and information security issues. The technology people at my company communicate clearly on how to prevent information security problems.	These two items were averaged to create our measure of security training and awareness.
The culture of my company encourages care and attention to information security issues. We feel empowered to follow our company's security policies and/or procedures.	These two items were averaged to create our measure of positive security culture.
My company seems well defended against problems related to information security. My company will probably successfully avoid future problems due to information security breaches.	These two items were averaged to create our measure of expected security outcomes for the organization.
My company lets workers know how their computer activities are monitored.	This item was used by itself to assess monitoring awareness.
My company consistently enforces an acceptable use policy that governs what employees can and cannot do with their work computers.	This item was used by itself to assess enforcement of acceptable use policies.

some output variable. One commonplace example to illustrate this is to think about how the weight of a vehicle and the size of its engine would predict its fuel economy: Heavier cars and cars with larger engines generally get lower mileage, but even working together, the two predictors can't predict a precise value for miles per gallon because of the many other unmeasured variables involved. Multiple regression analysis provides a picture of how well or poorly this prediction process works, as well as information on the goodness of each input or "predictor" variable. In our case we used employee-provided ratings of training and awareness, security self-efficacy, security culture, monitoring awareness, and enforcement of acceptable use policies as predictors and the expected success of information security as the outcome. A quantity called "R-squared" shows how successful this prediction is by describing the percentage of variation in the output variable that is accounted for by the predictors. Quantities known as beta weights help illustrate the comparative importance of each of the individual predictor variables in the analyses with a value that can range from -1 to +1. In the following analyses, we report only results that were statistically significant. Statistical significance is an idea that is closely related to probability. In this case statistical significance refers to quantities or values that were sufficiently large in the sample that the chances of their actually being nil in the population were quite small.

Because we knew which business unit each employee belonged to, we were able to conduct regression analyses that used a consensus of employee beliefs as the predictors. In these analyses we used aggregated ratings of training and awareness, security self-efficacy, security culture, monitoring awareness, and enforcement of acceptable use policies as predictors. To aggregate, we took the average score on each of those variables across all individuals who reported being in that business unit. In effect, these averages represented a group consensus about issues such as training. Because of the relatively small number of business units, we used a liberal statistical criterion (technically, $p<.10$, or a one-in-10 chance of reporting a false positive): This helps to compensate for the fact that this smaller number of cases in our analysis (i.e., 39 business units) adversely affected our ability to find statistically significant results.

In the first analysis, we used *expected* information security success as the outcome variable (that is, the employees' subjective, aggregated opinions about security success). Overall, the analysis was successful in predicting 64 percent of the variation in expected information security success, R-squared = .64, $F(5, 34) = 12.3$, $p<.001$. The two predictors that accounted for this variation were training and awareness (beta = .29) and positive security culture (beta = .55). That is, employees' beliefs about training and awareness in their organizations made strong showings as predictors of expected information security success. In the case of positive security culture, a follow-up analysis also showed that the level of agreement about how positive the group's security culture was had a strong relation to expected information security success ($r = .66$, $p<.001$). Here is a brief interpretation of these results: If many or all of the members of a business unit believed that they have received sufficient training about information security and/or they agreed that they have a culture of awareness and attention to security, they were more likely as a group to expect information security success for their business unit.

In the second analysis, we used the same set of predictor variables—aggregated measures of training and awareness, security self-efficacy, security culture, monitoring awareness, and enforcement of acceptable use policies—but we changed our focus to predicting the experts' rating of the security status of each organization. In this analysis, the predictors as a group accounted for 39 percent of the variation in the expert rating of the organizations' security status, R-squared = .39, $F(5,33)$ = 4.2, $p<.01$. The picture for the predictors was strikingly different, however. Unlike the first analysis, the aggregated ratings of training and awareness *did not* predict the experts' ratings of the organizations' security status. Instead, the level of monitoring awareness (beta = .35) and the consistent enforcement of acceptable use policies (beta = .53) predicted the experts' ratings. Perhaps more important, however, both self-efficacy (beta = -.25) and security culture (-.43) made *reversed* predictions of the experts' ratings. In other words, the more the employees believed they were empowered to deal with security and the more they felt they had a positive security culture in their groups, the *lower* the security experts rated their organization's information security.

As a closing analysis, we correlated the subjective and objective outcome measures: Experts' judgments of the organizations' security status correlated with the aggregated expectations of security success calculated from employees' survey responses. The small positive correlation ($r = .17$) was not statistically significant, confirming a notable lack of agreement between employees' collective judgments about their business unit's security and the judgments of the security experts.

What These Statistical Results Mean

The contrast between the employees' belief system about information security and the reality of an organization's actual security status was striking. Employees who are confident about their organization's security appear to have a self-consistent belief system in which the following kind of reasoning might typically occur: "We receive lots of information about security from our information technology people and we feel empowered to put that information to good use, making for a positive security culture and an expectation that we will be well defended against future attacks." Other individuals who hold the opposite beliefs seem to expect that their organization is not so likely to achieve success with information security. These beliefs probably have both logical and emotional appeal to employees: More training makes us better prepared; more empowerment makes our group feel good about security. Correspondingly, in certain other organizations, employees may think, "We don't get enough training on security and nobody seems to care about it, so there's no way that our organization is properly prepared to avoid a security crisis."

To the extent that one accepts the accuracy of the expert panel's ratings of the security success of these organizations, however, these beliefs appear to be false. Instead, what appears to set a positive stage for the effective enactment of information security are the firm's efforts to achieve *effective governance* over its user community. As the final regression analysis showed, if the employees in a business unit collectively reported that their organization "consistently enforces an acceptable use policy that governs what employees can and cannot do with their work computers," then that organization was more likely to have information security success as seen by the experts and documented in their audit report. Likewise, if the organization "lets workers know about how their computer activities are monitored," then the organization was also more likely to show information security success according to the experts. What these two issues have in common is a clear communication, in words and actions, that the organization's management takes information security seriously and backs up its words with relevant performance assessments and enforcement actions.

In interpreting all of these data together, it is important to note that these results do *not* say that providing training to enhance awareness, tools and techniques to enhance security, and encouragement of positive employee attitudes about security are bad. Rather, the data suggest that what was misleading was the employees' beliefs that these factors alone were sufficient to achieve success in information security. In other words, employees' beliefs about the status of "positive security culture" are not in themselves accurately predictive of whether the organization will have success with information security. Employees may have overconfident or misguided beliefs about this issue. In contrast, however, employees' perceptions of strong organizational governance in the form of monitoring and enforcement of acceptable use policies are good predictors of information security success.

Limitations to Keep in Mind

It is important to keep in mind that the foregoing results and discussion represent just one study of a handful of different firms, albeit drawing on the input of a substantial number of employees. Statistical analysis alone cannot ensure that these results are applicable to all types of employees or all types of organizations. We were not able to be systematic in our choice of participants in this study, either at the level of employee within the organization or with respect to the selection of organizations themselves. Both were what are technically known as "convenience" samples because they consisted of data that were readily available to us in the course of our project.

Another important caveat relates to the survey we used. In general, a survey that uses a larger number of high-quality items to capture its measurements provides more reliable results than a survey that uses a smaller number of items. We had to use a very brief survey in order to make our work palatable to the organizations we worked with, and this necessarily represents a compromise on the reliability of the data that we received. A longer survey with a large number of items capturing each of the individual measurements (e.g., training/awareness) would have provided more measurement precision and might have led to a somewhat different pattern of results.

At a more conceptual level, it is important to note that our "gold standard" outcome variable—the average expert ratings of each organization's security status—was itself an aggregation of subjective human judgments. Whether the reader should fully trust these expert judgments more than the collective judgments of the employees in these business units is not an absolute given. One might make plausible arguments that the employees, who frequently have had lengthy job experience within an organization, enjoy a more comprehensive view of the organization's security than do the expert auditors. In general, however (judging from the job titles they reported), most of the employees who responded to the survey had neither extensive technical knowledge of the organization's security processes nor a great deal of information regarding recent or current security threats, attacks, and breaches. The security auditing team did have both technical knowledge and background information and this may be taken as supporting the greater validity of their judgments. Each of these possible conclusions needs to be taken with a grain of salt.

To close this chapter, note how we have come full circle on the topic of monitoring. At the beginning of the chapter we showed survey results suggesting that a significant percentage of employees would try to "get around" monitoring systems if their organizations implemented them. In the interviews, we learned that in smaller companies employees believed that monitoring was unnecessary given the trust that everyone had in each other. In larger companies employees were often unaware of what existing monitoring activities the organization conducted and some were suspicious about monitoring on the basis that it would cause a loss of autonomy or would erroneously represent legitimate activities as inappropriate. Managers (as reported in Chapter 5) were unlikely to offer convincing rationales for monitoring, other than "we own the equipment, so we can do what we want." Together these results suggest that many organizations have failed to adequately justify the business necessity of monitoring to their employees. Besides the potential that this situation raises for poor management-labor relations, we believe that an important opportunity for enhancing information is also being lost here: The results of our final survey suggest that the organizations that make employees keenly aware of how their computer-related activities are monitored are more likely to succeed with information protection than those that do not.

In Chapter 8 we examine these findings in light of the complete set of data we collected in order to formulate an inclusive explanation of how employee monitoring, information security failures, and information security protections interact to create favorable or unfavorable conditions for information protection in organizations.

CHAPTER 8

Overall Analysis
and Interpretation

In this chapter we tie together the many nuggets of information we gleaned from managers, information technology professionals, and employees who are the end-users of information technology in organizations. Here we compare and contrast how the different groups think about their roles in the control and protection of information within the organization. We also want to understand their different perspectives on employee privacy as it relates to electronic monitoring and surveillance. It is obvious that managers, information technology professionals, and employees have a variety of ideas about what is good, right, and appropriate within the organization. Our goal is to find out which of those ideas can be reconciled and which of them are so far apart that they create a challenge in finding the common ground necessary for positive organizational change.

We have structured this chapter to focus on a number of key areas that roughly parallel those discussed in Chapters 5, 6, and 7. Although we have done our best to avoid overlap between these areas, it is inevitable that we will repeat ourselves at least a bit. On the other hand, by making each section of the chapter work independently of the others, we hope to make it easier for you to tackle this chapter in several different sittings rather than all at once. The five key issues we want to talk about are:

- Priorities for information security
- Computer-related behavior of employees/users
- Communication among different groups in the organization
- Policies, training, and other behavioral influences
- Electronic monitoring and surveillance rights

Priorities for Information Security

In the 1960s and 1970s, sociology researchers Bruce Biddle and Edwin Thomas energized the flowering of a research area called "role theory" (Biddle, 1986; Biddle & Thomas, 1979; note that the ideas behind role theory had existed diffusely for more than 50 years). The idea behind role theory is that an individual who occupies a particular position or role within an institution, organization, or society often adopts many of the attitudes and behaviors commonly associated with that role. Because of the influence of societal norms for behavior, the expectations of colleagues, the policies and other rules for behavior in an organizational setting, and a variety of other social influences, people who occupy a role—for example, the president of a company—often "follow the script" for how individuals in such positions should think and behave. In a variety of social settings, role-based influences may seemingly determine individuals' behavior almost to a greater degree than their own personality or values.

Evidence from our research suggests that managers, employees, and information technology professionals often think and act in accord with their respective organizational roles when it comes to information security and privacy, regardless of their own private beliefs and attitudes. Managers are stereotypically concerned with the "bottom line" in an organization—productivity, cash flow, and profitability. When managers think about the value of information in the organization, they often seem to reason in strategic business terms. In their view, compromise, loss, or destruction of customer data is bad because it may immediately or ultimately lead to the loss of customers and their associated revenue. Likewise, protecting employee data becomes important when its inappropriate dissemination might lead to adverse effects on employee morale or motivation. Ethical concerns about the "rightness" of protecting data or tactical concerns about the sufficiency of technical defenses may simply not enter the managerial "consciousness" on a regular basis or may take a backseat to pragmatic concerns. Perhaps as a result of this orientation, managers we interviewed generally had a very functional, business-focused perspective on information security: Their main questions revolved around how security measures would make a positive or negative impact on organizational outcomes of concern to them. Importantly, in some cases managers' abilities to think effectively about the trade-offs involved in information security seemed noticeably limited by their lack of technical understanding of how information technology works. This result hints at one of the negative implications highlighted by role theory: People can become constrained by their role perspective to the extent that they no longer consider it compelling to examine issues from another role perspective. An inability to walk in the shoes of someone who has a different job limits one's ability to see things from that person's perspective.

Turning now to information technology professionals, we often heard sentiments in keeping with that organizational role as well, although these respondents rarely reported the stereotypical affiliation of technical professionals strictly to their devices and software. In accord with their typical role, security professionals exhibited a substantial and justifiable penchant for preventing bad things from happening. Although bad things happen in some areas of technology as a result of mechanical failure or product defects, in the area of information security, bad things happen mainly as a result of the agency of people. While some of these people are shadowy, distant, and represented only in the results of their work—virus and worm writers come to mind as the primary examples—other "agents" of interest reside right in the same building. As a result, information technology professionals consistently reported a cogent and considerable concern for the behavior of employees and other users of the organization's network and computing facilities. Although some of our interviewees focused much of their attention on intentionally disruptive or malicious behavior, most of the information technology people we interviewed had a much greater concern for the possible adverse effects of employee mistakes and negligence. On a related note, these information technology people also recognized the attractiveness to employees of using Internet-connected computers as a launchpad for non-work use of the organization's information infrastructure.

Interestingly, the traditional role of the information technology professional as a service provider within the organization was a theme that also emerged from our interviewees' comments. The classic view of an information technology service provider is the friendly and (hopefully) competent voice at the help desk or that obliging but often incomprehensible individual who periodically drops by to install software or adjust computer settings. People who provide information technology services envisage their organizational role as helping others to get the most productivity and convenience out of their technology. We found that some information *security* people also seemed to think of themselves in a service-oriented role, even though the goals of information security operations may not always be entirely compatible with this orientation. For example, some security professionals we interviewed spoke of wanting to do things on a "trust basis," wanting to minimize the inconvenience of security for the users, and wanting to give users the benefit of the doubt when they made mistakes or visited inappropriate Web sites. Other respondents seemed to suggest that it was largely infeasible to try to combine the role of the security professional and the role of the information technology service provider.

For their part, members of the user community also seemed to think and act in accordance with their typical roles in the organization. Employees who use information technology to fulfill their roles do so within the context of their functional area and with concerns for serving their clients' and customers' best interests as well as getting their own jobs done foremost in their minds. Users appreciate security to the extent that it enhances their productive activities or protects others whom they care about. Viruses, worm attacks, and other nasty computer events always put a major crimp in productivity, and users who see the connections between, for example, keeping anti-virus software running and avoiding downtime due to virus infections generally expressed willingness to support the operation of security measures. At the same time, however, users were notably wary about any changes to security procedures or new security measures that had the potential to interfere with their productivity or tie a knot in existing work flow and communication patterns.

Although we have a long list of both negative and positive user actions as seen from the perspective of information technology professionals (see Appendix C), we noted that employees cited their major frustrations and barriers to greater security as falling in a different genre than many of the information technology professionals' concerns. While information technology people worry about strong passwords and acceptable network use, employees struggled with how to work securely off-site, keep paper records secure from prying eyes, and share data safely with legitimate outsiders. Again here, employees spoke from the perspective of the people who have to get the basic productive tasks of the organization done. As a result, they focused their expressions of frustration on insecurities that were a function of their everyday patterns of work.

Taken together, we hope it is not too obvious to observe that almost every member of the organization sees information security from their own unique but incomplete perspective. Perhaps less obviously, each perspective is strongly shaped by the operational goals and everyday activities associated with the organizational role that the person occupies. Further, these rigid, role-based points of view interfere with the ability to grasp the security priorities of those who occupy other roles. If, for a moment, we make the assumption that it would be a good thing for organizational members to also be able to see security priorities from other people's perspectives—for example, a human resource manager to see things from the information security manager's perspective—then it follows that a major challenge is to get people to shed, however temporarily, their role-based blinders.

Computer-Related Behavior of Employees/Users

When comparing views about user behavior, we found substantial divergences among the three perspectives. As we have already noted, information technology professionals tended to have security concerns about employees' network behavior, while employees' security concerns focused more holistically on the various combined challenges of getting work done and keeping data secure in both the "real" and digital worlds simultaneously. Both of these groups, at least, had a notion that employee behavior mattered: Managers sometimes failed to extrapolate from their own computer-related behavior that the activities of the larger community of computer users within the organization might also have a powerful impact on security. Recall that we made a gross distinction between the managers who had some degree of technical knowledge (tech-savvy) vs. those who were highly dependent on information technology professionals (tech-dependent). In the former group, an understanding of the importance of careful access control, effective password management, and related issues showed substantial understanding of the influence of user behavior on the status of the organization's information resources. In contrast, the tech-dependent managers appeared almost perversely trusting and naïve about other people's technology-related behavior. Particularly in smaller firms, tech-dependent managers often failed to imagine the possibility of scenarios in which employees—through dishonesty, maliciousness, or simply incompetence—might compromise, steal, or destroy the organization's information or information technology infrastructure. Many managers seemed to project beliefs about their own honesty onto others. Likewise, when managers lacked the knowledge or skill to obtain sensitive information (e.g., financial data) from some organizational system or server, they also frequently projected these characteristics onto the employees who worked for them. The net result was a distinct lack of appreciation, among a substantial subset of the managers we interviewed, of the potential influence of employee behavior on the protection of the organization's information assets. In the same vein, we found only rare mention of the value of setting a good example for employees to follow: Many managers seemed unconcerned that their behavior—for example, sharing their passwords with staff members—might set a poor example for others to follow.

Although information technology professionals also sometimes expressed reluctance to think the worst about the user community, we found this reluctance tempered by experience. Many information technology professionals—particularly those in larger organizations—had been seasoned by exposure to a wide range of behaviors with adverse effects on the organization's networks and data. Information technology professionals described for us a litany of lost files, damaged systems, slow networks, and information systems misuse in which employees had been involved. Despite their knowledge of the many possible problems that employees could cause, however, we found that information technology professionals often desperately wanted to attribute these problems to benign intentions (e.g., trying to help a co-worker), incompetence (e.g., not knowing how to construct a good password), or unintentional error (e.g., deleting a file that appeared to be unimportant), rather than maliciousness or malfeasance. In fact, some information technology professionals appeared to hold the belief that most employees were simply not sophisticated enough with information technology to cause a really important service disruption. From this perspective, employees' apparent unwillingness or inability to learn more about the operation of their information systems provided a source of both comfort and despair for information technology professionals. We heard the lament that "users don't want to learn" more about technology just a breath or two away from "We're glad they don't know enough to cause too much trouble." This contradiction may be problematic if it leads to a belief by information technology people that educating end-users about security is largely futile; it may also lead to an underestimation of the amount of damage employees might do under certain circumstances.

Note that the interview format of data collection is not conducive to obtaining frank admissions of cynicism about human nature, so it is likely that the managers and information technology professionals we interviewed had negative thoughts about their fellow organizational members that they were reluctant to reveal. In the same vein, our interviews were not designed, and were not conducted in the appropriate environment, to elicit admissions of wrongdoing or guilt from employees concerning their security-related behavior. As a result of these two considerations, it is important to note that the most negative things that managers, information technology professionals, and employees themselves might have said about employee behaviors were probably held back in most cases. Even keeping this in mind, however, it was evident from most managers and information technology professionals that their natural tendency was to trust the other people with whom they worked on a daily basis. Companies with fewer than about 50 or 100 employees have the advantage that this trust radiates throughout the organization by virtue of the many direct social ties among organizational members. We say advantage because research shows that trust improves communication about things like security and privacy priorities, even if we do not know whether such trust also facilitates achievement of those priorities. On this note, we turn next to a summary of our findings concerning communication among organization members.

Communication Among Different Groups in the Organization

Ask anyone whether their communication with business associates, children, friends, or relatives could be improved, and the answer is almost inevitably yes. Interpersonal communication is not a process that ever attains peak perfection but is rather an ongoing effort that achieves temporary successes and failures. Examined in retrospect and over time, these successes and failures may seem on the whole pretty good, pretty bad, or anything in between. The important aim is to prioritize the improvement of communications in those relationships that are most important. Evidence from our research suggests that communication between information technology professionals and other people and groups within the organization is certainly important. Information technology professionals have knowledge and skills that are relatively rare within the organization and generally quite valuable, if average salaries are any measure. If anything, the rarity of the skills and knowledge of those information technology professionals who specialize in security is even greater than for the more general body of system administrators, analysts, help-desk personnel, and so forth. Thus, most managers and employees with whom we spoke seemed to regard communications with information technology professionals as an area that needed improvement. Likewise, the information technology professionals we spoke to also cited communication with managers and employees as a substantial opportunity area.

Like any profession, information technology generates specialized terminology that insiders use to try to make their communications with each other more efficient (see, e.g., Gopen & Swan, 1990). As in any area of human endeavor, people also have a tendency to want to abbreviate, speak in shorthand, and turn key terms into acronyms. One major difference between information technology and other areas of human endeavor (for example, carpentry) is that the underlying technologies evolve at a dizzying rate. As a result, the shorthand, abbreviations, and acronyms tend to enter and exit the professional lexicon faster than even the smartest and most dedicated expert can possibly absorb. Given the difficulty that information technology experts have in keeping up, it is not surprising that the employees and managers we interviewed lamented the difficulty of comprehending technology jargon. In response to this difficulty, some managers mentioned that they use their position of power to force conversations back down to a level at which the audience can understand what is being said. In effect, if a manager outranked an information technology professional in the organizational hierarchy, the manager could take steps to ensure that presentations, discussions, and meetings avoided overuse of jargon and were kept at a comprehensible level. It was also evident from managers' responses that many managers failed to do this and would let incomprehensible jargon pass by, in all likelihood out of a fear of seeming foolish or ignorant to others who were participating in the conversation.

For their part, information technology professionals typically realized the communication barrier created by specialized knowledge and jargon. Although some of the individuals were dismissive, particularly when referring to members of the user community, and seemed to think that non-information-technology people were largely unwilling or unable to learn about information technology in any significant depth, other information technology professionals understood how to cross the jargon gap by using diagrams, drawings, analogies, and other techniques to help their audiences understand key technical concepts. Hints were sprinkled throughout the responses from employees, managers, and information technology professionals that the most respected and appreciated among the latter group were those who made a special effort to ensure that non-specialists understood key concepts and trade-offs.

A few of our respondents raised the interrelated issues of motivation and attention in the communication process. Researchers in organizational communication have clearly documented the importance of motivation in the communication process (see, e.g., Osterloh & Frey, 2000). In particular, for a message to be received and understood, the recipients must be ready to hear the message—they must have a reason for listening (Te'eni, 2001). Likewise, for communication to have a desired effect on subsequent behavior, it must garner the attention of the listener (see, e.g., Simons, 1991). Although it is almost trite to mention the topic of information overload, our respondents referred to it implicitly and explicitly as an important barrier to the communication of security priorities among organizational members. People need a reason to care about security before they will take the time to listen to information or warnings about it. Those organizations that successfully get employees and managers motivated to pay attention to information about security will have greater success in generating positive security behavior from the knowledge they gain. In the next section, we open up the topic of motivation in greater detail as we consider policy and other mechanisms that intend to influence security-related behavior.

Policies, Training, and Behavioral Influences

Policy means different things to different people. For a frontline information technologist, the idea of policy can sometimes be more akin to the common meaning of the word *rule*. Various methods of configuring devices, software, and systems involve the deployment of such rules, which are sometimes referred to by technology vendors as policies. Whole books have been written about security "policies" for popular operating systems (e.g., Moskowitz, 2001), but they are really all about the programming and configuration of rules for the internal operation of computers. On a related note, some information technology people with whom we spoke believed that it was important to develop as many of these rules as possible to constrain the range of user behavior.

At a somewhat higher level, those individuals who supervise the functioning of a business process often have written instructions and other documentation that indicate how to do certain tasks or complete certain activities. These instructions are also sometimes referred to as policy, but a more apt term might be *procedures*. Finally, from an even more general perspective, organizational managers who wish to influence the behavior and activities of groups of individuals in the organization will draft broad statements of goals, preferred strategies for achieving those goals, and possibly a set of pitfalls to be avoided in pursuit of those goals. Such statements are intended to influence the behavior of organizational members, not through constrictions on the capabilities of systems they use (rules), and not by giving them step-by-step instructions (procedures), but by documenting and communicating the behavioral norms and preferences of individuals in the organization who hold the power.

Thus, when we asked managers, information technology professionals, and employees about their take on information security policy, we always tried to guide the conversation toward a discussion of governance-oriented security policies—those documents that were intended as broad guides to the security-related behavior of information systems users, systems administrators, and other organizational members.

The first finding, which few will find surprising, was consistently reported among managers, information technology professionals, and employees alike: In many organizations, policies are frequently nonexistent and, in those cases where they have been written down, are frequently not disseminated, enforced, or updated. The rare exception to this gloomy diagnosis tended to occur in organizations in which new regulatory influences had heightened people's sensitivity to the importance of policies. For example, the recent focus on

HIPAA regulations has stirred up the status quo in healthcare organizations to a sufficient degree to ensure at least a temporary buzz of activity surrounding the development and deployment of policies. Likewise, some of the publicly traded organizations we visited had a similar buzz surrounding compliance with the federal Sarbanes-Oxley legislation.

Given our definition of policy, it should be evident that policies are largely a management construct, presumably developed in service of positively influencing behavior throughout the organization. Although some policies may certainly be amenable to further translation into procedures and rules, at heart an organizational policy is documentation concerning right behavior, where rightness is determined on the basis of the organization's mission and values. With this orientation in mind, we found it surprising that the connection between policy and motivation rarely garnered an explicit mention by managers. Although managers discussed policy with us and seemed to evince an understanding of how policy could benefit information security, the more concrete idea of motivating and influencing user behavior with policy did not seem to emerge from these discussions. In other words, while the concept of policy as a behavioral tool was not foreign, the idea that policies needed to *contain* motivational mechanisms was.

On a related note, little dialogue seemed to occur between information technology professionals and managers on the topic of policy. On several occasions we heard about the transom technique: Information technology people would write a policy and "throw it over the transom" to the managers, who would sign off on it (or not in some cases). Although it was less common, policies sometimes started on the managerial side and flew over the transom to the information technology side. In either case, however, it was evident to us that managers were learning little from information technology people about the detailed nature of information protection risks. Likewise, information technology people were learning little from managers about how to motivate employees to follow or comply with policies. As a result, we found that it was not uncommon for information technology people to think about policy compliance in simplistic, draconian terms— "my way or the highway." The phraseology of this mindset can be summarized in the following ubiquitous policy conclusion: "Any violation of this policy shall be grounds for immediate termination." Besides the legalistic tone of the statement, the lack of realism in this approach makes it evident to those who would be governed by the policy that it could probably not be enforced as written. Few managers have the desire or the stomach to fire a valued employee on the spot for a mild failure to follow policy (or even a major one in some circumstances). Thus, information technology professionals seem to have a naïve conviction concerning the power of punishments that makes their policy language unrealistic. As a result, employees may ignore policies because of the legalistic, punitively oriented language.

On a different tack, both managers and information technology people mentioned their beliefs that policies are expensive and time-consuming to create; they sometimes mentioned a similar rationale for why policies were difficult to maintain. For those organizations that had written policies, these reasons were also offered to explain why the policies had not been updated for a long time and sat in a binder on an obscure shelf in somebody's office. Part of the discussion on this topic focused on the committee nature of policy development: Committees struggled over the course of many meetings to find just the right wording, punctuation, and formatting for their policies. Another part of the discussion focused on the absence of sustained leadership commitment to policies. Although managers frequently initiated the development of policy, our respondents suggested that they did not always celebrate the completion of the working draft and even more rarely motivated the processes of education and updating needed to maintain policies as "living documents."

Evidently, the process of getting good, workable, enforceable, and motivating policies out into the workplace is a challenge that quite a few organizations are failing to meet. Perhaps for this reason, we often received negative feedback from employees about policy. Many employees did not know what their organization's security policies were, or were not even sure that they had policies. Other employees knew that their company had policies; they remembered reading and signing something at the time of hire, but they subsequently forgot anything and everything that the policy documents might have contained. At the few companies where policies were communicated to employees more frequently, workers sometimes felt that management was treating them in a condescending fashion by repeatedly spelling out a myriad of picky rules.

In light of this apparently sad state of policy affairs, our employee survey on policy, training, and monitoring was particularly illuminating. Recall that our study involved examining the responses of more than 700 employees in 39 different business units and connecting their beliefs to the results of security audits conducted in those organizations. Based on the survey, employees seemed to believe that the amount of information they receive about information security from information technology people corresponded to how secure their organization was. Likewise, the greater the feeling of empowerment they had about putting that security information to work, the more secure they felt their organization was. In contrast, employees seemed to see little connection between the monitoring that their organization did and its security status. In Chapter 7 we commented that these belief structures had both logical and emotional appeal to employees: More training makes us better prepared; more empowerment makes us feel that we can do something about security. Unfortunately, appealing as these beliefs may be, they did not seem to correspond well to the security realities of the organizations. Instead, the two measures that connected with security as quantified by external auditors were monitoring of user behavior and policy enforcement.

We believe the significance of these two issues lies in their association with making employees accountable for positive security behavior. Training is important, awareness is important, reminders are important, and rules are important, but they are all fundamentally prerequisites to the enactment of positive security behavior. This result dovetails perfectly with a study that we did a few years ago (Stanton & Julian, 2002). In the study, we told research participants (who were workers) one of two things: that we were monitoring the quality of their work *or* the amount they were producing. Sure enough, when we monitored the quality of their work, quality went up and quantity went down. When we monitored the quantity of their work, the opposite occurred. There is an old management saw that says, "You can't control what you can't measure." We would add to that a new maxim: You don't *motivate* what you don't measure. By finding out what employees are doing, holding employees accountable for their security behavior, and judiciously enforcing the policies that management has set, some organizations seemed to have greater success with security.

Electronic Monitoring and Surveillance Rights

So if monitoring is a key part of holding employees accountable for their security-related behavior—and it is also certainly a key ingredient in being able to enforce security policies—the question arises of how monitoring can be conducted in a fair and acceptable fashion. Both managers and information technology professionals expressed similar sentiments regarding the necessity for monitoring employees' computer and network activities. Information technology professionals perhaps had a higher degree of urgency to their beliefs about the necessity of monitoring because of their knowledge of the many problems that could arise in the organization's information systems. At the same time, however, some information technology professionals expressed a kind of squeamishness about their responsibilities with respect to monitoring. The closeness of the information technology people to the details of the monitoring process virtually ensures that they will encounter traces of employee behaviors— good, bad, and everywhere in between—and some of our respondents felt uncomfortable about their past experiences or future prospects with this.

Perhaps for this reason, information technology professionals often took pains to carefully explain to us their own ethicality and the kinds of controls they had in place to avoid misuse of the monitoring data. In addition, we saw several examples of *intentional* laxity in the enforcement of monitoring. Apparently, when information technology people found the organization's policies too harsh, they had a tendency to want to try to soften the actual monitoring practices in order to mollify their own concerns for fairness. In some of our previous research (Stanton & Stam, 2003), we found significant evidence that information technology people sometimes felt that they were caught in an ethical dilemma: Management demands for policy enforcement exerted pressure in one direction, while social ties and concerns for the well-being of employees (and perhaps their own reputations among employees) exerted pressure in the other direction. Although some might say that information technology people get paid to resolve such conflicts, it seems risky to have a substantial gap between stated policy and actual procedure that must be closed by means of the judgment calls of information technology people.

In contrast, managers expressed attitudes that suggested a sense of being insulated from the messy reality of monitoring techniques and data. When asked if monitoring was right, almost all managers reported the justification that the organization owned the equipment and therefore had rights to maintain records of all activities involving that equipment. This perspective is correct, in a purely legal sense, but seems unsubtle to us: "Because I said so" is a usable strategy with unruly children, but "because I own it" seems unproductive for use with employees. The tone of these conversations always created the sense that managers were following the "party line" and that they were reluctant to say what they really thought about justifications for monitoring (or perhaps, lamentably, they had just not given the matter much thought, particularly with respect to the specific technical benefits related to security). Although information technology people recognized this same ownership rationale, they were generally quick to temper the blanket statement of ownership with qualifications about fair and reasonable treatment of employees. For their part, employees with whom we spoke rarely if ever mentioned an awareness of the ownership rationale.

In fact, employees in some of the organizations we visited seemed relatively unconcerned about monitoring of their e-mail and Internet usage. A belief seemed to exist that such monitoring was customary; therefore the respondents had no major concerns about it. A few subtleties lingered under this calm surface, however. First, remembering the statistics presented in Table 7.1, it seems like a substantial percentage (9–25 percent, depending on the type of action proposed) of employees have quiet plans for escaping the monitoring thumb. From the simple and relatively benign step of using a free e-mail account for their personal correspondence to the more radical but less common notion of teaching co-workers how to subvert monitoring, it seems that employees may reveal their true feelings more freely in the context of an anonymous survey than in the interview format. Likewise, we heard several reports of the "nothing to hide" rationale: Employees indicated that they had no concerns about monitoring because they themselves were innocent of any wrongdoing.

Harking back to our discussion of monitoring and privacy in Chapter 4, it seems clear from these data that monitoring practices in the organizations we studied fit some of the ideas we raised about control, trust, fairness, and the zone of acceptance. In many organizations, employees' evaluations of their organizations' practices as typical within their respective industries created a situation in which they were unlikely to ruminate deeply about the fairness implications of those practices. The exceptions arose in situations where trust in the organization had been eroded by previous failures in the adoption of new information technology or where the proposed changes to monitoring practices looked to the employees like an attempt on the part of management to exert more control over their work schedules or procedures. The survey data reported in Table 7.1 evidence a similar underlying desire to avoid excessive control by the organization. Electronic monitoring becomes a threat to employee privacy when workers see it as controlling or unfair, when trust has eroded between employees and managers, and/or when abrupt changes to monitoring-related policies occur. We believe that it is possible for organizations to avoid these pitfalls.

Organizational Cycles of Monitoring and Security

So far in this chapter we have mostly recapped what came before. Next, we wish to tie everything together into a package that tells an interesting, and we believe plausible, story about information security, monitoring, and privacy within organizations. We say plausible because the ideas that follow represent what we believe is a logical extension of what our data had to say. We also recognize, however, that we are speculating about supposed or likely mechanisms that may explain how things are working in some organizations—what you might think of as a model of organizational activity and change as related to information security and monitoring. Although we recognize the danger of drawing implications from our data that are too strong, we also believe that to say anything truly useful in Chapter 9— where we make some practical recommendations—we must have a foundation upon which we can build, however preliminary.

Our story begins by pointing out the apparent rarity of major failures of information security. Like many of us, managers read the newspapers and see other companies' highly publicized losses of data, frauds, embezzlements, and so on, with their consequent legal actions, lost productivity, and ruined reputations. For most managers, however, problems of this magnitude never seem to occur within their own organizations. In small organizations, the firm might just not have had a long enough history with networked information technology to experience a major fraud or computer crime. In larger firms where security failures occur with moderate frequency, if not regularity, knowledge of information security failures may remain restricted to information technology departments and the functional areas in which they have occurred. Either way, we suspect that very few managers have an accurate sense of how often security failures occur or how bad the consequences might be. Psychologists and behavioral economists have documented such tendencies in a wide variety of areas; people everywhere have difficulty making accurate assessments of risk (e.g., Fischhoff et al., 1978). When considering events that occur infrequently, people are especially likely to be overly optimistic: They often think that an event with a beneficial outcome is more likely than it actually is and they often think that an event with an adverse outcome is less likely than it actually is. As a result of this so-called overconfidence bias, events that are both rare and adverse generally inspire little investment of time, money, and energy except in the immediate aftermath of a publicized disaster (Fischhoff, Slovic, & Lichtenstein, 1983; Slovic, Fischhoff, & Lichtenstein, 1985). We propose that when it comes to the protection of information, a systematic underinvestment in preventive measures and recovery resources results from a mistaken perception of risk and the consequences of risk.

In most organizations, decisions about how and where to invest the organization's resources arise from the thoughts, beliefs, and actions of managers. While an increasing number of organizations probably have individuals in positions of power who also have significant professional knowledge and experience in the area of information security, we take as a working assumption the idea that leaders in the great majority of organizations do not have such expertise at present. Both our survey and our interview data were consistent with this assumption. Relatedly, we believe that the owners and executives of small firms are also less likely to have information security expertise at hand when making decisions about security because of the relative lack of information technology specialization in such firms.

Kruger and Dunning (1999) researched one important outcome of the overconfidence bias: People with little domain expertise have an overinflated sense of their own competence and capabilities in the domain. Only by gaining some measure of expertise do they realize their incompetence. When we put these ideas together, we come up with what we jokingly call the "organizational insecurity shuffle." Some managers don't know enough about information protection to realize that they are very bad at judging security and privacy risks.

For their part, the information technology experts' difficulties with communicating technical concepts to managers make the process of educating managers about security and privacy concerns extra challenging. In an effort to avoid looking foolish, some managers don't question the jargon and abstruse concepts of the technology professionals and therefore don't get to the bottom of the complex trade-offs (e.g., between security and convenience, security and productivity, security and expenditures). In an effort to maintain professional pride and status within the organization, some information technology professionals may also guard their expertise to maintain their guru status by keeping managers in the dark.

The net result of this little informational power dance is that some managers misperceive the risks and some information technology professionals do not succeed in correcting these misperceptions. We believe that for an organization to be successful at information protection, the organization's information technology professionals must give the managers the knowledge and skills they need to judge risks accurately. In short, we propose that the capability of managers to accurately judge information protection risks correlates positively with the success of communication between the information technology world and the managerial non-information-technology world. As a corollary, we suggest that the poorer the communication between managers and information technology people, the more optimistic the managers are. On a related note, however, the need for this kind of clear communication is obviated in the wake of a security-related failure. By virtue of direct experience with the adverse consequences of the security failure, managers obtain a greatly heightened sense of information security risks following an information security failure, regardless of their knowledge of security or the quality of communications with the information technology department. In fact, we suggest that managers may swing in the opposite direction, becoming unduly pessimistic in the wake of a security failure.

Let us now add fuel to the fire: Most information technology available commercially today has not been designed with "security transparency" in mind. As you sit at your computer, you have essentially no information about what is contained in the stream of packets that flows in and out of it—unless you are an information technology professional armed with professional tools. In the past, a manager could look out on the factory floor and see who was working hard, who was shirking, and who was throwing a monkey wrench into the machinery. In the contemporary workplace—and particularly in information-based organizations—most managers do not have the foggiest idea about what employees are doing with their computers moment by moment. Managers have no tools available to let them overview the *processes* that employees are using to search for, create, manipulate, analyze, evaluate, and manage information. Managers only see the *outcomes*—in the form of documents, reports, spreadsheets, and so forth. The processes that employees use may be fraught with security vulnerabilities. In some cases the employees may be innocently causing security mistakes because of a lack of knowledge, a lack of training, or poor security "habits." In other cases, probably much rarer, employees may be intentionally manipulating information systems for personal gain or other malevolent motivations. In all cases, the inability of managers to visualize employee behavior interferes with the capability of accurately judging the information risks associated with that behavior.

To begin to address this specific but important problem with process transparency, information technology professionals recommend and managers agree to deploy computer monitoring and surveillance techniques. Unfortunately, many of the capabilities and products that provide these capabilities also fail to provide much transparency to managers. As we documented in an earlier article (Stanton & Stam, 2003), information technology professionals usually serve as intermediaries in this setup: Managers authorize the use of monitoring, and information technology people choose the products, install them, review the log files, and inform managers only if and when something goes wrong (for example, when an e-mail filtering system catches an employee sending documents to a competitor). As our responses from information technology people showed, minor issues are frequently and *intentionally* overlooked in order to give employees the benefit of the doubt and keep operations on a "trust basis." This is akin to intentionally designing a car with the gauges and warning lights underneath, so that the car has to be put up on a lift by a technician every few hundred miles to check for adequate oil pressure. In other words, we propose that a manager's appreciation of the information protection risks related to employee behavior correlates with the goodness of information about employees' information-related behaviors. In the worst cases, when data are absent because no monitoring exists or when data are highly scrubbed and predigested by information technology personnel, non-technical managers fail to develop a realistic sense of what is happening on their networks. The one exception is this: Immediately following an investment of resources into monitoring capabilities, information technology people are more likely to report to management any adverse events detected by monitoring as a form of justification for the investment.

As a result of being both more numerous and in lesser positions of power, employees magnify this same dynamic of risk ignorance. Employees take their cues about what is important from managers. Earlier in this chapter we mentioned our study about monitoring quantity and quality (Stanton & Julian, 2002): If you monitor something and employees know that you are monitoring it, it becomes important to employees. We also know, however, that the organization's strategy and methods for monitoring are not always adequately communicated to employees; managers also turn a blind eye to the softening of those policies by information technology professionals. In addition, we know that—with respect to password policies at a minimum—managers often fail to follow the best practices described to them by their own information technology people. As a result, managers transmit to employees their mistakes of perception of risk and consequences in at least five ways. First, by not setting visible examples of right behavior, managers impress employees with the idea that hidden unacceptable behavior is acceptable. Second, by leaving the job of monitoring to information technology professionals with obscure expertise, managers indicate the lack of importance attached to computer-related behavior. Third, by having monitoring apply only to employees and not to all managers, or by allowing that perception to manifest itself uncorrected, managers allow employees to believe that the monitoring is simply a way of controlling their behavior, rather than of ensuring the safety of the whole company. Fourth, in those cases where they under-invest in security training, managers communicate that the skills and knowledge involved in maintaining information security are not as important as other issues. Last of all, when managers recommend to employees that they circumvent security controls in order to get the job done or work more efficiently, they unsubtly communicate the relative importance of productivity and security.

These ideas lead to several additional proposals. First, the direction and occurrence of employees' security-related behavior are likely to follow from employees' beliefs about *their managers'* perceptions of risk. When managers inaccurately communicate the degree of information security risk (as too low) to employees through the five mechanisms just described, employees are likely to perform fewer positive security behaviors and more negative security-related behaviors. The opposite condition is likely to hold as well: When managers' words and actions work in harmony to reinforce the value of security relative to other priorities, employees are more likely to perform positive security behaviors and less likely to perform negative ones.

The net result of these dynamics may be an oscillation of monitoring and security that we call the organizational insecurity cycle (see Figure 8.1). Figure 8.1 shows a counterclockwise cycle in which an organization moves back and forth between a relatively strong degree of information protection (depicted at the bottom of the central circle) and a relatively weak degree of information protection (at the top). Note that we intentionally use the term "relative" because even at their peak of protection, some organizations may not be doing too great a job. Key events or mechanisms in the cycle are shown in boxes around the outside of the circle, with those events that have direct effects on information protection status designated by arrows pointing into the circle. Other boxes without such arrows are intermediary or precipitating events that have a later influence on security through some other mechanism. The plus signs before a label indicate an increasing amount of whatever is in the box, whereas a minus sign before a label indicates a decreasing amount.

Take any given organization and it might, at the present moment, fall at any point around the cycle, but we will begin our explanation at the box labeled "A: - Perceptions of Risk." At this point, we suggest that for a variety of reasons, managers in the organization have an excessively optimistic feeling about information security in the organization. As a result of this misperception that risk is declining or low, the managers decide to invest fewer resources in information protection (Box B). These resources need not be only money, or more specifically need not be expenditures purely for devices and software. Instead, we are speaking more generally of investments in protection of the organizations' information assets through such methods as staff development, policy development, training, monitoring, and enforcement, as well as investment in the devices and software needed to make computer and network behavior visible.

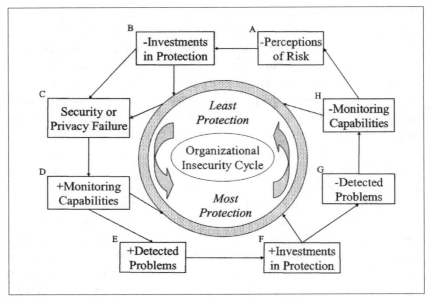

Figure 8.1 Key Events in the Organizational Insecurity Cycle

Given enough time and sufficient underinvestment in security controls, the likely eventual outcome is a security breach (Box C). Although we recognize that certain kinds of security breaches (e.g., virus infections, denial of service attacks) may trigger investments in purely technical defenses against outside intrusion, any problem or failure that can be traced to the innocent mistakes, negligence, or malfeasance of employees will result in an increased investment in monitoring capabilities (Box D). We suggest that in many cases the particular behaviors that led to the known security problem were probably more widespread than anyone thought. As a result, the increased capability for monitoring employee behaviors will probably begin to reveal a litany of inappropriate behaviors that range from minimal to substantial in terms of their significance to information protection (Box E).

Faced with evidence, provided in the form of reports from monitoring systems, that the original security problem was not the result of a "one bad apple" situation, managers will become willing to increase investments in various measures for protection (Box F). As already noted, these are not just investments in security software and devices, but also in policy development, deployment, communication, and enforcement; possible structural changes to the leadership, reporting lines, or responsibilities of departments; training and awareness programs; and possibly outside consultants to supervise or audit all of the new measures. With persistence, some or all of these measures will have their desired effect: Behavior will generally conform much more closely to the ideal set out in policies and the monitoring apparatus will begin to show fewer and fewer security-related problems (Box G).

At this point, managers, information technology people, and employees alike may begin to see little need for all of this monitoring, with its consequent overhead in productivity costs, generating and reading reports, maintenance of the technical infrastructure, and so forth. With these sentiments in mind, managers may begin to neglect the careful maintenance of policies, or information technology people may begin to soften their enforcement of the policies out of a desire to treat the employees fairly—after all, everyone is behaving admirably at this point. Likewise, with month after month of skimpy monitoring reports showing no activity, managers may begin to question their investment in the maintenance, upkeep, and staff time involved in these capabilities (Box H). At the same time, both employees and managers may begin to forget the original security breach(es) that triggered the investment in monitoring and protection capabilities; new employees and managers are hired who had no direct experience with the prior security problems at all. These people may also wonder why so much employee monitoring occurs, given that the organization seems to function so well on a "trust basis." In fact, everyone in the company seems so trustworthy that the perceptions of risks associated with the behaviors of employees begin to decline substantially (Box A), thus starting the whole cycle anew.

The full cycle may take years to unfold. Absent other mechanisms for preserving organizational knowledge over time, it is likely that collective memory of security events and the organization's response to them fades as people leave to find other jobs and new people come in to take their positions. A query of the U.S. Bureau of Labor Statistics private sector employment data finds that in any given month at least 1.5 percent of the labor force quits their current job. Extrapolated into a hypothetical private sector firm, this figure suggests that four years after a major security event, only half of the people in the company will have a direct personal memory of the event.

After six years only a third would have a personal memory, and this might not include anyone who had direct responsibility for dealing with the event. Given that most companies have at least an oral tradition for preserving company history, we might optimistically say that the whole organizational insecurity cycle takes eight to 10 years to unfold in a typical company, with the security event (Box C) triggering four or five years of relatively good information protection (Boxes D, E, F, and G), followed by four or five years of gradual decline (Boxes H, A, and B). The cycle rate probably also depends upon the size and type of company, as well as the ongoing intensity of security challenges in the company's environment. A constant rain of small security events may smooth and shorten the cycle.

Complex Security Risks in Organizations

In this chapter we reviewed the data presented in Chapters 5, 6, and 7 to provide an amalgamated overview of the thoughts, beliefs, and attitudes of three different groups within organizations: managers, information technology people, and regular employees. This overview suggested that several areas of organizational functioning may make an impact on information security operations. Evidence from our interviews and surveys suggested that non-technical employees— including managers—often have a poor grasp of the security vulnerabilities inherent in the technology that facilitates their work. Problems in communicating across the technical–non-technical boundary—particularly between managers and information technology people—exacerbate this information gap, as do most managers' inabilities to visualize what employees are doing with the organization's equipment. As a result, employees frequently fail to enact the kinds of behaviors that would help promote information protection in the organization.

Although so-called insider attacks have been documented in many organizations and highly publicized in a few notable cases, the majority of insecure employee behavior probably results from honest mistakes, lack of motivation, and/or negligence rather than from truly malicious intentions. Our results suggest that this situation can be rectified when managers take information security risks seriously enough to create mechanisms that establish accountability for security-related behavior in the organization. Employees who believe that their behavior matters to the collective welfare discern that someone is paying attention to how they use the organization's technology. They know that both proper and improper uses of the technology will have measured and appropriate consequences and are more likely to enact the range of behaviors that will enhance security within the organization. The main question raised by this chapter, then, is how to establish behavioral accountability in an environment of complex security risks. Chapter 9 addresses this question.

CHAPTER 9

Recommendations for Managers, Employees, and Information Security Professionals

In this chapter we offer a variety of ideas and recommendations that we hope will help improve the status of information protection through systemic changes to organizational behavior. If you have read all of the previous chapters, you are in a good position to critically evaluate our recommendations and conclusions. If you have skipped right to this chapter in order to get the most out of the least amount of reading, you'll have to take some of what we say on faith. We believe these are sensible suggestions based on our data, but we also believe in the idea of "equifinality": In any complex system—such as an organization—there are many different ways to go about solving a problem, and a number of these methods can lead to just about the same level of success. The recommendations we provide here make sense to us when thinking about the kinds of information protection situations we encountered in the course of our fieldwork. To achieve success in your organization, you will have to stretch and adjust our ideas in order to adapt them to local resources and politics.

As our data show, the influences that employees have over information security and information privacy can occur in a number of ways: creating secure passwords, maintaining anti-malware facilities (e.g., anti-virus protection), dealing with confidentiality challenges in the physical work environment, alerting information technology professionals about abnormal system functioning, caring for data brought outside of the organization, and following acceptable use policies. In our previous research, we argued that when employees perform these and related activities competently and consistently, it is likely that the overall security status of the organization improves (Stanton et al., 2005). The flip side of this argument is, of course, that failing to perform these duties and

253

actions, or worse, using the organization's equipment and network to perform negligent or malicious activities, puts the organization at greater risk for security problems and privacy breaches. Accepting these assumptions about end-user behavior then leads to a set of related questions about how constructive employee security behaviors can be encouraged and sustained, as well as how adverse employee security behaviors can be discouraged. Our summary and synthesis in Chapter 8 suggests that the optimal conditions for promoting positive security behaviors and suppressing negative ones involve establishing *accountability* for security-related behaviors. The unanswered question posed in Chapter 8 concerns what steps an organization might take to establish behavioral accountability in an environment of multiple, complex risks. The main message of this chapter contains our answer to that question: *transparent security governance*. In a nutshell, this approach involves removing communication barriers, employing consultative leadership, delegating policy development responsibilities, and involving the user community in monitoring and compliance. Now is a good time to buckle your seatbelt because this is going to require quite a bit of explanation.

The Main Message: Transparent Security Governance

If we examine organizations anywhere, we find that their members are struggling in many different areas with problems of risk similar to those encountered in the protection of information. For example, improving product safety comprises an analogous situation: Issues of significant human importance are at stake, a lot of money is involved, a complex regulatory environment surrounds the problems, no perfect solution exists, and all approaches to solving a problem must balance the ideal with the possible. Further, obtaining substantial, sustainable improvements to the situation almost certainly requires a prudent combination of technology and meaningful behavioral change. In this light, information protection represents a kind of microcosm of many other complex problems of time, money, technology, expertise, and behavior that organizations face. So if the idea of transparent security governance looks somewhat generic—something you could beneficially apply to a number of different problems of organizational change—that's because it is, and we believe justifiably so. We have outlined a continuing process for helping to establish security accountability in the user community rather than a one-size-fits-all security solution. The ongoing result of the process—the establishment and maintenance of judicious security and monitoring policies—will vary substantially in final details in every different organization where it is applied, but we believe the process itself is widely applicable in many different organizational contexts.

Chapter 8 suggests that some organizations are involved in an unhealthy cycle in which they veer from an insecure status into a security crisis, then move through a period of increased investment in security, followed by devolution into complacency, at which point the whole cycle starts again. To the extent that the behavior of the user community—i.e., the employees who do productive work using the organization's information systems—contributes to both the less secure and more secure phases of this cycle, both knowing about and influencing their behavior are important parts of breaking the pattern. In an information-based organization, electronic monitoring of computer and network behavior is the primary mechanism that managers have to find out about employee behavior. In the unhealthy cycle described in Chapter 8, the time lags between the deployment of programs for monitoring, detection, mitigation, and behavior change were an important contributor to the oscillation of the organization from relatively secure to relatively insecure status and back again. To dampen these extreme pendulum swings and help the information-based organization remain persistently in a viable state of information protection, we believe it is necessary to deploy electronic monitoring and surveillance in a prompt, judicious, fair, and sustainable fashion. Transparent security governance provides a process for realizing these goals. The following discussion outlines what we believe to be the key steps in transparent security governance.

Removal of Communication Barriers

The great thing about books and articles is that authors can say things like "remove communication barriers" and leave it up to others to actually face the challenges of accomplishing such directives. Removing communication barriers is probably the single most difficult step in the whole process we propose. As we documented in earlier chapters, specialized knowledge of information technology and the jargon that goes with it are significant barriers to clear communication among managers, employees, and information technology people. A general lack of information technology literacy, particularly among some older workers, is another significant barrier. Overloaded, over-committed, and time-strapped managers represent a third impediment to effective communication about information protection problems. One effect that we believe these barriers have is to make it difficult for managers to accurately assess risks associated with information protection and also to communicate those risks scrupulously to employees. As a result, a key first step in this process is to get everybody *speaking the same language* in regard to information technology and the risks surrounding information protection.

Fortunately this does not require each executive and every employee to go back to school for a graduate degree in information technology. Inevitably, many companies will have key decision makers and employees who simply do not have the time or background to become experts in information security and privacy risks. The goal is to get them to climb as high up the ladder as they can go, and then fill in the remaining distance with "bicultural technology translators." As any diplomat or foreign journalist might say, the best translators not only know both languages but also have an immersive knowledge of both cultures. The world of information technology professionals is truly a different occupational culture from the world of finance or sales or engineering, and to be an effective bridge between any of these worlds, a translator has to *culturally* be a competent member of both of them. If you are hiring and you want a bicultural person who can bridge the worlds of information technology and management, hire someone who has had a mid-career change from management into technology, who has obtained both an MBA and a technology degree, or who has worn both hats in a small company or start-up situation. If, instead, you want to grow your own talent, you can do this by giving employees cross-functional job assignments. These cross-functional assignments move a member of management into the technology department for 3, 6, or 12 months, or alternatively, move a member of the technology department into management for the same amount of time (or better yet, do both moves at once). Cross-functional work assignments are like study-abroad programs for college students: They have a similar salutary effect on broadening the horizons of the people who experience them. After a period of months, bring the employees back to their home department and put them in charge of communicating across the technology-management communications gap. Including these bicultural technology translators in all key discussions about security infrastructure, staffing, and policy will ensure that decision makers obtain the maximum possible benefit from the resident expertise of the technology people.

Consultative Leadership

Whichever strategy you use—training key executives in technology, hiring bicultural technology translators, or growing them internally—the fundamental condition for success is to get the people with the influence, the people who understand the technology, and the people who do the organization's essential work to sit down together and understand each other thoroughly as they have a frank discussion about information protection. Because executive management holds the purse strings, sets the mission, and creates the leadership example for others to follow, this discussion is effectively a consultation with the two most highly interested constituencies: technology people and the information systems user community. Some of this consultation can be conducted with representatives of each constituency separately, but there should also be at least a few opportunities for all three parties to sit down together.

Leadership consultation with employees serves several important goals. First, by asking employees how security affects them, how they deal with security, and how they attempt to balance security and productivity, leaders gain critical information about how to address these issues in the organization as a whole. Second, by evaluating the relative importance of the various issues that employees discuss during these consultations, leaders can make considered, explicit trade-offs that will reduce the incidence of unexpected consequences of security measures. Third, by letting employees make their concerns known, leaders can begin to establish an atmosphere of trust surrounding the deployment of security measures. When introducing techniques such as electronic monitoring, it is inevitable that not everyone will be happy with the changes, but if leaders cogently describe and justify how employees' expressed concerns were balanced against logistical and financial necessity, they are much more likely to achieve acceptance of the proposed new techniques.

The second consultation—equally important as the first—obtains the expertise of information security specialists on information protection risks. We believe that no one in the organization has an omniscient view of risk but that top leaders must strive to get as close to this ideal as they can. Information security specialists certainly do not have the full picture of risk: Almost by definition they know the risks associated with certain types of technology, configurations, security policies, and so forth, but they will not have a wide perspective on issues such as customer loyalty, regulatory constraints, industrial reputation, financial markets, or any of the other myriad areas in which managers must rely upon their own experience or on the knowledge of other specialists. In the area of information protection, however, information systems security specialists have the best information available, and leaders must have the tools and the language to absorb, question, critique, and evaluate that information.

Before completing this set of consultations, leaders should bring together their security experts and representatives of end-users in a room and repeat the information protection barriers, preferences, threats, and risks that they have learned. Leaders should try to verbalize the key trade-offs that they see embodied in these issues, and give all parties an opportunity to present final feedback before the work on formal security governance continues. Leaders should leave this meeting with a clear sense of how to proceed with devising a governance plan. Employees and information technology people should leave the meeting with an equally clear sense that the governance planning will lead to a fair, enforceable, and sustainable set of policies. The Information Systems Audit and Control Association (ISACA), a leading international professional organization in the area of information systems risk, refers to this process as "control risk self-assessment." In effect, the leaders with responsibility for the organization's information protection must undertake a collaborative effort with each and every relevant group in the organization to brainstorm the most critical risks in information protection as well as the range of possible measures to address these risks.

3D Security Governance: Devise, Document, Disseminate

Here we have reached a key turning point in the transparent governing process, and perhaps the one at which the greatest proportion of organizations may fail. By this stage, ideally, the organization has a well-informed leader, poised to balance the central trade-offs between time, money, productivity, and protection that can be effectively established only by executive decision. The leader has consulted with the constituencies and heard their perspectives. Everything stands in readiness for the issuance of new policy. One of several bad things often happens at this point: (1) Nothing happens— the leader tells an information technology person to buy something or tells a manager to get employees to do something, but nothing gets formalized into policy; (2) the leader delegates policy writing to someone in human resources who has no understanding of the technical issues or to someone in a technology department who has no grasp of the motivational or behavioral issues; or (3) the leader writes the policy in language that is unsatisfactory both to employees and technologists.

To avoid these unproductive paths, we advocate a separation of duties: The leader devises policy and the constituencies document it. To devise policy, the leader charts the course between what is prudent from a risk standpoint and what is feasible from a financial, ethical, and logistical perspective. The leader articulates decisions about what the policy should contain, but the actual policies—the wording, phrasing, structure, and details—are documented by a team consisting of one representative from each constituency. Optimally such a team should consist of two people, a knowledgeable information technology security person and an employee representative who is widely trusted by other employees. Don't expand this committee, at least not by much, and only if there is another constituency whose members will be directly affected by the policy. Nothing kills a policy development process more slowly and agonizingly than a large committee. Charge the policy writers with developing language that will seem sensible, readable, and comprehensible to those whose behavior is governed by it. We have provided two examples (in Appendices G and H) of security-related policies written in plain, non-punitive language that includes a straightforward explanation of monitoring and enforcement. Feel free to adapt these examples for your own purposes. If you must get a lawyer involved, choose one who feels capable of balancing the demands of legal defensibility with the necessity of having a document that will help regular people do the right thing.

Once these representatives finish documenting the policy and the attentive leader has reviewed it to make sure that it appropriately represents the original mandate, they should bring it to their constituencies. In an organization whose culture is amenable to wider participation, this process can include obtaining comments, feedback, and recommended changes to the document. Revisions based on feedback from affected constituencies are likely to help achieve buy-in later, when it is time to enforce the policy. In organizations where participation is not the norm, this phase can serve as

---

Hallmarks of Transparent Security Governance

- Everyone learns to speak the same language, or bicultural technology translators are engaged to ensure clear lines of communication, particularly on the topic of information protection risks.

- Leaders consult with employees to learn about barriers and preferences.

- Leaders consult with domain experts to find out about threats and risks.

- Leaders devise governance strategies—including how employees' computer-related activities will be monitored—and justify them within the organization.

- Employees and experts participate in documenting governance strategies and justifications in universally understood language.

- The organizational community monitors compliance with policy.

- The organizational community judiciously, swiftly, and publicly addresses successes and failures of compliance.

- An organizational historian documents the whole process to ensure the persistence of organizational memory.

- Leaders begin with a new policy or one that needs to be updated.

the initial distribution method. Policies are almost useless for behavioral change unless those individuals governed by them are well aware of their contents. Having the original authors of the policy involved in dissemination helps ensure that the strategies for monitoring and compliance built into the policy receive a supportive reception among members of the constituency.

Community-Based Monitoring and Compliance

Once policy authors have communicated the content and intentions of a policy to the individuals affected, the continuous process of obtaining and maintaining compliance begins. This point in the process of transparent security governance is where the transparency comes into play most strongly. Many organizations make the mistake of treating employee monitoring secretively. If anyone asks what kinds of data are collected, nobody knows. If anyone asks how the data are analyzed, who does the analysis, or where the reports end up, nobody knows. If anyone asks what happens when a violation of policy is detected, nobody knows. When discussing network technologies, security professionals routinely denigrate the idea of "security by obscurity"—the notion that you can keep something safe simply by making it hard to find or complicated to figure out. Yet the same professionals will sometimes act like pompous magicians when it comes to monitoring: "Sorry folks, we never reveal to the audience how our tricks are done." The problem is that this secretive approach makes employee monitoring the topic of rumor, mistrust, and inaccurate innuendo, thus increasing the likelihood that employees will look for ways of circumventing the system. If you are a manager and an information technology person tells you that employees cannot know how monitoring is accomplished because the employees might figure out how to beat the system, you need a new information technology person. In short, we argue that one key aspect of transparency in information security governance is making the methods of monitoring transparent, public, and widely understood in the organization's user community.

Making monitoring transparent occurs in three ways: publicizing the techniques, publicizing the results, and publicizing the enforcement outcomes. To begin with, employees should receive frequent, clearly worded notices about what aspects of their work are monitored, who conducts the monitoring, who views and analyzes the data, and who receives the reports. Many organizations have wisely adopted the idea of a sign-on message that informs employees about their expectations for privacy (or lack thereof) and lets them know how their uses of a system will be monitored. Such notices have an important legal implication because they typically indicate that the employees' decision to proceed with logging onto the system implies their consent to the policies related to system usage. These notices have another effect, although its value is not always so widely recognized. By reminding the employees that their system behavior will be logged, analyzed, and reported, the notice begins the process of transparent governance. The word "begins" is important here because reminders alone are not sufficient. We believe that there are two additional, important components to making monitoring transparent.

The next step in this process is to publicize the results of monitoring. This activity can occur in a variety of styles and by a variety of methods depending on the culture and norms of the organization, but the general principle is to continue to reinforce the idea that the organization is paying attention to and cares about what employees are doing with their information technology. At one extreme, imagine a large LCD monitor in the employee break room that has a continuous scroll of the Web sites currently being visited by employees. A tally of the hits on the top sites known to pertain directly to the productive business of the organization appears in one column, while a tally of the hits on questionable sites appears in the other column. To make it even more interesting, one might display the usernames of the individuals who were accessing the questionable sites. This highly public approach may not fit most organizations, but it almost certainly would tend to have a very powerful social effect on behavior. Most importantly, it involves the whole community of users in self-policing rather than making the processes of detection and enforcement shadowy and obscure. A less extreme approach would be to periodically broadcast e-mail reports to the whole user community showing similar kinds of overviews about appropriate and inappropriate usage, perhaps in a somewhat more scrubbed and summarized form. One could also imagine benchmarking these results week-by-week and developing a group reward for reaching certain targets for acceptable usage. Again, the important principle involves engaging the whole user community in the process of understanding what is occurring on the organization's

networks. This principle serves the dual purpose of making the monitoring mechanisms known and understood—thereby engendering
trust in the organization—and also utilizing community social influence to assist with the reduction of inappropriate behavior. This
reflects back to what some of our respondents in small companies
said: They trust each other because they can see each other all the
time—their behavior is mutually and constantly visible. Larger companies must work harder and figure out more innovative ways of
making behavior transparent and encouraging community-based
self-policing of acceptable systems use.

The final step in making monitoring transparent involves making
the enforcement process public. As with other aspects of transparency, the people in charge often feel squeamish about publicizing
details of problems that have occurred with employees, perhaps in
part because they feel it might make them look bad in their supervisory role. We recommend that you move past this squeamishness and
realize that policy enforcement carries no weight unless the rest of
the user community knows the organization cares about the policy.
Certainly in the extreme cases in which law enforcement must
become involved in the investigation of a fraud or other employee
malfeasance, those organizational members involved in the investigation may have a strict obligation to maintain the secrecy of the
case. For more minor infringements of policy, however, everyone in
the organization benefits from knowing—at least in broad outlines—
that a transgression was detected and that the individual involved
has received a warning or other enforcement measure. You can save
the rule breakers embarrassment (and you could save yourself possible legal problems later related to hostile workplace conditions) by
not revealing their identity to the larger user community; however, to
keep secret the successful detection of a transgression and the subsequent occurrence of the enforcement action itself is to fail to impress
upon the user community the reality that their behavior matters. For
monitoring to be effective, and for enforcement to be seen as consistent, fair, and justified, users must carry within them the sure knowledge that policy infractions will receive immediate, judicious, and
unbiased treatment by means of a reproducible organizational
process that applies equally to everyone. Keeping this part of the
process transparent can reassure everyone that nobody gets special
dispensations by virtue of their position in the organization's hierarchy. In other words, everyone must be subject to the same rules; the

visibility of enforcement processes must bolster the widespread belief that this is true.

One final note on this point again refers to the language, tone, and severity of policy documents: If formal policy is too harshly written, someone in the chain of enforcement will inevitably be highly tempted to soften the policy to give possibly innocent users "the benefit of the doubt." The need for such ad hoc softening results from badly written policy. Policies should have well-defined stages that define an escalating set of problems and consequences rather than black or white measures. A staged approach that builds in strategies for dealing with minor or unintentional transgressions will lessen the necessity for discretionary treatment and improve the likelihood of consistent administration of the enforcement process.

Collective Memory and Your Organizational Librarian

We have heard that some organizations do not have a librarian, historian, or archivist. This sad situation represents a final contribution to the unhealthy cycle depicted in Chapter 8. Throughout this chapter we have advocated the power of transparency as a method of getting key constituencies involved in the identification of information protection risks, of engendering trust by employees in the organization's monitoring processes, and of engaging the power of social influences in facilitating policy compliance in the community. All of these potential benefits are diminished by the ravages of time, however, unless the organization has an effective method of refreshing and maintaining its collective memory. Transparency produces powerful knowledge in the short term, but this knowledge fades quickly without constant reinforcement. People forget about the big security problem that happened last year, and the one that happened five years ago might just as well have never occurred. Because of turnover, retirement, and other forms of attrition in organizational membership, it is generally unreliable to leave remembering solely to people's memories. Even for those organizations with a very stable membership, human memory is such a fallible, malleable record of earlier events that it does not always serve as an accurate historical guide. Instead, more permanent forms of collective memory are needed, and these should be subject to the same transparency principles as everything else.

Something as simple as a quarterly security newsletter can serve this function in a smaller organization. Newsletters are relatively easy to put together, many people like to read them, and a few people may even archive them for later reference. Newsletters can provide reminders about policies, can chronicle recent performance improvements in acceptable use, and can note the occurrence of recent enforcement actions. For larger organizations, more complex approaches, such as knowledge bases and "wikis"—a type of server software that allows organization members to collectively maintain a Web page using simple, browser-based tools—can provide additional capabilities beyond a simple newsletter, such as threading and keyword searching. Whether the method chosen is complex or simple, expensive or cheap, the primary goal is to provide a compelling historical record of what was done: how the policies were developed, the feedback given by the community on the policies, the community's performance with respect to compliance, and a record of the enforcement actions taken. This historical record should be widely available to managers, technologists, and employees alike, rather than segregated for special access only by those "in the know." Lastly, the record should be frequently refreshed and publicized so that people have a reason to check in to see what else has happened. Someone in the organization has to be assigned responsibility.

Resistance to Organizational Change

In the previous section we outlined our vision for transparent security governance and rather blithely suggested a variety of actions that managers, information technologists, and regular employees ought to take in service of improving information protection. We recognize and acknowledge, however, that organizational change is difficult, usually happens slowly, and always requires substantial commitment on the part of those who would provoke change. We cannot hope to offer a universal prescription for overcoming resistance to change, and even if we tried, there are many dozens of books on the topic that do a better job than we could do. What we might beneficially do, however, is discuss some of the most commonly cited resistance factors specifically in terms of transparent security governance. To prioritize our discussion, we relied on an excellent list of sources of organizational resistance compiled by psychologists Jerry Hedge and Elaine Pulakos in their book *Implementing Organizational Interventions* (2002).

Political Resistance

First, Hedge and Pulakos describe two sources of political resistance: lack of top-level commitment/support and existing vested interests of organization members. Both of these issues arise from the power structure of the organization because the most significant disruptions to any program of information protection improvements will come from department leaders, directors, vice presidents, or chiefs who feel that the proposed changes will diminish their own power status or adversely affect the productivity of their constituencies. This kind of problem is exacerbated by the fact that information security threats are just that—threats and not (usually) realities—and it is easy to dismiss threats as improbable or unlikely to produce the kind of damage that security specialists claim. The "boy who cried wolf" syndrome also comes into play here: If any current or previous security personnel "oversold" an earlier threat that turned out to be insignificant, resistant managers will cite that incident as a justification for ignoring expert advice about future threats.

We suggest approaching managerial resistance through education that improves the accuracy of managers' assessments and judgments of information protection risks. First, recall from Chapter 8 that the (mis)perception of risk involves both thinking (cognitive) and emotional (affective) mental processes. Dry statistics about the incidence of virus infection alone will rarely convince a resistant person of the value of change; likewise, horror stories about security breaches will simply be viewed as scare tactics and dismissed. The combination of cognitive and affective approaches has the greatest likelihood of success: a visceral feeling for the negative impacts of a particular kind of security breach along with a realistic analysis of the scenarios leading to that breach. Author Paul Slovic (2001) has written extensively about the measurement and perception of risk, but his distilled wisdom has yet to percolate into the consciousness of managers and information technologists. In particular, familiarity, reversibility, and catastrophic potential are three of the several areas of risk perception he described that have a high degree of relevance to the issue of managerial resistance.

The familiarity aspect of risk perception focuses on the issue of clear communication. With the help of bicultural translators if necessary, managers must be educated to understand the nature and mechanisms through which information protection failures occur, even if those mechanisms are complex and technical. No individuals in high-level management positions should be permitted to keep making decisions unless they are willing, able, and ready to learn enough about information technology to be able to converse comfortably with experts. Knowledge of information technology is now as important as knowledge of finance as a basic substrate of business education and knowledge.

Reversibility refers to the issue of whether or how easily an information security failure can be undone and as such is intimately connected to questions of business continuity. Managers understand how certain types of resources, such as reputation and trust, cannot be readily restored, but they may lack understanding that some types of information losses also cannot be readily restored. In the realm of information security, reversibility addresses the key question of "can you fix it" or "how quickly can you fix it"; the answers to these questions have significant implications for managerial perception of risk. In our discussions with managers, we found that they often became quite reflective and thoughtful when asked how they would keep their business running if a particular information resource was made unavailable for a time. By repeating the question and varying the period of time from a few minutes to a few months, we were able to quickly assess how sensitive the resource was to reversibility.

Finally, catastrophic potential pertains to the concentration of adverse effects in time and space. In these cases managers need to be shown the extent to which the problem under consideration might cause massive, concentrated information security failures, ongoing but isolated problems, or something in between. To be eaten is a bad thing—whether quickly by piranhas or slowly by mosquitoes—but the protections one chooses to counter these hazards differ on a number of key dimensions, such as upfront investment, time to deploy, duration of exposure, the need for fallback strategies, and so forth. Managers need to have a clear sense of catastrophic potential in order to make good risk judgments. Note that Slovic and other scholars who have investigated the perception of risk also refer to a variety of other factors, such as controllability of threats, whether effects of problems manifest themselves quickly or slowly, voluntariness of exposure to threats, and uncertainty regarding threat mechanisms. Some of these factors may also be relevant in the process of engendering appropriate risk assessment by managers.

Employee Resistance

Next, Hedge and Pulakos describe three areas of resistance common among employees: fear of uncertainty, inconvenience, and social disruption. Fear of uncertainty is universal among human beings and reflects a fundamental drive to keep control over one's environment. In short, the way things are right now is often reasonably comfortable, and any of a variety of possible future situations represents the possibility of less comfort. When dealing with new technology, we found that a substantial part of employees' discomfort arose from a fear that they would not readily be able to learn the new technology or excel at the training offered. Second, in the same vein, every employee's comfort equation has evolved from an effort to make everything in the work environment as convenient and easy-to-use as possible. New security procedures, techniques, and technologies often seem to create inconveniences and hassles for employees; the burden of proof generally remains on information technology professionals to demonstrate that security steps will not interfere with the existing routine. Finally, these same security measures can also disrupt existing patterns of work flow, communication, and cooperation that employees have established over time. The "buddy system," reported in Chapter 7, is a perfect example of this: Employees often share passwords and account information with one another because there is a natural and legitimate need to "fill in" for people who are out sick, on vacation, or otherwise unable to fulfill their usual contribution to the work process. Thus, the social disruptions associated with security-related changes compose the third source of resistance among employees.

Transparent security governance offers two responses to these sources of employee resistance: Don't interfere or trade something for the interference. In the first case, we advocate that new security measures simply don't interfere with employees' convenience or social patterns. This idea may seem like a joke if one accepts the common assumption that security and convenience or security and productivity are always at odds with one another. Note the importance we gave in the previous section, however, to the inclusion of employee representatives in the governance development process. No one understands how the work of the organization gets done better than those people who do it, and their voices in the security governance process will help to ensure a minimum of disruption to existing productive patterns of work flow. Usually there are several different ways to implement a security control, and each of them is roughly equally effective from a security point of view. From a productivity point of view, however, these various approaches may be quite different: The only people who can accurately identify the least disruptive, least inconvenient approaches are the people who do the work.

In the second case, we suggest that security measures trade something of value to employees in exchange for the reduced convenience or changes to the social fabric of communication and collaboration. When risk becomes reality and an information protection problem occurs, some of those who are hardest hit are the employees who depend on information technology to get their work done. As several of our respondents mentioned, the feeling of helplessness one gets when information systems are "down" can be intensely frustrating and stressful. Good security controls help to minimize such disruptions, and as a result they have value to employees as well as security professionals. One key step here is to ensure that, like managers, employees have an appropriate sense of risk that includes both the cognitive and affective components.

The primary area where organizations fail in this regard is training: Training is usually long on facts, long on steps, and long on procedures but short on emotional impact. If employees take security training and all they get are statistics on virus infections and a series of clicks to check their subscription status, a major opportunity for engaging them as partners in security is lost. Instead, have each of them sit down at a specially configured training system and experience, firsthand, what it is like to have a virus take over your computer and delete all of your work. Training like this has emotional impact. It will help ensure that employees perceive the real value of security procedures and will in turn make it more likely that they will trade some convenience for better security.

Our conversations with employees identified two principal fears relative to new workplace monitoring or surveillance measures: The "dragnet" fear and the "sweatshop" fear. The dragnet fear refers to the feeling that the new measures will sweep up harmless or even productive behaviors, label them as counterproductive or counter to policy, and involve the employee in an enforcement action. The sweatshop fear, which is related, arises from a feeling that the employee has a right to a bit of recreational time during the workday and that monitoring and security measures that prevent any recreational use of computers will turn the workplace into a so-called electronic sweatshop.

These fears can be reduced through providing employees with the opportunity to use computers recreationally. Some employers subsidize home broadband connections as appeasement for more restrictive policies regarding non-business use of computers at work. Though this approach may lie beyond the means of most organizations, affordable alternatives such as the provision of a recreational "kiosk" (a workplace computer set aside for non-business use) and policies that permit the recreational use of desktop PCs during break periods may diminish employees' fears about and resistance to monitoring and related security measures.

Organization-Wide Resistance

Hedge and Pulakos describe three areas of resistance that have organization-wide implications: misunderstandings, organizational incompatibility, and rejection of outsiders. Misunderstandings generally refer to information gaps that exist between those who are setting new policies and those who will be governed by those policies. Often, inaccurate beliefs about the configuration or impact of new policies arise as a result of poor communication between managers and employees. Transparent security governance directly addresses these misunderstandings in two ways: (1) by ensuring that an employee representative is involved in the process of documenting new policies, and (2) by keeping implementation, detection, and enforcement processes open and visible. Having a trusted employee member of the user community involved in policy writing can help to allay fears that the governance system is rigged against the interests of employees and also provides a direct conduit for information from the policy development process into the employee community. Keeping implementation, detection, and enforcement processes open and visible ensures that no mysteries or secrets occur between the time when executive leadership decides on a new governance element and the time when that element has a tangible effect within the user community.

Organizational incompatibility refers to a situation in which a proposed organizational change simply fits poorly with the prevalent organizational culture or mission. If one reflects on how different a military organization is from a social service organization, or an educational setting from a retail setting, the importance of organizational culture in receptivity to a proposed change in security governance becomes evident. Because our proposal for transparent security governance always advocates a multiparty approach, however, the likelihood of developing a completely incompatible policy seems diminished. Still, such potential exists, particularly if the leader or decision maker in charge of policy development is relatively new to the organization. We counsel such new leaders to spend more time on the consultative leadership phase of new policy development and to choose constituency representatives with special care to ensure that any concerns they have about organizational incompatibility are accurate, well understood, and acted upon appropriately.

Finally, Hedge and Pulakos discuss the problem of rejection of outsiders, which they primarily frame as a problem for outside consultants or consulting firms. While we share their beliefs about the resistance that organizational outsiders may face when trying to spearhead policy changes, we also believe, based on our research, that "some insiders are outsiders." In an organization that is large enough to have separate wings in its headquarters, separate floors in its building, or any other physical or social barrier between different groups, it is likely that different subcultures exist within the organization and that members of these groups can mistrust and even fear each other. The common examples we found were mistrust and fear between information technology departments and human resources, between information technology departments and engineering departments, and, strangely enough, between information security functions and other groups with an interest in reducing the organization's risk.

In organizations in which these types of divisions exist, any efforts by members of one group to develop or implement policies that will affect another group may founder on resistance to the policies by the latter group. Clearly, any joint efforts at policy development among conflicting groups run the risk of failure because of these differences in subcultures. In these cases we advocate greater up-front investment in training bicultural technology translators, as suggested in the previous section. Following completion of their training, the bicultural translators are optimally equipped to navigate the hazards of the two conflicting subcultures and create the kind of détente needed for productive policy development.

One final consideration in this area pertains to cultural differences between information security groups and other groups with an interest in reducing the organization's risk. Depending upon the size of the organization, these groups may include departments involved in physical security, executive security, personnel security, self-insurance, facilities, and transportation. Over recent years the need for greater cooperation among these groups has increased as the complexity and scope of security problems has grown. Although the ideal solution at some organizations may involve putting all of these functions under the umbrella of a single executive leader, this ideal may be difficult for many organizations to reach, particularly in the short term. As an alternative to the kind of unity that can be enforced by having a strong single leader, transparent security governance offers bicultural translators, consultative leadership, and multiparty involvement in policy development as ways of helping to ensure that cultural resistance to policy changes does not interfere with the deployment of effective security controls.

Promoting Insider Integrity

We believe that the recommendations presented in this chapter comprise a useful starting point for improving information security in organizations, but we urge readers to interpret them as a work in progress rather than immutable truths. Organization leaders and information security practitioners may take our results as an indication that certain kinds of organizational interventions may succeed by improving the quality of information security governance within the organization, and more specifically by establishing organizational structures and mechanisms that promote behavioral accountability for information protection. The organizational mechanisms we believe will make the greatest impact on the quality of security-related behavior include user policies, behavioral monitoring, detection of unacceptable use, and enforcement of policies through application of fair and appropriate consequences. We strongly advocate transparent strategies for developing, disseminating, teaching, and implementing these measures. Without transparency we believe that some or all of these measures will fail in organizations as a result of employee resistance.

As a point of departure for future research on this topic, our results provide a hot list of factors to examine next but also clearly leave many new opportunities for worthwhile research on the behavioral aspects of security. The hot list of research topics should include examinations of what communication strategies work best for increasing security accountability, what makes acceptable use policies effective in influencing behavior, how to increase the accuracy and speed with which decision makers obtain information about security risks, how employees react to more or less restrictive security policies, methods of achieving fairness and consistency in the enforcement of security policies, and how to promote policy compliance without resorting to punitive measures.

A list of additional research topics should also include attention to the effectiveness of various strategies for monitoring employee compliance with security policies, for communicating monitoring strategies to employees, and for understanding employees' reactions to being monitored. As we put the finishing touches on this book, we realize that these questions all converge on one overriding goal: creating an organizational environment that promotes *integrity* in the use and treatment of information.

While some security researchers with an interest in employee behavior have focused on "insider threats"—the intentional malfeasance of employees and how to prevent it—the topic of insider integrity has received relatively little attention by either academic researchers or managerial practitioners. We define insider integrity as taking care of the collective well-being in the everyday conduct of work. Insider integrity differs from organizational citizenship behavior in that it can and should be formally rewarded by the organization even if its specific behaviors cannot be enumerated in advance in a job description. Insider integrity involves performing one's job both well and consistently with larger goods: the good of the business unit in which one is employed, the good of the organization as whole, and the good of the communities in which the organization operates. Insider integrity comprises acting thoughtfully and creatively to surpass the specific mission of a particular job title, to balance short-term solutions against long-term viability, and to maintain an appropriate equilibrium between personal achievement and group well-being.

With respect to information protection, insider integrity means looking out for a wide range of interests during the course of everyday work. The privacy and well-being of customers, other employees, and investors may depend upon the actions of a single person or a small group of people. One badly constructed password, one connection to a fake access point near a business hotel, or one key piece of information trustingly given to an impostor may make the difference between a close call and a major security breach. Creating an organization of accountability, in which employees know what to do and know that what they do matters, can promote the insider integrity needed to defend reliably and consistently against organizational insecurities. Creating an organization of accountability and integrity is also a colossal challenge in a business environment that emphasizes cost cutting, downsizing, and outsourcing over other objectives.

In our research we met many people—employees, managers, and information technologists—who apparently conducted their everyday work lives consistently with this vision of insider integrity. The care these people took for protecting the information of their patients, clients, customers, and co-workers was evidence of concern for information protection that transcended pure self-interest. We believe that organizational leaders should work at least as hard to recognize, reward, and reinforce these individuals' efforts as they do to reprimand or replace those individuals who cause failures of information protection. By working to establish an environment in which accountability and integrity can thrive, organizations can ensure that those individuals who handle and process the organization's informational lifeblood have the support they need to reduce the risks of organizational insecurity. Our research suggests that organizations can take steps toward this ideal through developing the processes of transparent security governance.

References

9 to 5, Working Women Education Fund. (1990). *Stories of mistrust and manipulation: The electronic monitoring of the American workforce*. Cleveland, OH: Author.

Adams, J. S. (1965). Inequity in social exchange. In L. Berkowitz (Ed.), *Advances in experimental social psychology* (Vol. 2). New York: Academic Press.

Adler, P. A., Parson, C. K., & Zolke, S. B. (1985, Winter). Employee privacy: Legal and research developments and implications for personnel administration. *Sloan Management Review*, 13–25.

Agre, P. E. (1997). Introduction. In P. E. Agre & M. Rotenberg (Eds.), *Technology and privacy, the new landscape* (pp. 1–28). Cambridge, MA: MIT Press.

Ajzen, I. (1991). The theory of planned behavior. *Organizational Behavior and Human Decision Processes, 50*, 179–211.

Alder, G. S. (1998). Ethical issues in electronic performance monitoring: A consideration of deontological and teleological perspectives. *Journal of Business Ethics, 17*, 729–743.

Alder, G. S., & Tompkins, P. K. (1997). Electronic performance monitoring: An organizational justice and concertive control perspective. *Management Communication Quarterly, 10*, 259–288.

Allen, A. (1988). *Uneasy access: Privacy for women in a free society*. Totowa, NJ: Rowman and Littlefield.

Altman, I. (1975). *The environment and social behavior*. Monterey, CA: Brooks/Cole.

Altman, I. (1976). Privacy: A conceptual analysis. *Environment and Behavior, 8*, 7–29.

Altman, I., Vinsel, A., & Brown, B. B. (1981). Dialectic conceptions in social psychology: An application to social penetration and privacy regulation. *Advances in Experimental Social Psychology, 14*, 107–160.

American Management Association & ePolicy Institute. (2004, July). *2004 workplace e-mail and Instant Messaging survey summary.* New York: Author. Available at www.epolicyinstitute.com/survey/survey04.pdf

Arkin, R. M., & Shepperd, J. A. (1989). Strategic self-presentation: An overview. In M. J. Cody & M. L. McLaughlin (Eds.), *The psychology of tactical communication* (pp. 175–193). Clevedon, U.K.: Multilingual Matters.

Attewell, P. (1987). Big brother and the sweatshop: Computer surveillance in the automated office. *Sociological Theory, 5,* 87–99.

Attewell, P., & Rule, J. (1984). Computing and organizations: What we know and what we don't know. *Communications of the Association for Computing Machinery, 27,* 1184–1192.

Averill, J. R. (1973). Personal control over aversive stimuli and its relationship to stress. *Psychological Bulletin, 80,* 286–303.

Bain, P., & Taylor, P. (2000). Entrapped by the "electronic panopticon"? Worker resistance in the call centre. *New Technology, Work and Employment, 15*(1), 2–18.

Baird, J., Kadue, D. D., & Sulzer, K. D. (1995). *Public employee privacy: A legal and practical guide to issues affecting the workplace.* Chicago: American Bar Association.

Ball, K. (2002). Elements of surveillance: A new framework and future directions. *Information, Communication, and Society, 3.*

Bandura, A. (1977). *Social learning theory.* Englewood Cliffs, NJ: Prentice-Hall.

Barrett, R. (1964). Outside consultants to industry: Strengths, problems and pitfalls (A symposium): VI. Comments on the Symposium. *Personnel Psychology, 17,* 128–133.

Bellotti, V. (1997). Design for privacy in multimedia computing and communication environments. In P. E. Agre & M. Rotenberg (Eds.), *Technology and privacy, the new landscape* (pp. 63–98). Cambridge, MA: MIT Press.

Bennahum, D. S. (1999, May). Daemon seed: Old e-mail never dies. *Wired,* 100–111.

Beynon-Davies, P. (1997). Ethnography and information systems development: Ethnography of, for, and within IS development. *Information and Software Technology, 39,* 531–540.

Biddle, B. J. (1986). Recent developments in role theory. *Annual Review of Sociology, 12,* 67–92.

Biddle, B. J., & Thomas, E. J. (Eds.). (1979). *Role theory: Concepts and research.* Huntington, NY: Robert E. Krieger Publishing Co.

Bies, R. J. (1985). Individual reactions to corporate recruiting encounters: The importance of fairness. Unpublished manuscript.

Bies, R. J. (1987). The predicament of injustice: The management of moral outrage. In L. L. Cummings & B. M. Staw (Eds.), *Research in organizational behavior* (Vol. 9, pp. 289–319). Greenwich, CT: JAI Press.

Bies, R. J., & Moag, J. S. (1986). Interactional justice: Communication criteria of fairness. In R. J. Lewicki, B. H. Sheppard, & M. Baxerman (Eds.), *Research on negotiation in organizations* (Vol. I, pp. 43–55). Greenwich, CT: JAI Press.

Bies, R. J., Shapiro, D. L., & Cummings, L. L. (1988). Causal accounts and managing organizational conflict: Is it enough to say it's not my fault? *Communication Research, 15,* 381–399.

Blau, P. M. (1964). *Exchange and power in social life.* New York: Wiley.

Block, L. K., & Stokes, G. S. (1989). Performance and satisfaction in private versus non-private work settings. *Environment and Behavior, 21,* 277–297.

Boon, S. D., & Holmes, J. G. (1991). The dynamics of interpersonal trust: Resolving uncertainty in the face of risk. In R. A. Hinde & J. Groebel (Eds.), *Co-operation and Prosocial Behaviour* (pp. 190–211). Cambridge: Cambridge University Press.

Bowers, J. K. (1979). Privacy, territoriality, personal space, and personality. *EDRA: Environmental Design Research Association, 10,* 51–62.

Brigham, T. A. (1979). Some effects of choice on academic performance. In L. C. Perlmuter & R. A. Monty (Eds.), *Choice and perceived control* (pp. 131–141). Hillsdale, NJ: Erlbaum.

Brockner, J. & Higgins, E. T. (2001). Regulatory focus theory: Implications for the study of emotions at work. *Organizational Behavior & Human Decision Processes, 86*, 35–66.

Bruce, A., & Formisano, R. (2003). *Building a high-morale workplace.* New York: McGraw Hill.

Cangelosi, V. E., & Lemoine, L. F. (1988). Effects of open versus closed physical environment on employee perception and attitude. *Social Behavior and Personality, 16* (1), 71–77.

Carkenord, D. M. (1996). A group exercise to explore employee ethics in business-related psychology courses. *Teaching of Psychology, 23*(2), 100–102.

Carlopio, J., & Gardner, D. (1995). Perceptions of work and workplace: Mediators of the relationship between job level and employee reactions. *Journal of Occupational and Organizational Psychology, 68*, 321–326.

Chang, C. Y. (1997). Using computer simulation to manage the crowding problem in parks: A study. *Landscape and Urban Planning, 37*, 147–161.

Clement, A. (1996). Considering privacy in the development of multi-media communications. In R. Kling (Ed.), *Computerization and controversy* (pp. 848–869). San Diego: Academic Press.

Cohen, J. (1992). A power primer. *Psychological Bulletin, 112*, 155–159.

Cook, K. S., Molm, L. D., & Yamagishi, T. (1993). Exchange relations and exchange networks: Recent developments in social exchange theory. In J. Berger & M. Zelditch (Eds.), *Theoretical research programs: Studies in the growth of theory* (pp. 296–322). Stanford, CA: Stanford University Press.

Cropanzano, R., & Konovsky, M. A. (1995). Resolving the justice dilemma by improving the outcomes: The case of employee drug screening. *Journal of Business & Psychology, 10*(2), 221–243.

Culnan, M. J. (1993, September). How did they get my name? An exploratory investigation of consumer attitudes toward secondary information use. *MIS Quarterly*, 341–361.

Dallas v. England, 846 S.W.2d 957, 1993 Tex.App. LEXIS 643 (Tx.Ct.App 1992), rev'd, 849 S.W.2d 941, 1994 Tex. LEXIS 17 (Tex. 1994).

Davis, F. D. (1989). Perceived usefulness, perceived ease of use, and user acceptance of information technology. *MIS Quarterly, 13,* 319–339.

deCharms, R. (1968). *Personal causation: The internal affective determinants of behavior.* New York: Academic Press.

Deal v. Spears. (1992). 980 F.2d 1153 (8th Cir. 1992); 1992 U.S. App. LEXIS 31203; 8 I.E.R. Cas. (BNA) 105.

Deci, E. L., & Ryan, R. M. (1991). Intrinsic motivation and self-determination in human behavior. In R. M. Steers & L. W. Porter (Eds.), *Work motivation.* New York: McGraw-Hill.

Ditton, J. (2000, January). Do we expect too much of open-street CCTV? *CCTV Today, 7*(1), 20–24.

Dunlop, C., & Kling, R. (1991). *Computers and controversy.* Boston: Academic Press.

Duvall-Early, K., & Benedict, J. O. (1992). The relationships between privacy and different components of job-satisfaction. *Environment & Behavior, 24,* 670–679.

Eddy, E. R., Stone, D. L., & Stone, E. F. (1999). The effects of information management policies on reactions to human resource information systems: An integration of privacy and procedural justice perspectives. *Personnel Psychology, 52,* 335–358.

Ehn, P. (1989). *Work-oriented design of computer artifacts.* Stockholm: Arbetlivscentrum.

Eisenhardt, K. M. (1989). Agency theory: An assessment and review. *Academy of Management Review, 14,* 57–74.

Emerson, R. M. (1972). Exchange theory part I: A psychological basis for social exchange. In J. Berger, M. Zeldich, Jr., & B. Anderson (Eds.), *Sociological theories in progress* (Vol. 2). Boston: Houghton–Mifflin.

Ernst and Young LLP. (2002). *Global information security survey.* U.K.: Presentation Services.

Ethics Officer Association. (1997). *Sources and consequences of workplace pressure: Increasing the risk of unethical and illegal business practices.* Belmont, MA: Author.

Ferrell, O. C., & Gresham, L. G. (1985). A contingency framework for understanding ethical decision making in marketing. *Journal of Marketing, 49,* 87–96.

Fischhoff, B., Slovic, P., & Lichtenstein, S. (1983). The "public" vs. the "experts": Perceived vs. actual disagreement about the risks of nuclear power. In V. T. Covello, J. Flamm, J. Rodericks, & R. Tardiff (Eds.), *Analysis of actual versus perceived risks* (pp. 235–249). New York: Plenum.

Fischhoff, B., Slovic, P., Lichtenstein, S., Read, S., & Combs, B. (1978). How safe is safe enough? A psychometric study of attitudes towards technological risks and benefits. *Policy Sciences, 8,* 127–152.

Flynn, G. (1997, October). How much medical disclosure is too much? *Workforce, 76*(10), 89, 92.

Flynn, N. (2004). *Instant messaging rules: A business guide to managing policies, security, and legal issues for safe IM communication.* New York: AMACOM Books.

Foddy, W. H. (1984). A critical evaluation of Altman's definition of privacy as a dialectical process. *Journal for the Theory of Social Behavior, 14,* 297–307.

Foddy, W. H., & Finighan, W. R. (1981). The concept of privacy from a symbolic interaction perspective. *Journal for the Theory of Social Behavior, 10,* 1–17.

Freedman, W. (1987). *The right of privacy in the computer age.* New York: Quorum.

French, J. R. P. (1956). A formal theory of social power. *Psychological Review, 63,* 181–194.

French, J. R. P., & Raven, B. (1959). Bases of social power. In D. Cartwright (Ed.), *Studies in social power* (pp. 150–167). Ann Arbor: University of Michigan.

Frey, B. S. (1993). Does monitoring increase work effort? The rivalry with trust and loyalty. *Economic Inquiry, 31,* 663–670.

Fusilier, M. R., & Hoyer, W. D. (1980). Variables affecting perceptions of invasions of privacy in a personnel selection situation. *Journal of Applied Psychology, 65,* 623–626.

Futrell, C. M., & Jenkins, O. C. (1978). Pay secrecy versus pay disclosure for salesmen: A longitudinal study. *Journal of Marketing Research, 15,* 214–219.

Garrett, R. (1974). The nature of privacy. *Philosophy Today, 89,* 421–472.

Gavison, R. (1980). Privacy and the limits of law. *Yale Law Journal, 89,* 421–471.

Giacalone, R., & Rosenfeld, P. (1991). *Applied impression management: How image-making affects managerial decisions.* Newbury Park, CA: Sage.

Goffman, E. (1959). *The presentation of the self in everyday life.* Garden City, NY: Doubleday.

Goffman, E. (1963). *Behavior in public places: Notes on the social organization of gatherings.* New York: Free Press.

Gopen, G. D., & Swan, J. A. (1990, Nov–Dec). The science of scientific writing. *American Scientist, 78,* 550–558.

Grant, R. A., Higgins, C. A., & Irving, R. H. (1988). Computerized performance monitors: Are they costing you customers? *Sloan Management Review, 29,* 39–45.

Greenberg, J. (1986a). Determinants of perceived fairness of performance evaluations. *Journal of Applied Psychology, 71,* 340–342.

Greenberg, J. (1986b). Organizational performance appraisal procedures: What makes them fair? *Research on Negotiation in Organizations, 1,* 25–41.

Greenberg, J. (1986c). The distributive justice of organizational performance evaluations. In H. W. Bierhoff, R. L. Cohen, & J. Greenberg (Eds.), *Justice in social relations* (pp. 337–351). New York: Plenum Press.

Greenberg, J. (1987). Using diaries to promote procedural justice in performance appraisals. *Social Justice Research, 1,* 219–234.

Greenberg, J. (1993). The social side of fairness: Interpersonal and informational classes of organizational justice. In R. Cropanzano (Ed.), *Justice in the workplace: Approaching fairness in human resource management.* Hillsdale, NJ: Erlbaum.

Greenberger, D. B., & Strasser, S. (1986). The development and application of a model of personal control in organizations. *Academy of Management Review, 11,* 164–177.

Greenberger, D. B., Strasser, S., Cummings, L. L., & Dunham, R. B. (1989). The impact of personal control on performance and satisfaction. *Organizational Behavior and Human Decision Processes, 43,* 29–51.

Greene, R. W. (1998, September). Internet addiction: Is it just this month's hand-wringer for worry-warts, or a genuine problem? *Computerworld, 32,* 78–79.

Greengard, S. (1999, February). Web-based training yields maximum returns. *Workforce, 78*(2), 95–96.

Gross, H. (1971). Privacy and autonomy. In J. R. Pennock & J. W. Chapman (Eds.), *Privacy: Nomos XIII* (pp. 169–181). New York: Atherton Press.

Grossman, M. (1998, September 7). Pithy answers to important questions: Just what can employers do when it comes to monitoring their employees' cyber activity? *The Connecticut Law Tribune,* 1.

Hacker, S. L. (1987). Feminist perspectives on computer based systems. In G. Bjerknes, P. Ehn, & M. Kyng (Eds.), *Computers and democracy* (pp. 177–190). Aldershot, U.K.: Avebury.

Haggerty, K. D., & Ericson, R. V. (2000, December). The surveillant assemblage. *British Journal of Sociology, 51*(4), 605–622.

Hale, R. (1998, December 28). Keeping the firm's network safe requires more than passwords. *New York Law Journal,* 5.

Hammitt, W. E. (1982). Cognitive dimensions of wilderness solitude. *Environment and Behavior, 14,* 478–493.

Hammitt, W. E., & Brown, G. F. (1984). Functions of privacy in wilderness environments. *Leisure Sciences, 6,* 151–166.

Hammitt, W. E., & Madden, M. A. (1989). Cognitive dimensions of wilderness privacy: A field test and further explanation. *Leisure Sciences, 11*, 151–166.

Harris, L. and Associates, & Westin, A. F. (1981). *The dimensions of privacy.* New York: Garland.

Hatch, D. D., & Hall, J. E. (1997, August). Video surveillance presents HR challenges. *Workforce, 76*(8), 67.

Hawk, S. (1994). The effects of computerized performance monitoring: An ethical perspective. *Journal of Business Ethics, 13*, 949–957.

Hedge, J. W., & Pulakos, E. D. (2002). Grappling with implementation. In J. W. Hedge & E. D. Pulakos (Eds.), *Implementing organizational interventions: Steps, processes, and best practices.* San Francisco: Jossey-Bass.

Heider, F. (1944). Social perception and phenomenal causality. *Psychological Review, 51*, 358–374.

Higgins, E. T. (1997). Beyond pleasure and pain. *American Psychologist, 52*(12), 1280–1300.

Higgins, E. T. (1998). Promotion and prevention: Regulatory focus as a motivational principle. *Advances in Experimental Social Psychology, 30*, 1–16.

Homans, G. C. (1958). Social behavior as exchange. *American Journal of Sociology, 63*, 597–606.

Hoofnagle, C. J., & Honig, E. (2005). *Victoria's Secret and financial privacy.* Washington, DC: Electronic Privacy Information Center. Available at www.epic.org/privacy/glba/victoriassecret.html

Hoylman, F. (1975). The effect of personal control and instrumental value on the experience of invasion of privacy. Unpublished doctoral dissertation. Purdue University, West Lafayette, IN.

Ingulli, E., & Halbert, T. (1998, September). Electronic monitoring of employees: An ethical analysis. *Employment Testing: Law & Policy Reporter*, 129.

Inness, J. C. (1992). *Privacy, intimacy, and isolation.* New York: Oxford University Press.

International Labour Office. (1993). *Workers' privacy. Part 2: Monitoring and surveillance in the workplace, 12*(1). Geneva: Author.

Iwata, O. (1980). Territoriality orientation, privacy orientation and locus of control as determinants of the perception of crowding. *Japanese Psychological Research, 22,* 13–21.

Jenero, K. A., & Mapesriordan, L. D. (1992, Summer). Electronic monitoring of employees and the elusive right to privacy. *Employee Relations Law Journal, 18,* 71–102.

Jewett, T., & Kling, R. (1997). *Teaching social issues of computerization.* San Diego: Academic Press.

Johnson, C. A. (1974). Privacy as personal control. In D. H. Carson (General Ed.) & S. T. Margulis (Vol. Ed.), *Man-environment interactions: Evaluations and applications: Vol. 6. Privacy* (pp. 83–100). Washington, DC: Environmental Design Research Association.

Johnson, C. A. (1976). Privacy as personal control. In D. H. Carson (Ed.), *Man-environment interactions: Selected papers presented at EDRA 5* (pp. 83–100). Stroudsberg, PA: Dowden, Hutchinson, & Ross.

Jones, G. R. (1984). Task visibility, free riding, and shirking: Explaining the effect of structure and technology on employee behavior. *Academy of Management Review, 9,* 684–695.

Jones, T. M. (1991). Ethical decision making by individuals in organizations: An issue contingent model. *Academy of Management Review, 16,* 366–395.

Kahin, B., & Nesson, C. R. (1997). *Borders in cyberspace: Information policy and the global information infrastructure.* Cambridge, MA: MIT Press.

Kalven, H. (1966). Privacy and tort law: Were Warren and Brandeis wrong? *Law and Contemporary Problems, 326,* 327–348.

Kanfer, R., Sawyer, J., Earley, P. C., & Lind, E. A. (1987). Fairness and participation in evaluation procedures: Effects on task attitudes and performance. *Social Justice Research, 1,* 235–249.

Keeney, M., Cappelli, D., Kowalski, E., Moore, A., Shimeall, T., & Rogers, S. (2005). *Insider threat study: Computer system sabotage in critical infrastructure sectors*. Pittsburgh, PA: CERT Program, Software Engineering Institute, Carnegie Mellon University. Available at www.cert.org/archive/pdf/insidercross051105.pdf

Kirchner, W. K. (1966). A note on the effect of privacy in taking typing tests. *Journal of Applied Psychology, 50,* 373–374.

Kling, R. (1987). Computerization as an ongoing social and political process. In G. Bjerknes, P. Ehn, & M. Kyng (Eds.), *Computers and democracy* (pp. 117–136). Aldershot, U.K.: Avebury.

Kling, R. (1994). Organizational analysis in computer science. In C. Huff & T. Finholt (Eds.), *Social issues in computing: Putting computing in its place* (pp. 18–37). New York: McGraw-Hill.

Kling, R. (1996a). *Computerization and controversy.* San Diego: Academic Press.

Kling, R. (1996b). Beyond outlaws, hackers, and pirates: Ethical issues in the work of information and computer science professionals. In R. Kling (Ed.), *Computerization and controversy* (pp. 848–869). San Diego: Academic Press.

Kling, R., & Star, S. L. (1998, March). Human centered systems in the perspective of organizational and social informatics. *Computers and Society, 28* (1), 22–29.

Klitzman, S., & Stellman, J. M. (1989). The impact of the physical environment on the psychological well being of workers. *Social Science Medicine, 29,* 733–742.

Kraut, R. E. (1987). Predicting the use of technology: The case of telework. In R. Kraut (Ed.), *Technology and the transformation of white collar work* (pp. 113–133). Hillsdale, NJ: Erlbaum.

Kruger, J., & Dunning, D. (1999). Unskilled and unaware of it: How difficulties in recognizing one's own incompetence lead to inflated self-assessments. *Journal of Personality and Social Psychology, 77,* 1121–1134.

Kupritz, V. W. (1998). Privacy in the work place: The impact of building design. *Journal of Environmental Psychology, 18,* 341–356.

Landy, F. J., Barnes, J. L., & Murphy, K. R. (1978). Correlates of perceived fairness and accuracy of performance evaluation. *Journal of Applied Psychology, 6,* 751–754.

LePoire, B. A., Burgoon, J. K., & Parrott, R. (1992). Status and privacy restoring communication in the workplace. *Journal of Applied Communication Research, 20*, 419–436.

Leventhal, (1980). What is to be done with equity theory? New approaches to the study of fairness in social relationships. In K. J. Gergen, M. S. Greenberg, & R. H. Willis (Eds.), *Social exchange: Advances in theory and research* (pp. 27–55). New York: Plenum.

Lewicki, R. J., McAllister, D. J., & Bies, R. J. (1998). Trust and distrust: New relationships and realities. *Academy of Management Review, 23*, 438–458.

Lind, E. A., & Tyler, T. R. (1988). *The social psychology of procedural justice.* New York: Plenum.

Lombard, M. (1995). Direct responses to people on the screen: Television and personal space. *Communication Research, 22*, 288–324.

Lyon, D. (2001). *Surveillance society: Monitoring everyday life.* London: Routledge.

Macaulay, S. (1963). Non-contractual relations in business: A preliminary study. *American Sociological Review, 28*, 55–67.

MacQueen, K. M., McLellan, E., Kay, K., & Milstein, B. (1998). Codebook development for team-based qualitative analysis. *Cultural Anthropology Methods, 10*, 31–36.

Marshall, N. J. (1974). Dimensions of privacy preferences. *Multivariate Behavioral Research, 9*, 255–272.

Martinko, M. J., & Gardner, W. L. (1982). Learned helplessness: An alternative explanation for performance deficits. *Academy of Management Review, 7*, 195–204.

Marx, G. T. (1998). An ethics for the new surveillance. *The Information Society, 14.*

Marx, G. T., Moderow, J., Zuboff, S., Howard, B., & Nussbaum, K. (1990, March/April). The case of the omniscient organization. *Harvard Business Review, 68* (2), 12–30.

Mayer-Schönberger, V. (1999). Generational development of data protection in Europe. In P. E. Agre & M. Rotenberg (Eds.),

Technology and privacy: The new landscape (pp. 219–241). Cambridge, MA: MIT Press.

Mead, G. H. (1962). *Mind, self, & society.* Chicago: University of Chicago Press.

Milberg, S. J., Burke, S. J., Smith, H. J., & Kallman, E. A. (1995). Values, personal information, privacy and regulatory approaches. *Communications of the ACM, 38,* 65–74.

Molm, L. D. (1991). Affect and social exchange: Satisfaction in power dependence relations. *American Sociological Review, 56* (4), 475–493.

Molm, L. D. (1994). Dependence and risk: Transforming the structure of social exchange. *Social Psychology Quarterly, 57,* 163–176.

Moorman, R. H., & Podsakoff, P. M. (1992). A meta-analytic review and empirical test of the potential confounding effects of social desirability response sets in organizational behaviour research. *Journal of Occupational and Organizational Psychology, 65,* 131–149.

Morrison, E. W., & Bies, R. J. (1991). Impression management in the feedback-seeking process: A literature review and a research agenda. *Academy of Management Review, 16,* 522–541

Moskowitz, J. (2001). *Windows 2000: Group policy, profiles, and IntelliMirror.* Alameda, CA: Sybex, Inc.

Mumford, E. (1987). Sociotechnical systems design: Evolving theory and practice. In G. Bjerknes, P. Ehn, & M. Kyng (Eds.), *Computers and democracy* (pp. 59–76). Aldershot, U.K.: Avebury.

Newell, P. B. (1995). Perspectives on privacy. *Journal of Environmental Psychology, 13,* 87–104.

O'Neill, M. J. (1994). Work space adjustability, storage, and enclosure as predictors of employee reactions and performance. *Environment and Behavior, 26,* 504–526.

Orthmann, R. (1998, December). Workplace computer monitoring rose in 1998. *Employment Testing: Law & Policy Reporter,* 182.

Osterloh, M., & Frey, B. S. (2000). Motivation, knowledge transfer, and organizational forms. *Organization Science, 11* (5), 538–550.

Panko, R. R., & Beh, H. G. (2002). Monitoring for pornography and sexual harassment. *Communications of the ACM, 45* (1), 84–87.

Parent, W. A. (1983). Recent work on the concept of privacy. *American Philosophical Quarterly, 20,* 341–354.

Pedersen, D. M. (1997). Psychological functions of privacy. *Journal of Environmental Psychology, 17,* 147–156.

Perlmuter, L. C., & Monty, R. A. (Eds.). (1979). *Choice and perceived control.* Hillsdale, NJ: Erlbaum.

Perlmuter, L. C., Scharff, K., Karsh, R., & Monty, R. A. (1980). Perceived control: A generalized state of motivation. *Motivation and Emotion, 4,* 35–45.

Perrault, N., Stanton, J. M., & Barnes-Farrell, J. L. (1998a, April). Fairness in supervisory behavior: Two experimental investigations. Poster presentation at the annual meeting of the Society for Industrial and Organizational Psychology, Dallas, TX.

Perrault, N., Stanton, J. M., & Barnes-Farrell, J. L. (1998b, August). Reactions to organizational policies: Intrusiveness and conse-quences as determinants of need for justification. Poster presenta-tion at the 24th International Congress of Applied Psychology, San Francisco, CA.

Petronio, S. (1991). Communication boundary management: A theo-retical model of managing disclosure of private information between marital couples. *Communication Theory, 1,* 311–335.

Petronio, S., & Chayer, J. (1988). Communicating privacy norms in a corporation: A case study. Paper presented at the International Communication Association, New Orleans, LA.

Pincus, L. B., & Trotter, C. (1995). The disparity between public and private sector employee privacy protections: A call for legitimate privacy rights for private sector workers. *American Business Law Journal, 33,* 51–89.

Powers, M. (1996). A cognitive access definition of privacy. *Law and Philosophy, 15,* 369–386.

Preston, D. (1998, December). Business ethics and privacy in the workplace. *Computers and Society,* 12–18.

Priest, S., & Bugg, R. (1991). Functions of privacy in Australian wilderness environments. *Leisure Sciences, 13*, 247–255.

Proshansky, H., & Altman, I. (1979). Overview of the field. In W. P. White (Ed.), *Resources in environment and behavior* (pp. 3–36). Washington, DC: American Psychological Association.

Proshansky, H., Ittelson, W. H., & Rivlin, L. G. (Eds.). (1970). *Environmental psychology.* New York: Holt, Rhinehart & Winston.

Prosser, W. (1984). Privacy: A legal analysis. In F. D. Schoeman (Ed.), *Philosophical dimensions of privacy* (pp. 107–142). Cambridge: Cambridge University Press.

Reese Bros. Plastics Limited vs. Hamon–Sobelco Australia Pty Limited. See Butterworth's Property Reports #97235 (1988). Supreme Court of New South Wales Court of Appeal (Appeal #414 of 1988, decided December 23, 1988).

Rehnquist, W. H. (1974). Is an expanded right to privacy consistent with fair and effective law enforcement? *Kansas Law Review, 23*, 1–15.

Rempel, J. K., Holmes, J. G., & Zanna, M. P. (1985). Trust in close relationships. *Journal of Personality and Social Psychology, 49*, 95–112.

Robinson, S. L., & Rousseau, D. M. (1994). Violating the psychological contract: Not the exception but the norm. *Journal of Organizational Behavior, 15*, 245–259.

Ross-Flanigan, N. (1998, March/April). The virtues (and vices) of virtual colleagues. *MIT's Technology Review, 101* (2), 52–59.

Rosse, J. G., Miller, J. L., & Stecher, M. D. (1994). A field-study of job applicants' reactions to personality and cognitive-ability testing. *Journal of Applied Psychology, 79*, 987–992.

Rousseau, D. M. (1989). Psychological and implied contracts in organizations. *Employee Responsibilities & Rights Journal, 2*, 121–139.

Rousseau, D. M., Sitkin, S. B., Burt, R. S., & Camerer, C. (1998). Not so different after all: A cross discipline view of trust. *Academy of Management Review, 23*, 393–404.

Rule, J., McAdam, D., Stearns, L., & Uglow, D. (1980). *The politics of privacy: Planning for personal data systems as powerful technologies.* New York: Elsevier.

Rustemli, A., & Kokdemir, D. (1993). Privacy dimensions and preferences among Turkish students. *Journal of Social Psychology, 133,* 807–814.

Sanders v. Robert Bosch Corp. (1994). 38 F.3d 736; 1994 U.S. App. LEXIS 30314; 10 I.E.R. Cas. (BNA) 1.

Sandhu, R. W., Coyne, E. J., Feinstein, H. L., & Youman, C. E. (1996). *Role-based access control models.* Los Alamitos, CA: IEEE Computer Society Press.

Sasse, M., Brostoff, S., & Weirich, D. (2001). Transforming the "weakest link": A human/computer interaction approach to usable and effective security. *BT Technology Journal, 19,* 122–131.

Schein, V. E. (1977). Individual privacy and personnel psychology: The need for a broader perspective. *Journal of Social Issues, 33,* 154–167.

Schwartz, B. (1968). The social psychology of privacy. *American Journal of Sociology, 73,* 741–752.

Security Wire Digest. (2000, March 27). *CSI/FBI study says: Security breaches on the rise.* Author. Available at www.lexias.com/1.0/securitywiredigest_27MAR2000.html

Seifman, D. H., & Trepanier, C. W. (1996, Winter). Evolution of the paperless office: Legal issues arising out of technology in the workplace. 1. E–mail and voicemail systems. *Employee Relations Law Journal, 21,* 5–36.

Seligman, M. E. P. (1975). *Helplessness: On depression, development, and death.* San Francisco: W. H. Freeman.

Shahar v. Bowers, 836 F. Supp. 859, 1993 U.S.Dist. LEXIS 14206 (N.D.Ga., 1993).

Shapiro, D. L., Buttner, E. H., & Barry, B. (1994). Explanations: What factors enhance their perceived adequacy. *Organizational Behavior and Human Decision Processes, 58,* 346–368.

Simon, H. A. (1965). *The shape of automation: For men and management.* New York: Harper and Row.

Simons, R. (1991). Strategic orientation and top management attention to control systems. *Strategic Management Journal, 12* (1), 49–62.

Sipior, J. C., & Ward, B. T. (1995). The ethical and legal quandary of e-mail privacy. *Communications of the Association for Computing Machinery, 38* (12), 8–54.

Sipior, J. C., Ward, B. T., & Rainone, S. M. (1998). Ethical management of employee e-mail privacy. *Information Systems Management, 15,* 41–47.

Skoudis, E., & Zeltser, L. (2003). *Malware: Fighting malicious code.* Upper Saddle River, NJ: Prentice Hall.

Slovic, P. (2001). *The perception of risk.* London: Earthscan Publications.

Slovic, P., Fischhoff, B., & Lichtenstein, S. (1985). In R. Kates, C. Hohenernser, & J. Kasperson (Eds.), *Perilous progress: Managing the hazards of technology* (pp. 91–125). Boulder CO: Westview.

Smith, H. J. (1993, December). Privacy policies and practices: Inside the organizational maze. *Communications of the Association for Computing Machinery, 36* (12), 105–122.

Smith, H. J., Milberg, S. J., & Burke, S. J. (1996, June). Information privacy: Measuring individual's concerns about organizational practices. *MIS Quarterly,* 167–195.

Smith, M. J., Carayon, P., Sanders, K. J., Lim, S. Y., & LeGrande, D. (1992). Employee stress and health complaints in jobs with and without electronic performance monitoring. *Applied Ergonomics, 23,* 17–28.

Society for Human Resource Management. (2001). *Workplace Privacy Survey, 2000.* Alexandria, VA: West Group.

Somerville, P. (1997). The social construction of home. *Journal of Architectural and Planning Research, 14,* 226–245.

Soroka v. Dayton Hudson Corp., I Cal.Rptr.2d 77, 1991 Cal.App. LEXIS 1241 (Cal.Ct.App. 1st Dist. 1991).

Spector, P. E. (1981). *Research designs.* Beverly Hills, CA: Sage.

Stanton, J. M. (1997, April). A multi-organization, procedural justice analysis of performance monitoring. In B. P. Niehoff (Chair), Recent research in performance monitoring. Symposium conducted at the annual meeting of the Society for Industrial and Organizational Psychology, St. Louis, MO.

Stanton, J. M. (1998a). An empirical assessment of data collection using the Internet. *Personnel Psychology, 51,* 709–725.

Stanton, J. M. (1998b). Validity and related issues in Web-based hiring. *The Industrial-Organizational Psychologist, 36* (3), 69–77.

Stanton, J. M. (2000). Traditional and electronic monitoring from an organizational justice perspective. *Journal of Business and Psychology, 15,* 129–147.

Stanton, J. M. (2002). Information technology and privacy: A boundary management perspective. In S. Clarke, E. Coakes, G. Hunter, & A. Wenn (Eds.), *Socio-technical and human cognition elements of information systems* (pp. 79–103). London: Idea Group.

Stanton, J. M., & Barnes-Farrell, J. L. (1996). Effects of electronic performance monitoring on personal control, task satisfaction and task performance. *Journal of Applied Psychology, 81,* 738–745.

Stanton, J. M., & Julian, A. L. (2002). The impact of social cues about an EPM system on performance quality and quantity. *Computers in Human Behavior, 18,* 85–101.

Stanton, J. M., & Stam, K. R. (2003). Information technology, privacy, and power within organizations: A view from boundary theory and social exchange perspectives. *Surveillance and Society, 2,* 152–190.

Stanton, J. M., & Weiss, E. M. (2000). Electronic monitoring in their own words: An exploratory study of employees' experiences with new types of surveillance. *Computers in Human Behavior, 16,* 423–440.

Stanton, J. M., & Weiss, E. M. (2003). Organisational databases of personnel information: Contrasting the concerns of human resource managers and employees. *Behaviour and Information Technology, 22* (5), 291–304.

Stanton, J. M., Stam, K. R., Mastrangelo, P., & Jolton, J. (2005). An analysis of end user security behaviors. *Computers & Security, 24,* 124–133.

Steptoe, R. M., & Johnson, S. E. (1999, January). Seeing and hearing evil. *West Virginia Employment Law Letter, 4* (1).

Stone, D. L. (1986). Relationship between introversion/extraversion, values regarding control over information, and perceptions of invasion of privacy. *Perceptual and Motor Skills, 62,* 371–376.

Stone, D. L., & Kotch, D. A. (1989). Individuals' attitudes toward organizational drug testing policies and practices. *Journal of Applied Psychology, 74,* 518–521.

Stone, D. L., & Stone, E. F. (1987). Effects of missing application blank information on personnel selection decisions: Do privacy protection strategies bias the outcome? *Journal of Applied Psychology, 72,* 452–456.

Stone, D. L., & Vine, P. (1989, April). Some procedural determinants of reactions to drug testing. Paper presented at the annual conference of the Society for Industrial and Organizational Psychology, Boston, MA.

Stone, E. F. (1980). *Testimony presented at U. S. Labor Department hearings on workplace privacy (Working Paper 7).* West Lafayette, IN: Purdue University, Information Privacy Research Center.

Stone, E. F., & Stone, D. L. (1990). Privacy in organizations: Theoretical issues, research findings and protection mechanisms. *Research in Personnel and Human Resources Management, 8,* 349–411.

Stone, E. F., Guetal, H. G., Gardner, D. G., & McClure, S. (1983). A field experiment comparing information privacy values, beliefs, and attitudes across several types of organizations. *Journal of Applied Psychology, 68,* 459–468.

Stone, E. F., Stone, D. L., & Hyatt, D. (1989, April). Personnel selection procedures and invasion of privacy. In R. Guion (Chair), Privacy in organizations: Personnel selection, physical environment, and legal issues. Symposium conducted at the annual conference of the Society for Industrial and Organizational Psychology, Boston, MA.

294 **The Visible Employee**

Strickland, L. (1958). Surveillance and trust. *Journal of Personality*, *26*, 245–250.

Surowiecki, J. (2004). *The wisdom of crowds*. New York: Doubleday.

Taylor, G. S., & Davis, J. S. (1989). Individual privacy and computer-based human resource information systems. *Journal of Business Ethics*, *8*, 569–576.

Te'eni, D. (2001). Review: A cognitive-affective model of organizational communication for designing IT. *MIS Quarterly*, *25* (2), 251–312.

Tepper, B. J., & Braun, C. K. (1995). Does the experience of organizational justice mitigate the invasions of privacy engendered by drug testing? An empirical investigation. *Basic and Applied Social Psychology*, *16*, 211–225.

Thibaut, J., & Walker, L. (1975). *Procedural justice: A psychological analysis*. Hillsdale, NJ: Erlbaum.

Thibaut, J. W., & Kelley, H. H. (1959). *The social psychology of groups*. New York: Wiley.

Thomson, J. J. (1975). The right to privacy. *Philosophy & Public Affairs*, *4*, 295–314.

Thorne v. El Segundo, 726 F.2d 456 (9th Cir. 1983), cert. denied, 469 U.S. 979 (1984).

Thurston, R. J., & Jones, J. R. (1994, May). Health-care reform warrants HRIS updates. *Personnel Journal*, *73* (5), 42–46.

Tolchinsky, P. D., McCuddy, M., Adams, J., Ganster, D. C., Woodman, R., & Fromkin, H. L. (1981). Employee perceptions of invasion of privacy: A field simulation experiment. *Journal of Applied Psychology*, *66*, 308–313.

Trevino, L. K. (1986). Ethical decision making in organizations: A person–situation interactionist model. *Academy of Management Review*, *11*, 601–617.

Turkington, R. C. (1990). Legacy of the Warren and Brandeis article: The emerging unencumbered Constitutional right to informational privacy. *Northern Illinois University Law Review*, *10*, 479–520.

Tyler, T. R., & Caine, A. (1981). The influence of outcomes and procedures on satisfaction with formal leaders. *Journal of Personality and Social Psychology, 41*, 642–655.

Tyler, T. R., Rasinski, K. A., & Spodick, N. (1985). The influence of voice upon satisfaction with leaders: Exploring the meaning of process control. *Journal of Personality and Social Psychology, 48*, 72–81.

U.S. Congress, Office of Technology Assessment. (1987). *The electronic supervisor: New technology, new tensions.* OTA–CIT–333. Washington, DC: U.S. Government Printing Office.

Vangelisti, A. L. (1994). Family secrets: Forms, functions and correlates. *Journal of Social & Personal Relationships, 11*, 113–135.

Vest, J. M., Vest, M. J., Perry, S. J., & O'Brien, F. (1995). Factors influencing managerial disclosure of AIDS health information to coworkers. *Journal of Applied Social Psychology, 25*, 1043–1057.

Wagner, I. (1996). Confronting ethical issues of systems design in a web of social relationships. In R. Kling (Ed.), *Computerization and controversy* (pp. 889–902). San Diego: Academic Press.

Warren, S. D., & Brandeis, L. D. (1890). The right to privacy: The implicit made explicit. Reprinted in F. D. Schoeman (Ed.), (1984), *Philosophical dimensions of privacy: An anthology* (pp. 75–103). Cambridge: Cambridge University Press.

Westin, A. F. (1967). *Privacy and freedom.* New York: Atheneum.

Westin, A. F. (1992). Two key factors that belong in a macroergonomic analysis of electronic monitoring: Employee perceptions of fairness and the climate of organizational trust or distrust. *Applied Ergonomics, 23*, 35–42.

Whitener, E. M., Brodt, S. E., Korsgaard, M. A., & Werner, J. M. (1998). Managers as initiators of trust: An exchange relationship framework for understanding managerial trustworthy behavior. *Academy of Management Review, 23*, 513–530.

Woodman, R. W., Ganster, D. C., McCuddy, M. K., Tolchinsky, P. D., & Fromkin, H. (1982). A survey of the perceptions of information privacy in organizations. *Academy of Management Journal, 25*, 647–663.

Zweig, D., & Webster, J. (2002). Where is the line between benign and invasive? An examination of psychological barriers to the acceptance of awareness monitoring systems. *Journal of Organizational Behavior, 23*, 605–633.

Recommended Reading

Here is a list of books that readers may find helpful for in-depth research on the major topics examined in this book. In addition to the volumes listed below, readers can find a complete list of the source materials we used in preparation of this book by consulting the References section. We have organized the following list in order of topics covered and chapters in the book. Suggestions relevant to Chapters 1 through 4 include books on information security, privacy, data laws, and employment law. Suggestions corresponding to Chapters 5 through 7 include books on research methods, interviewing, surveying, and statistics. Suggestions relevant to Chapters 8 and 9 include books on information technology governance, organizational interventions, and organizational change.

Chapters 1–4: Information Security, Privacy, Ethics, and Law

Information Security

Bidgoli, H. (2005). *Handbook of information security*. New York: John Wiley and Sons.

Conklin, W. A., White, G. B., Cothren, C., Williams, D., & Davis, R. (2005). *Principles of computer security: Security+ and beyond*. Dubuque, IA: McGraw-Hill.

Dhillon, G. (2005). *Information system security: A management challenge*. New York: John Wiley and Sons.

Hitchcock, J. A. (2006). *Net crimes and misdemeanors: Outmaneuvering Web spammers, stalkers, and con artists, 2nd ed*. Medford, NJ: Information Today, Inc.

Kairab, S. (2004). *A practical guide to security assessments*. Totowa, NJ: Auerbach.

Mitnick, V. (2002). *The art of deception*. Indianapolis: Wiley.

Petersen, J. K., & Zamir, S. (2000). *Understanding surveillance technologies: Spy devices, their origins & applications.* Boca Raton, FL: CRC Press.

Stamp, M. (2005). *Information security: Principles and practice.* New York: John Wiley and Sons.

Volonino, L., & Robinson, S. (2004). *Principles and practice of information security.* Upper Saddle River, NJ: Prentice Hall.

Winkler, I. (1997). *Corporate espionage.* Rocklin, CA: Prima Publishing.

Privacy

Agre, P., & Rotenberg, M. (1997). *Technology and privacy: The new landscape.* Cambridge, MA: MIT Press.

Banisar, D., & Schneier, B. (1997). *The electronic privacy papers.* New York: John Wiley and Sons.

Etzioni, A. (1999). *The limits of privacy.* New York: Basic Books.

Garfinkel, S. (2000). *Database nation: The death of privacy in the 21st century.* Beijing: Cambridge University Press.

Hunter, R. (2002). *World without secrets: Business, crime, and privacy in the age of ubiquitous computing.* New York: John Wiley and Sons.

Lyon, D. (2002). *Surveillance as social sorting: Privacy, risk and digital discrimination.* New York: Routledge.

Lyon, D., & Zureik, E. (1996). *Computers, surveillance, and privacy.* Minneapolis: University of Minnesota Press.

Petronio, S. (2002). *Boundaries of privacy: Dialectics of disclosure (SUNY series in communication studies).* Albany: State University of New York Press.

Schneier, B. (2004). *Secrets and lies: Digital security in a networked world.* New York: Wiley.

Shoeman, F. (1984). *Philosophical dimensions of privacy: An anthology.* New York: Cambridge University Press.

Smith, J. M. (1997). *Private matters.* New York: Addison-Wesley.

Solove, D. (2004). *Digital person: Technology and privacy in the information age.* New York: NYU Press.

Electronic Monitoring and Privacy in the Workplace

Boreham, P., Parker, R., & Thompson, P. (2006). *New technology @ work.* New York: Routledge.

Hearn, J., & Heiskanan, T. (2003). *Information society and the workplace: Spaces, boundaries and agency.* New York: Routledge.

Lane, C. A. (2002). *Naked in cyberspace: How to find personal information online, 2nd ed.* Medford, NJ: CyberAge Books.

Lane, F. S. (2003). *The naked employee: How technology is compromising workplace privacy.* New York: American Management Association.

Rothke, B. (2003). *Computer security: 20 things every employee should know.* Dubuque, IA: McGraw-Hill.

Taras, D. G., Bennett, J. T., & Townsend, A. M. (2004). *Information technology and the world of work.* New Brunswick, NJ: Transaction Publishers.

Weckert, J. (2004). *Electronic monitoring in the workplace: Controversies and solutions.* Hershey, PA: Idea Group Publishing.

Sarbanes-Oxley, Gramm-Leach-Bliley, and HIPAA

Beaver, K., & Herold, R. (2003). *The practical guide to HIPAA privacy and security compliance.* Totowa, NJ: Auerbach.

Dinkins, C., & Gilbreath, A. (2003). *HIPAA in daily practice.* Memphis, TN: Kerlak Enterprises.

Green, S. (2004). *Manager's guide to the Sarbanes-Oxley act: Improving internal controls to prevent fraud.* New York: Wiley.

Lander, G. (2003). *What is Sarbanes-Oxley?* Dubuque, IA: McGraw-Hill.

Moore, D. (2004). *Gramm-Leach-Bliley act.* Hunt Valley, MD: Training Pro.

Sanjay, A. (2005). *The Sarbanes-Oxley guide for finance and information technology professionals.* Clifton, NJ: Sarbanes-Oxley Group LLC.

Silverman, L., Becker, D., Rosen, E. J., Fisher, J. L., Braverman, D. A., Sperber, S. R., & Greene, E. F. (2003). *The Sarbanes-Oxley act: Analysis and practice.* Frederick, MD: Aspen.

Information Ethics

Azari, R. (2003). *Current security management and ethical issues of information technology.* Hershey, PA: Idea Group Publishing (IRM Press).

Bowyere, K. W. (2000). *Ethics and computing: Living responsibly in a computerized world.* Hoboken, NJ: Wiley-IEEE Press.

Johnson, D. (2001). *Computer ethics* (3rd ed.). Upper Saddle River, NJ: Prentice Hall.

Tavani, H. (2003). *Ethics and technology: Ethical issues in an age of information and communication technology.* Hoboken, NJ: Wiley.

Employment Law

Covington, R., & Decker, K. (2002). *Individual employee rights in a nutshell.* Eagan, MN: West Publishing Company.

Delpo, A., & Guerin, L. (2002). *Federal employment laws: A desk reference.* Berkeley. CA: Nolo.

Chapters 5–7: Research Methods, Interviewing, Surveying, and Basic Statistics

General, Mixed, and Qualitative Methods

Creswell, J. W. (2002). *Research design: Qualitative, quantitative, and mixed method approaches.* London: Sage.

Denzin, N., & Lincoln, Y. (2003). *The SAGE handbook of qualitative research.* London: Sage.

Kling, R., Rosenbaum, H., & Sawyer, S. (2005). *Understanding and communicating social informatics: A framework for studying and teaching the human contexts of information and communication technologies.* Medford, NJ: Information Today.

Maxwell, J. A. (2004). *Qualitative research design: An interactive approach (Applied social research methods).* London: Sage.

Warren, C. A. B., & Karner, T. X. (2004). *Discovering qualitative methods: Field research, interviews, and analysis.* Los Angeles: Roxbury.

Methodology for Organizational Research

Cassell, C., & Symon, G. (2004). *Essential guide to qualitative methods in organizational research.* London: Sage.

Grey, C. (2005). *Very short, fairly interesting and reasonably cheap book about studying organizations.* London: Sage.

Schwab, D. P. (2005). *Research methods for organizational studies.* Mahwah, NJ: Lawrence Erlbaum.

Interviewing

Rubin, H., & Rubin, I. (2004). *Qualitative interviewing: The art of hearing data.* London: Sage.

Weiss, R. S. (1993). *Learning from strangers: The arts and method of qualitative interview studies.* New York: Free Press.

Statistics

Berinstein, P. (2003). *Business statistics on the Web: Find them fast—at little or no cost.* Medford, NJ: Information Today, Inc.

Moore, D. S. (2003). *The basic practice of statistics.* New York: W. H. Freeman & Company.

Urdan, T. C. (2005). *Statistics in plain English.* Mahwah, NJ: Lawrence Erlbaum Associates.

Vaughan, L. (2001). *Statistical methods for the information professional.* Medford, NJ: Information Today, Inc.

Surveys

Fowler, J., Jr. (2001). *Survey research methods (Applied social research methods).* London: Sage.

Nardi, P. M. (2002). *Doing survey research: A guide to quantitative research methods.* Boston: Allyn and Bacon.

Chapters 8–9: Information Technology Governance in Organizations

Information Technology Governance

Broadbent, M. (2004). *The new CIO leader: Setting the agenda and delivering results.* Boston: Harvard Business School Press.

Lutchen, M. (2003). *Managing IT as a business: A survival guide for CEOs.* New York: John Wiley and Sons.

van Grembergen, W. (2003). *Strategies for information technology governance.* Hershey, PA: Idea Group Publishing.

Weill, P., & Ross, J. *IT governance: How top performers manage IT decision rights for superior results.* Boston: Harvard Business School Press.

Organizational Interventions

Desman, M. B. (2001). *Building an information security awareness program*. Miami: Assurant Group (Auerbach).

Hedge, J., & Pulakos, E. (2002). *Implementing organizational interventions: Steps, processes, and best practices (J-B SIOP professional practice series)*. San Francisco: Pfeiffer.

Trust

Curtin, M., & Neumann, P. (2001). *Developing trust: Online privacy and security*. Berkeley, CA: Apress L.P.

Kramer, R. M., & Tyler, T. R. (1995). *Trust in organizations: Frontiers of theory and research*. London: Sage.

Lane, C., & Bachmann, R. (2001). *Trust within and between organizations: Conceptual issues and empirical applications*. Oxford: Oxford University Press.

Writing Policies

Barman, S. (2001). *Writing information security policies*. Indianapolis, IN: New Riders Publishing (SAMS, Pearson Education).

Peltier, T. R. (2001). *Information security policies, procedures, and standards: Guidelines for effective information security management*. Southgate, MI: Peltier and Associates (Auerbach).

Organizational Culture

Cameron, K. S., & Quinn, R. E. (1999). *Diagnosing and changing organizational culture: Based on the competing values framework*. Upper Saddle River, NJ: Prentice Hall.

Fisher, K. E., Erdelez, S., & McKechnie, L. (E. F.) (2005). *Theories of information behavior*. Medford, NJ: Information Today, Inc.

Schein, E. (1985). *Organizational culture and leadership*. San Francisco: Jossey-Bass.

Organizational Change

Beitler, M. (2003). *Strategic organizational change*. Practitioner Press International.

Burke, W. (2002). *Organization change: Theory and practice (Foundations for organizational science)*. London: Sage.

Choo, C. W. (2001). *Information management for the intelligent organization*. Medford, NJ: Information Today, Inc.

Harrison, M. I. (2004). *Diagnosing organizations: Methods, models, and processes (Applied social research methods)*. London: Sage.

Koenig, M. E. D., & Srikantaiah, T. K. (Eds.). (2004). *Knowledge management lessons learned: What works and what doesn't*. Medford, NJ: Information Today, Inc.

Langley, G. J., Nolan, K. M., Norman, C. L., Provost, L. P., & Nolan, T. W. (1996). *The improvement guide: A practical approach to enhancing organizational performance*. San Francisco: Jossey-Bass.

Discussion Questions

Chapter 1: An Introduction to Information Protection and Employee Behavior

1. Who should care about information security? Why?
2. What is the role of information technology in an organization?
3. What do the authors mean by "behavioral information security?"
4. Discuss the various ways in which technology has played a role in imposing control on unruly environments and in stabilizing business processes.
5. What arguments do critics and privacy advocates have against monitoring and surveillance and where were these critiques initiated?
6. In this chapter we refer to the two formidable monsters, Scylla and Charybdis, from Greek mythology. How is the navigation between a menacing six-headed monster and a treacherous whirlpool nearby a good analogy for the path between information insecurity and employee mistreatment?

Chapter 2: How Employees Affect Information Security

1. What roles do employees play in keeping information secure?
2. Using the list of behaviors in Appendix C, write down the numbers of the behaviors that you have personally observed or heard about happening in the organizations where you have worked. Are there a lot? A few? How important or significant were those behaviors to information security in your organization? Do you agree with the ratings of the expertise needed and likely intentions described for those behaviors?

3. In some cases, providing excellent customer service can be at odds with the main objectives of the security department. Discuss this paradox. In what other ways might security measures interfere with the overall mission of an organization and vice versa?

4. Social engineering, in which an employee is tricked into giving more information than policy allows, is frequently noted as being one of the greatest threats to any security system. How can increased knowledge of different perspectives of security (e.g., the views and experiences of leaders, technology professionals, employees) help an organization protect against this threat?

5. Drawing from your experience as an employee, list the security vulnerabilities that you have seen violated most frequently. In general, what types of employee behavior do you think have the potential to cause the greatest damage to your company or employer?

6. What range of motivations for human behavior cause security transgressions? Do these behaviors require different strategies to prevent their causing security problems? Provide examples and discuss.

7. Why might information technology departments tend to focus on external threats rather than the internal threats that could be posed by employees or contractors with trusted access to the company's information and technology? Who in the organization "owns" the responsibility for employee behavior?

Chapter 3: Information Security Technologies and Operations

1. In your opinion, who in the organization needs to understand the technological solutions to problems? Why?

2. Which kinds of technological security solutions can work effectively in spite of uncooperative behavior on the part of people?

3. What does CIA stand for and why do these elements make up the basic triad? What does non-repudiation mean? In what types of transactions is non-repudiation an especially important issue?

4. Identify several key security technologies that support CIA+NR for information and information systems. For each, list what the technology must do and what the human beings using the technology must do to make the tool effective.

5. If you wanted to become better versed in information technology and security terminology, where would you start? How can increased familiarity with technical jargon help the typical employee or an organizational leader?

6. Imagine that you were the network security consultant who installed a network filtering device and found that three-quarters or more of your client's bandwidth was taken up with non-business uses of the Internet, such as shopping, reading the news, downloading music, and viewing pornography. What would you be able to do with that information? What would be an appropriate first step?

Chapter 4: Employee Monitoring, Surveillance, and Privacy

1. What laws or regulations govern workplace monitoring and surveillance in your state, region, or country?

2. Do employee reactions to monitoring and surveillance matter to an organization's success? Why or why not?

3. Is privacy a process, an event, or state of being? Explain.

4. In the discussion of control, how is the concept of "social access" important? Make up a story about the installation of new surveillance technology in an organization and describe the variety of possible employee reactions.

5. How do you think monitoring and surveillance affect the status of trust between managers and employees?

6. What kinds of changes in monitoring policies are most likely to evoke consideration by employees concerning the status of their relationship with the organization?

Chapter 5: Managerial Perspectives

1. What are the major technology and security concepts with which managers need to be concerned?

2. How does the industrial sector in which an organization operates affect its approach to security? How about its approach to regulating user behavior? In some types of sectors (e.g., military, nonprofit), are the trade-offs between security and regulation of behavior different from those in a typical organization?

3. What do you think about the designation of some managers as "tech-dependent" and others as "tech-savvy"? What are some of the key characteristics that seem to differentiate these two clusters? Both kinds of managers seem to rely on the advice and assistance of technical experts in order to make important decisions, so what difference is there between them?

4. What experiences or personal characteristics do you think lead some managers to believe in "security by obscurity"?

5. Describe an example or two from your own employment history of situations in which the use of technical jargon seemed to interfere with communication between technical staff and non-technical managers.

6. Why do you think the managers in this study were so concerned about protecting leakage of information outside the company rather than about particular security technologies or specific security mechanisms?

7. In your experience, are employees "part of the problem" of information security or part of the solution? Is there any danger in thinking of employees as primarily one or the other? If so, what is it?

8. What do you think about some managers' explanations that they were monitoring because of "one bad apple" in the organization? Were they sincere in saying that only a tiny minority of employees ever caused problems or was it a public relations ploy to suggest how virtuous their organizations were overall?

Chapter 6: Information Technology Professionals' Perspectives

1. In response to questions about what employees do to compromise security, what kinds of answers were provided by the information technology professionals? Which of these actions might not be considered dangerous by the typical non-information-technology employee?

2. How did information technology professionals understand the tensions of balancing information access for employees?

3. The authors wrote that some information technology professionals seemed to think that people are basically good and have to be given opportunities to behave as they should, while other information technology professionals think that people are basically bad and have to be controlled by threats. Which side do you fall on and why?

4. If you believe that people are basically good, what do you have to do, if anything, to make sure that they enact positive security behaviors? Answer the same question under the assumption that people are basically bad.

5. How are the authors using the term *policy*? What other kinds of controls within an organization might also be called policy? What do these types of policies have in common? What danger is there, if any, in calling all of these different things by the same name?

6. Some information technology professionals described in this chapter choose to build scripts, privilege mechanisms, and other types of automated controls to impose constraints on user behavior. In your experience, is this a highly effective strategy? When might it work best? When might it not work well?

Chapter 7: Employee Perspectives on Information Security and Privacy

1. In this chapter, users sometimes came across as being quite trusting. They seemed to project their own motivations and interests onto their co-workers. How do you think this tendency affects the overall efficiency of the organization? How do you think this tendency affects the information security of an organization?

2. Many of the employees admitted to having given the topic of information security little thought or time for discussion. What kinds of changes would have to happen in the organization in order for the typical employee to place a higher priority on information security?

3. How do you personally decide whether a particular file or piece of information is valuable?

4. What do employees believe contributes to having a secure organization? Training? Knowledge? Positive security culture? Or something else? Are these beliefs correct in your opinion or in light of the data presented in this chapter?
5. What were some of the main barriers to positive security behaviors as viewed by employees? Why do you think they understood their work world in this way? In what ways was a long-term or comprehensive view of security available or unavailable to employees?
6. In terms of monitoring, managers had both positive and negative views about what their employees were doing. Describe the various perspectives presented in this chapter. Which of them were surprising to you?

Chapter 8: Overall Analysis and Interpretation

1. How do the perspectives of various constituencies in an organization differ with respect to security? What common ground do you see between them? In other words is there any overriding goal or principal upon which everyone's concerns for security converge?
2. Can you think of situations from your own work experience in which managers, employees, and information technology people reactively implemented technologies in response to one perceived crisis after another?
3. How does the "organizational insecurity cycle" in Figure 8.1 function? At the peak of protection, is it possible that organizations are still not doing a particularly good job? Have you ever seen a cycle like this in an organization where you worked? If so, what period of time elapsed between two major security crises?
4. Why do the authors say that "policy" is a slippery word? How are policies and procedures different? Why is it so common in organizations that policies are nonexistent, not disseminated, not enforced, or not updated?
5. Discuss the authors' new maxim, "You don't motivate what you don't measure."
6. What do you think of the notion that the organization "owns the equipment," so it has a right to control its use? Who might be impressed by this argument and who might not be?

Chapter 9: Recommendations for Managers, Employees, and Information Security Professionals

1. What elements do you think all information security programs should have in common?

2. The authors state that they believe in "equifinality," that in any complex system, such as an organization, there are many different ways to go about solving a problem, and a number of these can lead to just about the same level of success. What's your take on this? True or not?

3. Why is it both difficult and important to take a set of ideas for organizational change and adapt them to local conditions?

4. The first step of "transparent security governance" is to remove communication barriers. Do you agree that this is the most difficult step in the process? Why or why not?

5. What do you think employees can learn from cross-functional work assignments? Increasing the number of in-house people who are able to translate between the technical domain and the managerial domain (or any other pair of constituencies) sounds like a great idea on paper, but are there any downsides?

6. The authors suggest that the fundamental condition for success is to get the people with the influence, the people who understand the technology, and the people who do the organization's essential work to sit down together and discuss information protection. Do you think this could work in the organizations in which you have experience? What obstacles to this process might be present and how can they be overcome?

7. The second part of the consultative leadership process is for leaders to bring together their security experts and representatives of end-users and summarize information protection barriers, preferences, threats, risks, and trade-offs. If you were an organizational leader, how would you find this prospect: exhilarating, intimidating, or perhaps a bit of both?

8. If you were one of the employee representatives charged with the responsibility of writing policy, where would you start? What resources might you look to for help? How would you check to make sure that the language you used was comprehensible to the other people with whom you work?

9. When publicizing monitoring results, one extreme described was to display results on a large LCD monitor in the employee

break room. In what settings might this be appropriate, and in what others is this idea problematic?

10. Imagine you were given the task of designing the first issue of an internal security newsletter. What topics would it include and why?

11. When we suggest that "transparent security governance" does not have to interfere with employees' convenience or social patterns, why does this idea seem like a joke?

12. Are employees' voices important in the security governance process? Why or why not in your opinion?

13. What elements would you include in security training to help ensure that it makes an emotional impact and makes it more likely that employees will want to "trade" some convenience in return for better security?

14. How would you help ensure that a new policy is not "rigged" against the interests of employees and provides a direct conduit for information from the policy development process into the employee community?

Employee Security-Related Behavior List

Employee Security-Related Behavior	Expertise Needed	Likely Intentions
1. Employee transmitted a harassing message using the company's e-mail	Lower	Negative
2. Employee harassed a colleague by sending many, lengthy pager messages	Lower	Negative
3. Someone pretending to be a systems administrator called and said there was a problem with his account and asked for his password, which employee gave with no verification of the caller's credentials	Lower	Negative
4. Employee provided information or a list of staff members to someone outside the organization	Lower	Negative
5. Employee sent an obscene joke using company e-mail	Lower	Negative
6. Employee copied and distributed copyrighted material including digitizing photographs from magazines and books	Lower	Negative
7. Employee sent a harassing e-mail to someone in her company from an anonymous outside e-mail account	Lower	Negative
8. Employee sold cosmetics with the use of the company e-mail system	Lower	Negative
9. Employee used the Internet for activities that interfered with her work-related productivity	Lower	Negative
10. Employee forwarded a chain letter that contained a "pyramid" (get rich quick) scheme	Lower	Negative
11. Employee chose a password that was "1234.	Lower	Negative
12. Employee transferred a lot of files to a personal notebook computer that got stolen	Lower	Negative
13. Employee left confidential data out on his desk at night	Lower	Negative
14. Employee shared her company access codes with others in her family so that they could use her high speed Internet connection	Lower	Negative
15. Employee played network games on the company's computers	Lower	Negative
16. Employee sent e-mail from someone else's account	Lower	Negative
17. Employee sent unsolicited e-mail messages in the form of "junk mail" advertising material to individuals who did not specifically request such material	Lower	Negative
18. Employee did not change her password for over two years	Lower	Negative
19. Employee shared her account information with a friend	Lower	Negative
20. Employee wrote her password on a sticky tape and put it on her monitor	Lower	Negative
21. Employee taped his password to the bottom of his keyboard	Lower	Negative
22. Employee used his social security number as a password	Lower	Negative
23. Employee transmitted her personal opinions about politics on the company's group collaboration tool.	Lower	Hard to tell
24. Employee sent out e-mails in order to compile a list of others' e-mail addresses.	Lower	Hard to tell
25. Employee chose an easily guessable password.	Lower	Hard to tell

26. Employee questioned the need and applicability of organizational security policies.	Lower	Hard to tell
27. Employee complained about the inconvenience of organizational security policies to his boss.	Lower	Hard to tell
28. Employee told customers over the phone that they could rest assured that hackers would not steal their customer information.	Lower	Hard to tell
29. Employee followed the terms of a software license.	Lower	Positive
30. Employee signed compliance statements after review of information security policies.	Lower	Positive
31. Employee changed her password every six months.	Lower	Positive
32. Employee signed all the way out to the sign-out screen whenever he left his desk.	Lower	Positive
33. Employee notified an appropriate administrator when she copied organizational information resources for use in off-site work (e.g., at client site, business trip).	Lower	Positive
34. Employee logged off whenever he left his cubicle.	Lower	Positive
35. Employee shredded her old paper documents.	Lower	Positive
36. Employee locked her tapes, disks, and documents in a file cabinet when she was away from her desk.	Lower	Positive
37. Employee refused to release non-public company data/information to a reporter.	Lower	Positive
38. Employee accessed files that she should not have had access to by using a colleague's user ID because she wanted to avoid filling out the paperwork to increase her access level.	Middle	Negative
39. Employee accessed data for which she was not an intended recipient.	Middle	Negative
40. Employee mailed an encryption software CD to a foreign country in violation of international or regional export control laws.	Middle	Negative
41. Employee posted a cartoon containing an ethnic slur on the company's internal Web site.	Middle	Negative
42. Employee used the company's information resources for personal commercial profit.	Middle	Negative
43. Employee distributed someone else's copyrighted materials using the company's network.	Middle	Negative
44. Employee used an unauthorized file-sharing program on a company computer without written consent from the relevant authority.	Middle	Negative
45. Employee installed pirated software.	Middle	Negative
46. Employee loaded an unauthorized application onto her PC.	Middle	Negative
47. Employee created and mailed a chain letter containing a "pyramid" (get rich quick) scheme.	Middle	Negative
48. Employee installed some software from a CD and didn't know where the CD came from or who wrote the software.	Middle	Negative
49. Employee installed shareware with a restricted license agreement on her company PC and did not pay the shareware fee.	Middle	Negative
50. Employee installed some software on his PC for which the company did not have a license.	Middle	Negative
51. Employee exchanged digital movies and songs (peer-to-peer sharing of files) using company equipment.	Middle	Negative
52. Employee mistakenly introduced a malicious worm program into the network.	Middle	Negative
53. Employee used unsolicited e-mail to advertise a service offered by the organization.	Middle	Hard to tell
54. Employee used her company PC to post non-business-related messages to large numbers of Usenet newsgroups.	Middle	Hard to tell
55. Employee used a modem to dial out to the Internet from a computer connected to a secure LAN.	Middle	Hard to tell

56. Employee constructively criticized organizational security policies to her boss.	Middle	Positive
57. Employee obtained authorization for the connection of his portable computer with an appropriate system administrator.	Middle	Positive
58. Employee released sensitive data to other staff only on a need-to-know basis.	Middle	Positive
59. Employee activated his screensavers with password protection to protect his data when left unattended.	Middle	Positive
60. Employee backed up her data on a regular basis.	Middle	Positive
61. Employee used excellent access codes (passwords and usernames) and changed them periodically.	Middle	Positive
62. Employee reported a discovered security vulnerability to the appropriate authorities.	Middle	Positive
63. Employee intentionally introduced a Trojan horse program into the network.	Higher	Negative
64. Employee used a file decryption program to discover the contents of a file containing trade secrets.	Higher	Negative
65. Employee forged routing information to make it seem like someone else had sent some packets.	Higher	Negative
66. Employee forged her e-mail header information to make it look like her boss had sent a message.	Higher	Negative
67. Employee logged into a server account he was not expressly authorized to access.	Higher	Negative
68. Employee deleted a colleague's account information so that he would not be able to access his files.	Higher	Negative
69. Employee intentionally put a logic bomb in her code.	Higher	Negative
70. Employee built a special script that disabled another user's terminal session.	Higher	Negative
71. Employee used the company's information resources to help a colleague erase her performance reviews.	Higher	Negative
72. Employee created a denial of service attack on a competitor's Web site using the company's computers.	Higher	Negative
73. Employee created a security breach by disrupting network communications.	Higher	Negative
74. Employee used a "ping flood" attack to see what would happen to the company's network.	Higher	Negative
75. Employee turned off the user authentication function on the console of a Web host system.	Higher	Negative
76. Employee found and saved trade secret information about other companies using the Internet.	Higher	Negative
77. Employee brought a wireless gateway device into his office and installed it on the network without authorization.	Higher	Negative
78. Employee encrypted some of her files even though this was against company policy.	Higher	Negative
79. Employee set up a network monitoring device, which intercepted data not intended for his system, to assess how well the network was running.	Higher	Hard to tell
80. Employee set up a packet spoofing application just to test out her programming ability.	Higher	Hard to tell
81. Employee used a "steganography" software tool to store organizational information in a JPEG file.	Higher	Hard to tell
82. Employee attached a modem to her office computer so that she could dial in from home and do work.	Higher	Hard to tell
83. Employee used an intrusion detection program on the company's network even though that was not part of his job.	Higher	Hard to tell
84. Employee used a password-cracking program to unlock a file for which a colleague had lost the password.	Higher	Hard to tell
85. Employee used a port-scanning program to look for vulnerabilities on company computers even though this was not part of her job.	Higher	Hard to tell

86. Employee used a network sniffer to diagnose a problem with the company's network.	Higher	Positive
87. Employee removed access rights data from a user who was leaving the company.	Higher	Positive
88. Employee scanned his files and software for malicious code prior to execution.	Higher	Positive
89. Employee taught others about appropriate and acceptable user policies within the organization.	Higher	Positive
90. Employee participated in advanced security training designated by the organization.	Higher	Positive
91. Employee conducted random/periodic auditing of different departments' security status.	Higher	Positive
92. Employee attended a training program to become familiar with indicators of virus infection and learn how to report operational anomalies to resource administrators.	Higher	Positive
93. Employee attended a training program to learn about the sensitivity/criticality of special company files so that he could apply appropriate protective measures when handling the information.	Higher	Positive

Notes: This behavior list was compiled from two sources: 1) brainstorming exercises conducted with approximately 12 information security experts; 2) interview transcripts from approximately 70 information technology professionals. Subject matter experts (n=50) provided ratings of the necessary expertise and positive vs. negative intentions of the employee on five–point scales. Mean expertise ratings from the experts were divided into three categories representing the level of needed expertise: 1 −2.5=lower, 2.6 −3.1=middle, 3.2 −5=higher. Mean intentionality ratings from the experts were divided into three categories representing the likely intentions of the actor: 1 −2.5=negative, 2.6 −3.1=hard to tell, 3.2 −5=positive.

Leadership Interview Protocol

Authors' note: Semi-structured interview guides give the interviewer a general overview of the path to take in a discussion but do not dictate that interviewers follow the exact wording or sequence of questioning. One hallmark of a good interviewer is the ability to follow an interesting lead, regardless of whether it is in the protocol. As a result, the interview queries shown in Chapter 5 differ in some cases from those presented in the material below.

Before we begin, I need to mention a couple of formalities about this interview. I am working with Dr. Jeffrey Stanton at Syracuse University on a project that has been funded by the National Science Foundation. This research has been approved by Syracuse University's institutional review board and given project number 01123. In this research we are looking at information security in the workplace. We would like to get your perspectives on these issues during this 30-minute interview.

All of your responses will remain confidential. We will aggregate information from many individuals to develop our research conclusions. Neither you personally nor your organization will be identified in any of our research. We will protect your identity in any reports that are provided as feedback to your organization.

With your agreement, we would like to tape-record this interview. For this reason we ask that you try to avoid naming specific individuals associated within your organization. Remember that your participation is voluntary and you are free to not answer any question that does not fit your circumstances or that you feel is inappropriate; you may also withdraw from the interview at any time. If you wish to participate, please read and sign the attached informed consent forms. Please keep one signed copy of the form for your records.

General Questions

1. Could you give me a **quick overview** of your history in this organization?
2. In what other **settings have you worked** as an organizational leader?
3. How do you **feel about your job**?
4. How do you think your employees would **describe you** as a leader of the organization?
5. What are your **biggest concerns** for your organization? What do you spend the most time thinking/worrying about?

Information Protection Questions

6. What is the most **sensitive information** that your organization works with?
7. What are **your concerns or priorities** in terms of information security?
8. How well do you think your employees understand the **information security priorities** of the organization?
9. How much of your **time and energy is spent on efforts to communicate** these priorities to your employees?
10. At present, what are the main incentives or **motivational structures** for your employees? How much **leeway** do you have to **change these incentives**?
11. How closely do you **communicate with IT employees**? What do you usually communicate with them about?
12. In addition to yourself, who **plays the most important role in ensuring information security in** your organization?
13. How much have your **employees participated in the planning** and design of the information security infrastructure? Which employees in particular? What will their roles be in the future?

Monitoring Questions

14. In what ways do you keep track of what your employees are doing?
15. Do you have the **ability to monitor** your employees' work activities? Do you use it? How do you feel about this?

16. Have you experienced any information security problems or crises in this organization in the past? What did you do about them?

17. **What things do non-information-technology employees do** in organizations that affect information security? Can you think of any stories in which something an employee did affected an organization's information security? (Could be an adverse effect or a beneficial effect.)

Closing Questions

18. I would guess that you're involved in **setting or mandating the policies for information technology** security in this organization. Is everyone following these policies to the degree that you would like? Can you discuss how effective you believe existing policies are in helping maintain information security? If you could change anything about policies, enforcement, incentives, etc., what would you change?

19. Along the same lines, if you had a **big pile of money** that you could spend on people or equipment or training or whatever, how would you spend it to enhance information security?

Thank you very much for your participation. Do you have any questions for me?

Information Security Professional Interview Protocol

Authors' note: Semi-structured interview guides give the interviewer a general overview of the path to take in a discussion but do not dictate that interviewers follow the exact wording or sequence of questioning. One hallmark of a good interviewer is the ability to follow an interesting lead, regardless of whether it is in the protocol. As a result, the interview queries shown in Chapter 6 differ in some cases from those presented in the following material.

Before we begin, I need to mention a couple of formalities about this interview. I am working with Dr. Jeffrey Stanton at Syracuse University on a project that has been funded by the National Science Foundation. This research has been approved by Syracuse University's institutional review board and given project number 01123. In this research we are looking at information security in the workplace. We would like to get your perspectives on these issues during this 30-minute interview.

All of your responses will remain confidential. We will aggregate information from many individuals to develop our research conclusions. Neither you personally nor your organization will be identified in any of our research. We will protect your identity in any reports that are provided as feedback to your organization.

With your agreement, we would like to tape-record this interview. For this reason we ask that you try to avoid naming specific individuals associated within your organization. Remember that your participation is voluntary and you are free to not answer any question that does not fit your circumstances or that you feel is inappropriate; you may also withdraw from the interview at any time. If you wish to participate, please read and sign the attached informed consent forms. Please keep one signed copy of the form for your records.

1. WARM-UP QUESTIONS

   A. Could you give me a **quick overview** of your history in this organization?

   B. In what other **settings have you worked**? How did they differ from this organization?

2. WHAT IS HAPPENING HERE WITH RESPECT TO INFORMATION SECURITY?

   A. Could you give a **broad overview** of the information systems for which you have responsibility?

   B. What kinds of information in your organization are particularly **sensitive** (for example, information about clients, patients, your products or services)?

   C. What are your **biggest security concerns** for your organization? What do you spend the most time thinking/worrying about?

   D. Are there any **events** that have happened in your organization that have affected your information security activities?

   E. What are **your own priorities** in terms of information security?

   F. What are the **priorities of your organization's leaders** in terms of information security? How do you get information about their priorities?

   G. Are there any **outside regulations or policies** that affect **you and your organization** in terms of information security (e.g., HIPAA, GLB, SarBox)? How do you feel about them? How do they affect you and your job?

3. PEOPLE AND SECURITY ISSUES

   A. Who are the **main people who affect information security** in your organization (e.g., users, clients, managers, organizational leaders)?

   B. What's happening in your organization with respect to **information security policy?** How do users know or find out about acceptable uses of information systems?

C. What has been **your involvement** in the **development and enforcement of policy?**

D. How well do you think your co-workers and other staff **follow proper information security procedures?** Please explain.

E. Do you feel that **other precautions** can be taken **to improve security** issues organization wide? Can you give a few examples?

4. COMMUNICATION

A. How do you find **communicating** with non-technical folks about information security issues? Can you think of any ways that communication could be improved?

B. Are there any **barriers to communication** within your organization that you would like to remove if you could?

C. How well do you think your **staff understands the security goals, strategies, and vision** of the organization?

D. What are the **main incentives or motivational structures for your staff?**

Do you have any questions for me? Thank you very much for your assistance!

Employee Interview Protocol

Authors' note: Semi-structured interview guides give the interviewer a general overview of the path to take in a discussion but do not dictate that interviewers follow the exact wording or sequence of questioning. One hallmark of a good interviewer is the ability to follow an interesting lead, regardless of whether it is in the protocol. As a result, the interview queries shown in Chapter 7 differ in some cases from those presented in the material below.

Before we begin, I need to mention a couple of formalities about this interview. I am working with Dr. Jeffrey Stanton at Syracuse University on a project that has been funded by the National Science Foundation. This research has been approved by Syracuse University's institutional review board and given project number 01123. In this research we are looking at information security in the workplace. We would like to get your perspectives on these issues during this 30-minute interview.

All of your responses will remain confidential. We will aggregate information from many individuals to develop our research conclusions. Neither you personally nor your organization will be identified in any of our research. We will protect your identity in any reports that are provided as feedback to your organization.

With your agreement, we would like to tape-record this interview. For this reason we ask that you try to avoid naming specific individuals associated within your organization. Remember that your participation is voluntary and you are free to not answer any question that does not fit your circumstances or that you feel is inappropriate; you may also withdraw from the interview at any time. If you wish to participate, please read and sign the attached informed consent forms. Please keep one signed copy of the form for your records.

1. WARM-UP QUESTIONS

   A. Could you give me a **quick overview** of your history in this organization?

   B. In what other **settings have you worked**? How did they differ from this organization?

   C. Could you give a **quick overview** of how you **use information systems**?

2. WHAT IS HAPPENING HERE WITH RESPECT TO INFORMATION SECURITY?

   A. What are your **biggest security concerns** for your organization?

   B. Are there any **big events** that have happened in your organization that have affected the operation or reliability of the computer/information systems you use?

   C. What kinds of information in your organization are particularly **sensitive** (for example, information about clients, patients, your products or services)?

   D. What aspects of **your job** pertain to **maintaining information security**?

3. WHAT DO YOU HEAR FROM *INFORMATION TECHNOLOGY PEOPLE* ABOUT INFORMATION SECURITY?

   A. How do information technology people **communicate** information security **priorities** to you?

   B. What are the rules for **acceptable uses** of information systems? How did you learn them?

   C. What's happening in your organization with **information security policy**?

   D. **How are information technology people involved** in **security policy**? Do they **monitor compliance**?

   E. How do you think information security **policies** or procedures could be **adjusted** to help people work more effectively?

   F. What kind of **training programs** does your organization have in information security? Who gives the training? What's your feeling about the training's effectiveness?

4. WHAT'S THE LEADERSHIP SITUATION IN YOUR ORGANIZATION?

    A. What are the priorities of your organization's leaders in terms of information security? How do you **learn about** your leaders' **priorities** with respect to information security?

    B. **How are leaders involved** in **motivating** security policy compliance?

    C. How do **regulations or laws** affect **your organization's handling of information**?

5. HOW DO YOUR PEERS/COLLEAGUES HANDLE INFORMATION SECURITY?

    A. How well do you think your **co-workers and other staff follow** proper information security procedures?

    B. What kinds of **security issues** are **discussed** among workers and managers?

    C. What **new steps** might be taken to **improve** security issues in your group?

6. IF YOU SUPERVISE, HOW DO YOU APPROACH SECURITY WITH YOUR WORKERS?

    A. How well do you think your **staff buys into security goals** of the organization?

    B. How do you motivate **your staff**? How much leeway do you give them on security issues?

    C. What is your customary or **preferred mode of communication with your staff**?

    D. How do you find **communicating** with non-technical folks about security issues?

    E. How well do you think your **staff communicates with each other**?

Do you have any questions for me? Thank you very much for your assistance!

Straightforward Acceptable Use Policy

Disclaimer: The following material is provided "as is" to serve as an example of policy language that a small business might adapt to help regulate employee behavior. This document is not legal advice; competent human resources and legal professionals should review all matters pertaining to employment practices and actions.

Title: Acceptable Use of Company Information Systems and Data

Date Last Updated: _____

Purpose and Scope: This document defines the range of acceptable and unacceptable employee behavior pertaining to the use of information systems and data in possession of the company. The behavioral rules in this document apply to all employees and contractors of the company.

Justification: Every employee's actions when using company information systems and data can affect the privacy and security of our employees, customers, and business partners. Certain kinds of misuses, whether intentional or not, may create liabilities for our company that could put us out of business. State and federal laws have created civil and criminal penalties for mishandling of financial records, student data, and healthcare data. To preserve all of our livelihoods it is imperative that we collectively adhere to a set of rules for computer usage that will keep our company in business and each of us personally out of trouble.

Permitted Activities: Each employee may use his or her computer for certain personal activities during break periods: The personal activities are limited to online shopping, obtaining news reports, conducting research (e.g., on personal health matters), and exchanging plain text e-mails or messages with family members and/or friends. During non-break periods employees must limit their information systems usage to legitimate business purposes.

Prohibited Activities: In general, employees may not conduct any activities prohibited under law. Employees may never perform the following behaviors while on company premises and/or using company-possessed equipment and systems:

- Gambling;

- Examining or downloading pornography or any material in violation of sexual harassment or hostile work environment laws;

- Downloading or installing executable software programs of any type except as specifically authorized by cognizant information technology personnel;

- Receipt, storage, or transmission of unlicensed intellectual property (e.g., MP3s, shareware);

- Introduction of malicious software into the company's information systems;

- Making fraudulent offers of products or services or making unauthorized offers of warranties;

- Revealing protected information (including your username and password) to unauthorized individuals;

- Interfering with the performance of company information systems or the service of other users.

Required Activities: In general, employees should take all reasonable steps to ensure the security and privacy of the company's systems and data. Employees should frequently or regularly perform the following behaviors:

- Choose difficult-to-guess passwords containing at least eight characters including numbers and punctuation, and change passwords at least twice a year;

- Keep username, password, and sensitive data secure; do not share accounts or access; encrypt data as needed;

- Take special precautions when taking laptops, electronic storage devices, or removable media off premises;

- Ensure that protections on your computer (e.g., anti-virus) remain updated and operational;

- Use extreme caution when opening attachments or removable media;

- Bring unusual information systems behavior to the immediate attention of someone who can help with it.

Monitoring and Enforcement: Positive security behavior benefits all of us and may enhance our collective success and the safety of our customers and co-workers. Because of the importance of this policy, the information technology department has implemented systems that help to monitor compliance with it. Records of your computer activities will regularly be reviewed by the manager of information systems, who will in turn discuss any concerns with your supervisor. Using these monitoring data as a guide, the company will periodically recognize and reward individuals and groups who consistently demonstrate compliance with this policy. The detection of prohibited activities will lead to loss of information technology privileges, informal reprimands, and/or disciplinary action up to and possibly including dismissal.

Straightforward Password Policy

Disclaimer: The following material is provided "as is" to serve as an example of policy language that a small business might adapt to help regulate employee behavior. This document is not legal advice; competent human resources and legal professionals should review all matters pertaining to employment practices and actions.

Title: Policy for Creating and Maintaining Good Passwords

Date Last Updated: _____

Purpose and Scope: This document defines the range of acceptable and unacceptable employee behavior pertaining to the use of usernames and passwords to access information systems and data in possession of this organization. The behavioral rules in this document apply to full-time, part-time, temporary, and contract employees of this organization.

Justification: Usernames and passwords are strings of characters assigned to users of information systems in the organization as a means of identification and authentication. Each username and password pair is associated with the one person to whom it was assigned. If someone other than the legitimate owner uses a username and password, with either good or bad intentions, this action represents a kind of "identity theft" and it puts the legitimate owner at risk. To prevent this kind of problem, it is imperative that we collectively adhere to a set of rules for password usage that will inhibit security problems.

Required Activities: Compose each of your passwords by employing a method that will help you remember them. For example, if your favorite nursery rhyme is "Jack and Jill," you might compose a password that looks like this: J&J^H2fpw. (Please don't use this specific password, however. Make one up based on your own favorite phrase.) Your password must satisfy the following rules:

- Your passwords must contain at least eight characters.

- Your passwords must contain at least one punctuation character and one digit.

- Change your password at least twice per year. Use daylight savings time as a reminder: Change your password when the clocks change.

- Immediately request a password reset or manually change any password you believe may have been stolen or inadvertently revealed. Report such issues to the information systems staff within one business day.

Prohibited Activities: In general, all individuals must keep their username/password private. Users must avoid the following behaviors related to usernames/passwords for information systems:

- Never create passwords that are words in the dictionary or proper names (e.g., the word "password," date of birth, names of relatives or pets, the name of the company).

- Never use your social security number, phone number, or other account numbers in a password.

- Never reveal your password to another person; even information technology personnel should never request your password; never reveal a password to someone on the phone. In an emergency or life-threatening situation, you may reveal your username and password to an appropriate authority (e.g., your supervisor).

- Never write down or record your password unless you place the resulting record in a locked area.

- Never send a password using e-mail or other unencrypted methods.

Recommended Practices: In general, users of information systems of our organization should take all reasonable steps to ensure the security of their passwords. Please remember to:

- Choose passwords for organizational information systems that differ from the ones you use for personal activities, such as your personal e-mail account;

- Choose passwords for use with Internet services that are different from the ones you use for internal information systems;

- Request disabling of your user account during the periods when you know you will not need to use your username and password (e.g., vacation, leave).

Monitoring and Enforcement: Positive security behavior benefits our whole company and may enhance our collective success and the safety of our customers' and co-workers' data. Because of the importance of this password policy, the information technology department has implemented a program that monitors system log ons and password changes. Records of these activities will be reviewed regularly by the manager of information systems, who will in turn discuss any concerns with your supervisor. Using these monitoring data as a guide, the company will periodically recognize and reward individuals and groups who consistently demonstrate good password and account information handling practices. Inappropriate activity related to the security of your user account will result in the temporary suspension of your user privileges and a reset of your password.

About the Authors

Jeffrey M. Stanton, PhD (University of Connecticut, 1997), is an associate professor in the School of Information Studies at Syracuse University and Director of the Syracuse Information Security Evaluation Project. Dr. Stanton also holds a bachelor's degree in computer science from Dartmouth College and has nine years of professional experience as a software engineer. Dr. Stanton has published more than 50 articles, proceedings, and chapters on research topics at the intersection of organizational behavior and technology. His work has been published in top behavioral science journals, such as the *Journal of Applied Psychology, Personnel Psychology*, and *Human Performance*, as well as technology-oriented publications, such as *Communications of the Association for Computing Machinery, Computers and Security*, and *Lecture Notes in Computer Science*. Dr. Stanton has also presented his work at leading scholarly conferences, including the Society for Industrial-Organizational Psychology, the Academy of Management, and the Americas Conference for Information Systems. Dr. Stanton's research has been supported through grants and supplements from the National Science Foundation, including its prestigious CAREER award, as well as grants and contracts from the Society for Industrial-Organizational Psychology Research Foundation, Procter and Gamble, Brush Wellman, the National Society of Black Engineers, and the American Library Association. Dr. Stanton is also a GIAC Certified Information Security Officer and was on the advisory boards of the SANS Institute's GSLC and GISF certifications in 2004 and 2005. Dr. Stanton is an associate editor for the *Journal of Information Systems Security* and *Human Resources Management*.

Kathryn R. Stam, PhD (Syracuse University, 1999), is an assistant professor of Anthropology at the SUNY Institute of Technology in Utica, New York, where she teaches courses in anthropology, sociology, cultural diversity, and the social and ethical aspects of information technology. She earned her PhD in Social Science (Anthropology and Sociology) from Syracuse University's Maxwell School of Citizenship and Public Affairs. She is a founding member and the Associate Director of the Syracuse Information Security Evaluation project at Syracuse University's School of Information Studies. Her main research interests are related to information technology, health and social services, ethnographic methods, and organizational culture. She has published a range of qualitative research on the topics of information technology, health communications, and teaching in the *Journal of Digital Information, Journal of Information Systems Education*, and *World Health Forum*. She has received financial support for her research from the National Science Foundation and the State of New York/UUP Professional Development Committee. Dr. Stam's background also includes learning, writing, and teaching about Thai and Lao culture. After serving as a Peace Corps volunteer in northeast Thailand, she continued to work there for more than a decade as a translator, teacher, and program manager in the field of health communications. She presented her research in this area at conferences of the American Anthropological Association and the Northeast Anthropological Association.

Index

J

jargon, 90–95, 142, 234–235, 256. *see also* culture gaps
job function classification, 6
job satisfaction, 73, 218
Johnson, Carl, 71
justification
governance strategies, 260
for monitoring, 78, 114, 116, 214, 241

K

Kazaa, 33
keychain devices, 48
keyloggers, 36, 55
keys, encryption, 42
knowledge bases, 265

L

labor unions. *see* unions
laptops
file storage on, 22
information carried on, 128
personal, 29
security of data on, 192–194
theft of, 131
lawsuits. *see also* legal liability
by employees, 4, 63
records management and, 104
leased lines, 41
legal liability. *see also* lawsuits
copyrighted materials and, 30
for employee communications, 26
employee concerns for, 172, 180
employee misbehavior and, 112

illegal data on organization computers, 23
legislation, 105. *see also* regulations, external
librarians, 264–265
log files
of file modifications, 50
volume of, 53
logging off, 110
logging on, 47
acceptable use policies, 140–141
failed, 50
repeated attempts, 112–113
sign-on messages, 262

M

malevolency, 28
malware, 31, 35–36
management
attitudes of, 191
behaviors of, 191
communication barriers, 256
consultative leadership, 257–258, 271
contact with, 162
policy design, 259
styles of, 73
support from, 156
trust in, 209
management-labor relationships, 4, 6, 226
managers
concern with outcomes, 245
definition of, 9
on employee monitoring, 111–117
enforcement of policies, 140
on information security, 95–111
interview protocols, 84
mistrust of employees, 75

More Great Books from
Information Today, Inc.

Net Crimes & Misdemeanors, 2nd Edition
Outmaneuvering Web Spammers, Stalkers, and Con Artists

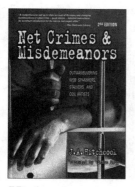

By J. A. Hitchcock
Foreword by Vint Cerf

In this revised and expanded edition of her popular
book, cybercrime expert J. A. Hitchcock offers
practical and easy-to-follow methods for dealing
with spam, viruses, hack attacks, identity theft, and
other online dangers. The book covers a broad
range of abusive practices and features dozens of
firsthand anecdotes and success stories. A one-time
victim of cyberstalking who fought back and won,
Hitchcock went on to become a leading victim's advocate. Her readable
and reassuring book is loaded with tips, strategies, and techniques as well
as pointers to the laws, organizations, and Web resources that can aid
victims and help them fight back. Supported by a Web page.

496 pp/softbound/ISBN 0-910965-72-2 $24.95

Naked in Cyberspace, 2nd Edition
How to Find Personal Information Online

By Carole A. Lane
Foreword by Beth Givens

In this second edition of her bestselling guide,
author Carole A. Lane surveys the types of
personal records that are available on the
Internet and online services. Lane explains how
researchers find and use personal data, identifies
the most useful sources of information about
people, and offers advice for readers with privacy
concerns. You'll learn how to use online tools
and databases to gain competitive intelligence, locate and investigate people,
access public records, identify experts, find new customers, recruit
employees, search for assets, uncover criminal records, conduct genealogical
research, and much more.

586 pp/softbound/ISBN 0-910965-50-1 $29.95

Web of Deception
Misinformation on the Internet

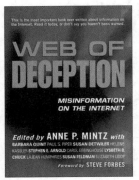

Edited by Anne P. Mintz
Foreword by Steve Forbes

Intentionally misleading or erroneous information on the Web can wreak havoc on your health, privacy, investments, business decisions, online purchases, legal affairs, and more. Until now, the breadth and significance of this growing problem for Internet users have yet to be fully explored. In *Web of Deception*, Anne P. Mintz (Director of Knowledge Management at Forbes, Inc.) brings together 10 information industry gurus to illuminate the issues and help you recognize and deal with the flood of deception and misinformation in a range of critical subject areas. A must-read for any Internet searcher who needs to evaluate online information sources and avoid Web traps.

304 pp/softbound/ISBN 0-910965-60-9 $24.95

Yahoo! to the Max
An Extreme Searcher Guide

By Randolph Hock
Foreword by Mary Ellen Bates

With its many and diverse features, it's not easy for any individual to keep up with all that Yahoo! has to offer. Fortunately, Randolph (Ran) Hock—"The Extreme Searcher"—has created a reader-friendly guide to his favorite Yahoo! tools for online research, communication, investment, e-commerce, and a range of other useful activities. In *Yahoo! to the Max*, Ran provides background, content knowledge, techniques, and tips designed to help Web users take advantage of many of Yahoo!'s most valuable offerings—from its portal features, to Yahoo! Groups, to unique tools some users have yet to discover. The author's Web page helps readers stay current on the new and improved Yahoo! features he recommends.

256 pp/softbound/ISBN 0-910965-69-2 $24.95

Millenium Intelligence
Understanding and Conducting Competitive Intelligence
in the Digital Age

By Jerry P. Miller and the
Business Intelligence Braintrust

With contributions from the world's leading busi-
ness intelligence practitioners, *Millenium
Intelligence* offers a tremendously informative and
practical look at the CI process, how it is changing,
and how it can be managed effectively in the
Digital Age. Loaded with case studies, tips, and
techniques, chapters include: What Is Intelligence?;
The Skills Needed to Execute Intelligence
Effectively; Information Sources Used for Intelligence; The Legal and
Ethical Aspects of Intelligence; Small Business Intelligence; Corporate
Security and Intelligence; ... and much more!

276 pp/softbound/ISBN 0-910965-28-5 $29.95

Assessing Competitive Intelligence Software
A Guide to Evaluating CI Technology

By France Bouthillier and Kathleen Shearer
Foreword by Chun Wei Choo

As commercial software products for Competitive
Intelligence (CI) emerge and gain acceptance,
potential users find themselves overly dependent on
information supplied by the software makers. This
book is the first to propose a systematic method
firms can use to evaluate CI software independently,
allowing them to compare features, identify
strengths and weaknesses, and invest in products
that meet their unique needs. Authors Bouthillier and Shearer demonstrate their 32-step methodology through an evaluation of four popular
CI software packages. In addition, they identify important sources of
information about CI software, map information needs to intelligence
outcomes, and describe key analytical techniques.

216 pp/hardbound/ISBN 1-57387-173-7 $39.50

Information Management for the Intelligent Organization, 3rd Edition

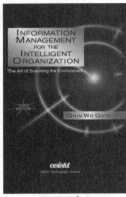

By Chun Wei Choo

The intelligent organization is one that is skilled at marshaling its information resources, transforming information into knowledge, and using it to sustain and enhance its performance in a restless environment. This updated and expanded monograph shows how an organization may manage its information processes more effectively in order to achieve these goals. It includes new sections on information culture, information overload, and organizational learning; a new chapter on Knowledge Management (KM) and the role of information professionals; and extended case studies of environmental scanning by organizations in Asia, Europe, and North America.

272 pp/hardbound/ISBN 1-57387-125-7 $39.50

Evaluating Networked Information Services
Techniques, Policy, and Issues

Edited by Charles R. McClure and John Carlo Bertot

As information services and resources are made available in the global nerworked environment, there is a critical need to evaluate their usefulness, impact, cost, and effectiveness. This monograph brings together an introduction and overview of evaluation techniques and methods, information policy issues and initiatives, and other critical issues related to the evaluation of networked information services.

300 pp/hardbound/ISBN 1-57387-118-4 $44.50

Understanding and Communicating Social Informatics

A Framework for Studying and Teaching the Human Contexts of Information and Communication Technologies

By Rob Kling, Howard Rosenbaum, and Steve Sawyer

Here is a sustained investigation into the human contexts of information and communication technologies (ICTs), covering both research and theory. The authors demonstrate that the design, adoption, and use of ICTs are deeply connected to people's actions as well as to the environments in which ICTs are used. They offer a pragmatic overview of social informatics, articulating its fundamental ideas for specific audiences and presenting important research findings.

240 pp/hardbound/ISBN 1-57387-228-8 $39.50

Knowledge Management Lessons Learned
What Works and What Doesn't

Edited by Michael E. D. Koenig and T. Kanti Srikantaiah

A follow-up to Srikantaiah and Koenig's ground-breaking *Knowledge Management for the Information Professional* (2000), this new book surveys recent applications and innovation in KM. More than 30 experts describe KM in practice, revealing what has been learned, what works, and what doesn't. Includes projects undertaken by organizations at the forefront of KM, and coverage of KM strategy and implementation, cost analysis, education and training, content management, communities of practice, competitive intelligence, and much more.

624 pp/hardbound/ISBN 1-57387-181-8 $44.50

Theories of Information Behavior

Edited by Karen E. Fisher, Sanda Erdelez, and Lynne (E. F.) McKechnie

This unique book presents authoritative overviews of more than 70 conceptual frameworks for understanding how people seek, manage, share, and use information in different contexts. Covering both established and newly proposed theories of information behavior, the book includes contributions from 85 scholars from 10 countries. Theory descriptions cover origins, propositions, methodological implications, usage, and links to related theories.

456 pp/hardbound/ISBN 1-57387-230-X $49.50

Intelligent Technologies in Library and Information Service Applications

By F. W. Lancaster and Amy Warner

Librarians and library school faculty have been experimenting with artificial intelligence (AI) and expert systems for 30 years, but there has been no comprehensive survey of the results available until now. In this carefully researched monograph, authors Lancaster and Warner report on the applications of AI technologies in library and information services, assessing their effectiveness, reviewing the relevant literature, and offering a clear-eyed forecast of future use and impact. Includes almost 500 bibliographic references.

214 pp/hardbound/ISBN 1-57387-103-6 $39.50